STARGATE ATLANTIS™

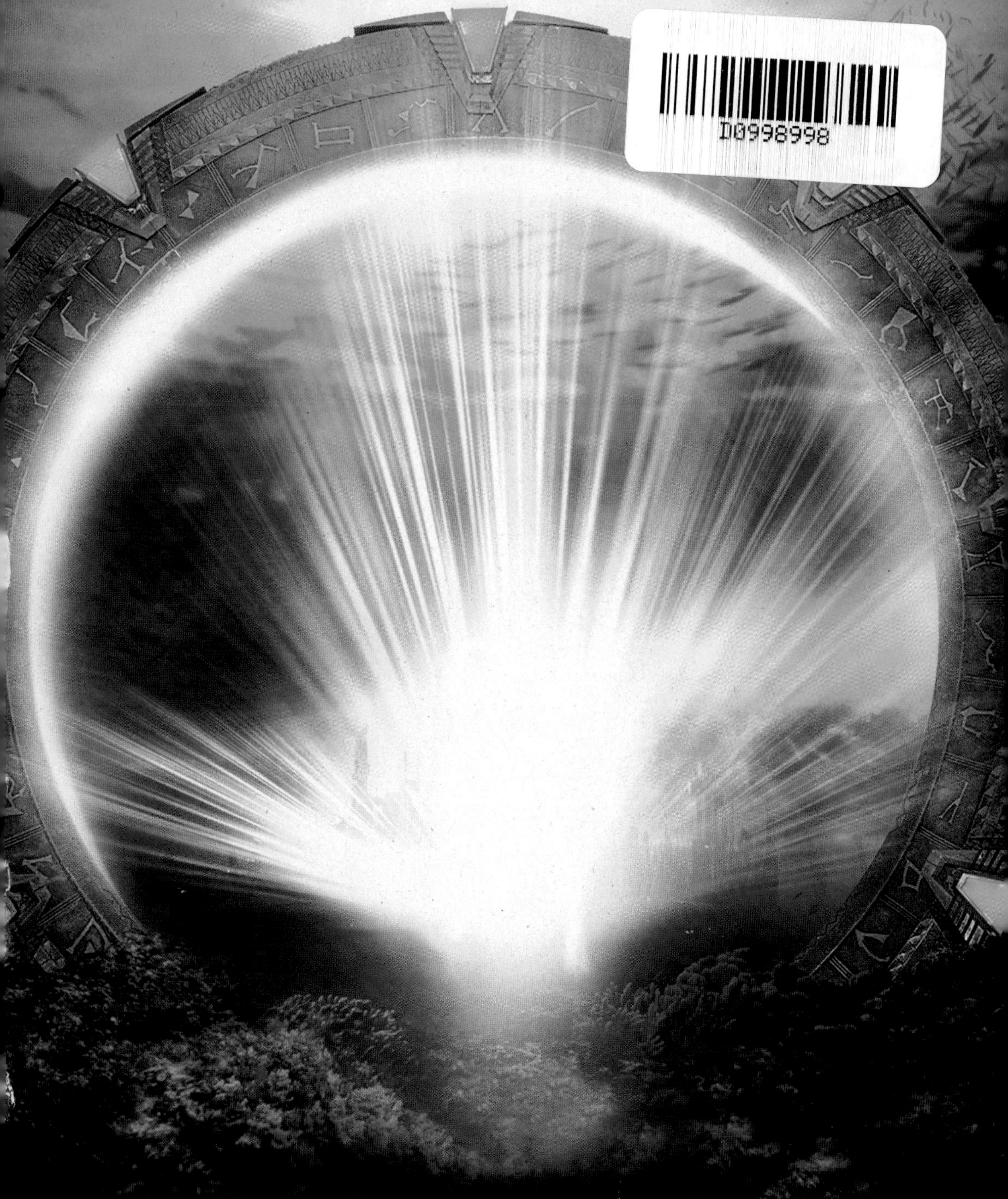

VOLUME TWO

STARGATE ATLANTIS

HEARTS & MINDS
SINGULARITY

STARGATE ATLANTIS
Created by Brad Wright
& Robert C. Cooper

HEARTS & MINDS
ISSUES #1-3
Written by Mark L. Haynes & J.C. Vaughn
Art by Greg LaRocque
Color by Gene / Emmanuel Ordaz Torres
Lettering by James Dufendach

SINGULARITY ISSUES #1-3
Written by Mark L. Haynes & J.C. Vaughn
Art by Gordon Purcell / Greg LaRocque
Color by Emmanuel Ordaz Torres
Lettering by Natalie Jane

COVER GALLERY
Greg LaRocque
Dan Parsons
Clint Hilinski

Vol. 2 Cover Art- *Greg LaRocque*
Production & Design- *Mike Wolfer*
Publisher- *Michael Bornstein*
Marketing Manager- *Barlow Jones*

Editors-
James Kuhoric, Mike Wolfer
Managing Editor-
S.A. Check

VOLUME TWO

STARGATE ATLANTIS™ Volume Two Trade Paperback. First Printing. Published by American Mythology Productions, LLC, P.O. Box 325, Bel Air, MD 21014
www.americanmythology.net. STARGATE ATLANTIS is a trademark of Metro-Goldwyn-Mayer Studios Inc. ©2004-2018 MGM Global Holdings Inc. All Rights Reserved.
METRO-GOLDWYN-MAYER is a trademark of Metro-Goldwyn-Mayer Lion Corp ©2018 Metro-Goldwyn-Mayer Studios Inc. All Rights Reserved. American Mythology
logo ™ American Mythology Productions, LLC. All names, characters, events and locales in this publication are entirely fictional. Any resemblance to actual persons
(living or dead), events or places without satiric intent is coincidental. No portion of this publication may be reproduced by any means (digital or print) without the written

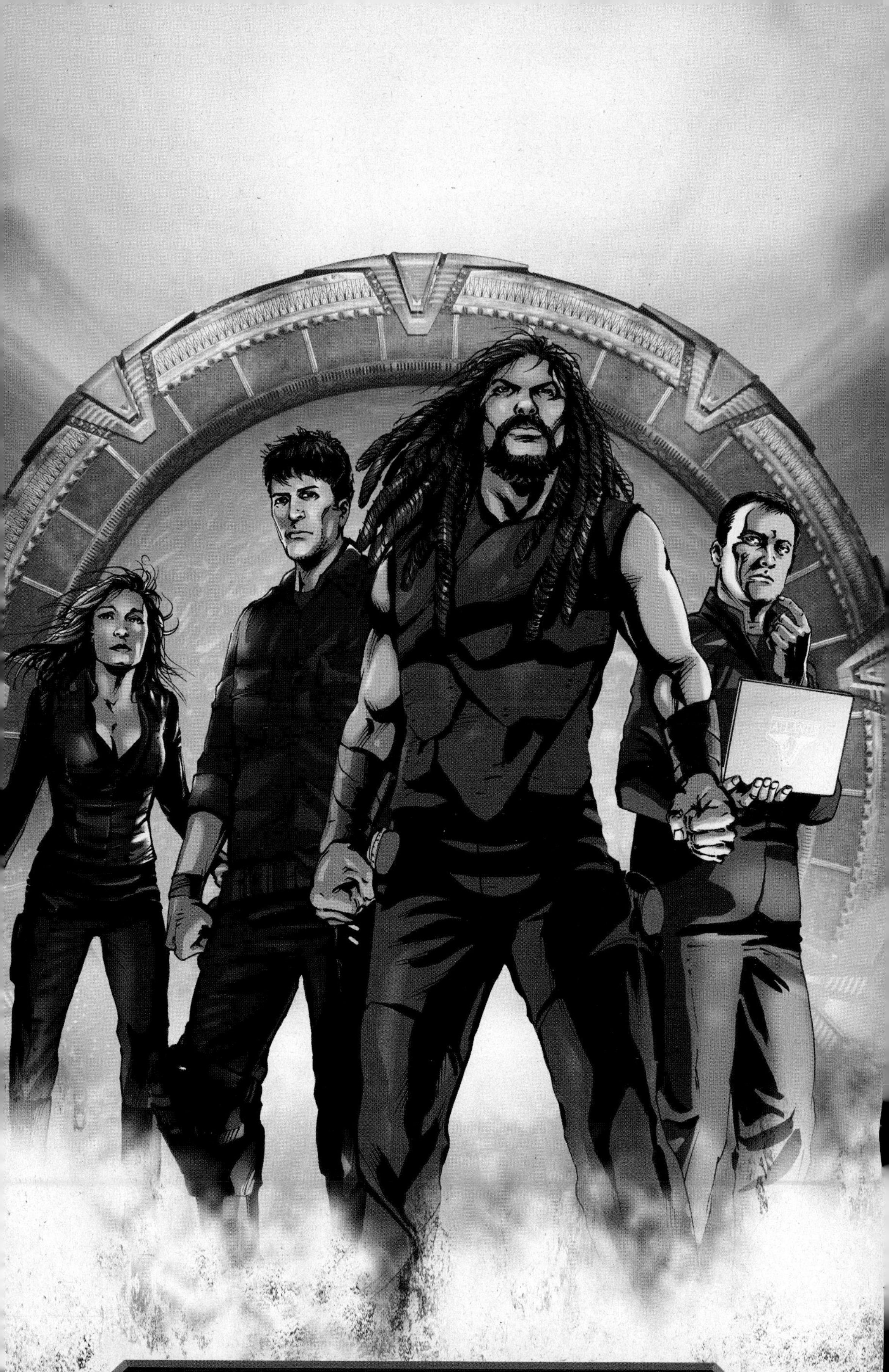

COVER GALLERY
HEARTS & MINDS #1 MAIN COVER

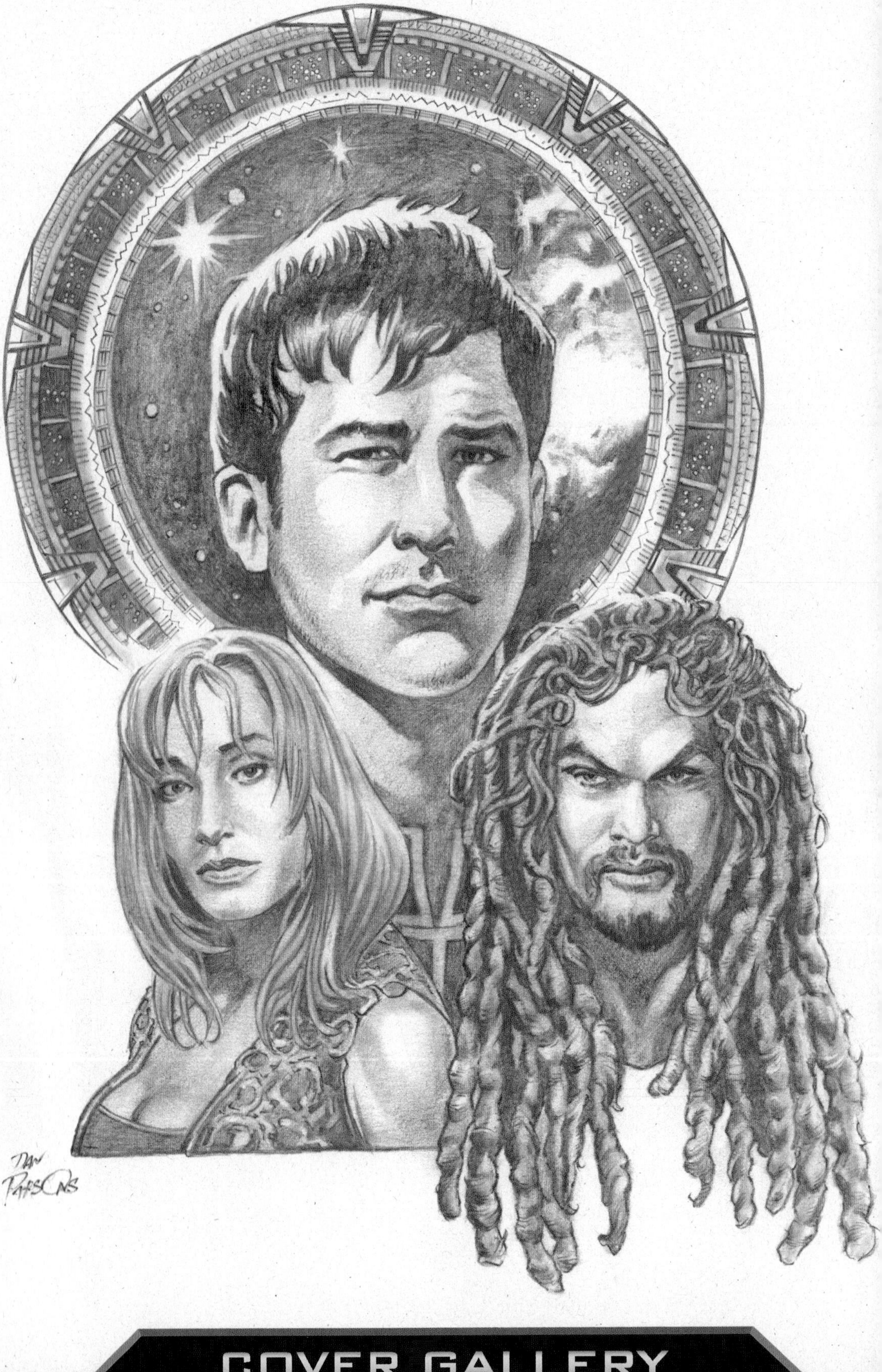
DAN PARSONS

COVER GALLERY

HEARTS & MINDS #1 LTD COVER

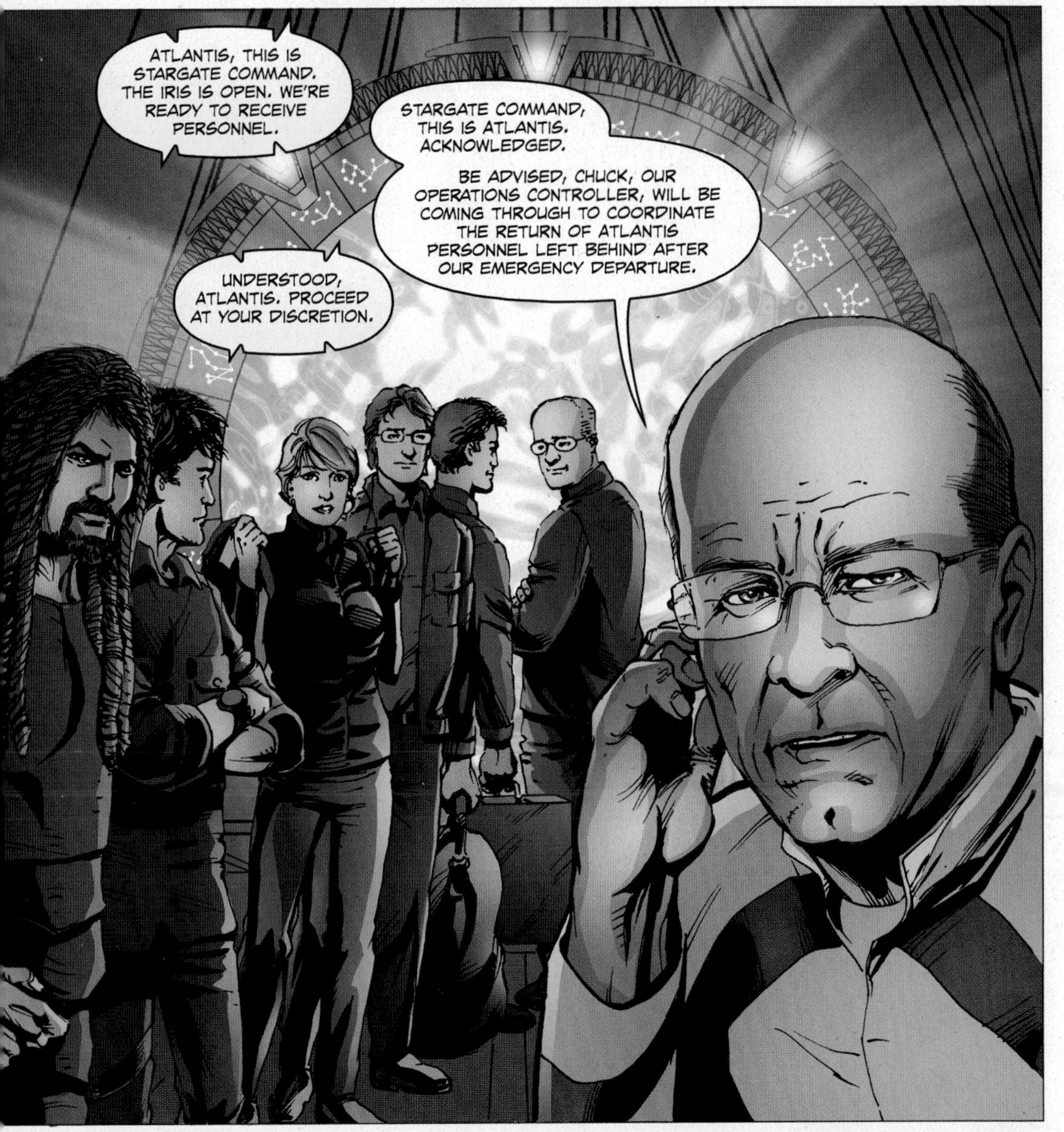
ATLANTIS, THIS IS STARGATE COMMAND. THE IRIS IS OPEN. WE'RE READY TO RECEIVE PERSONNEL.
STARGATE COMMAND, THIS IS ATLANTIS. ACKNOWLEDGED.
BE ADVISED, CHUCK, OUR OPERATIONS CONTROLLER, WILL BE COMING THROUGH TO COORDINATE THE RETURN OF ATLANTIS PERSONNEL LEFT BEHIND AFTER OUR EMERGENCY DEPARTURE.
UNDERSTOOD, ATLANTIS. PROCEED AT YOUR DISCRETION.

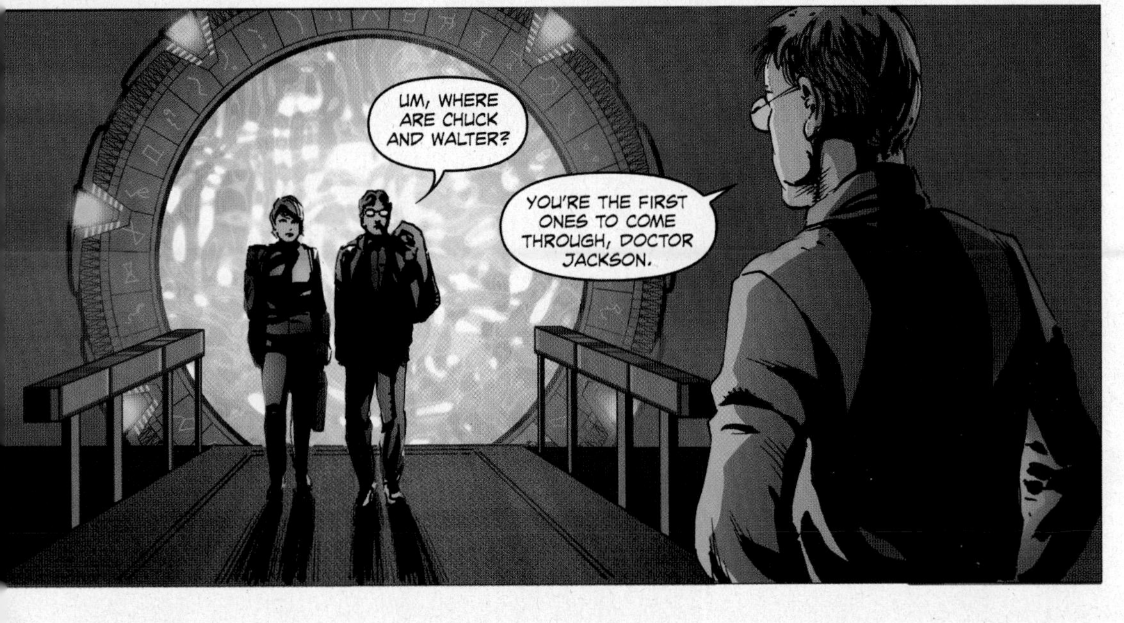
UM, WHERE ARE CHUCK AND WALTER?
YOU'RE THE FIRST ONES TO COME THROUGH, DOCTOR JACKSON.

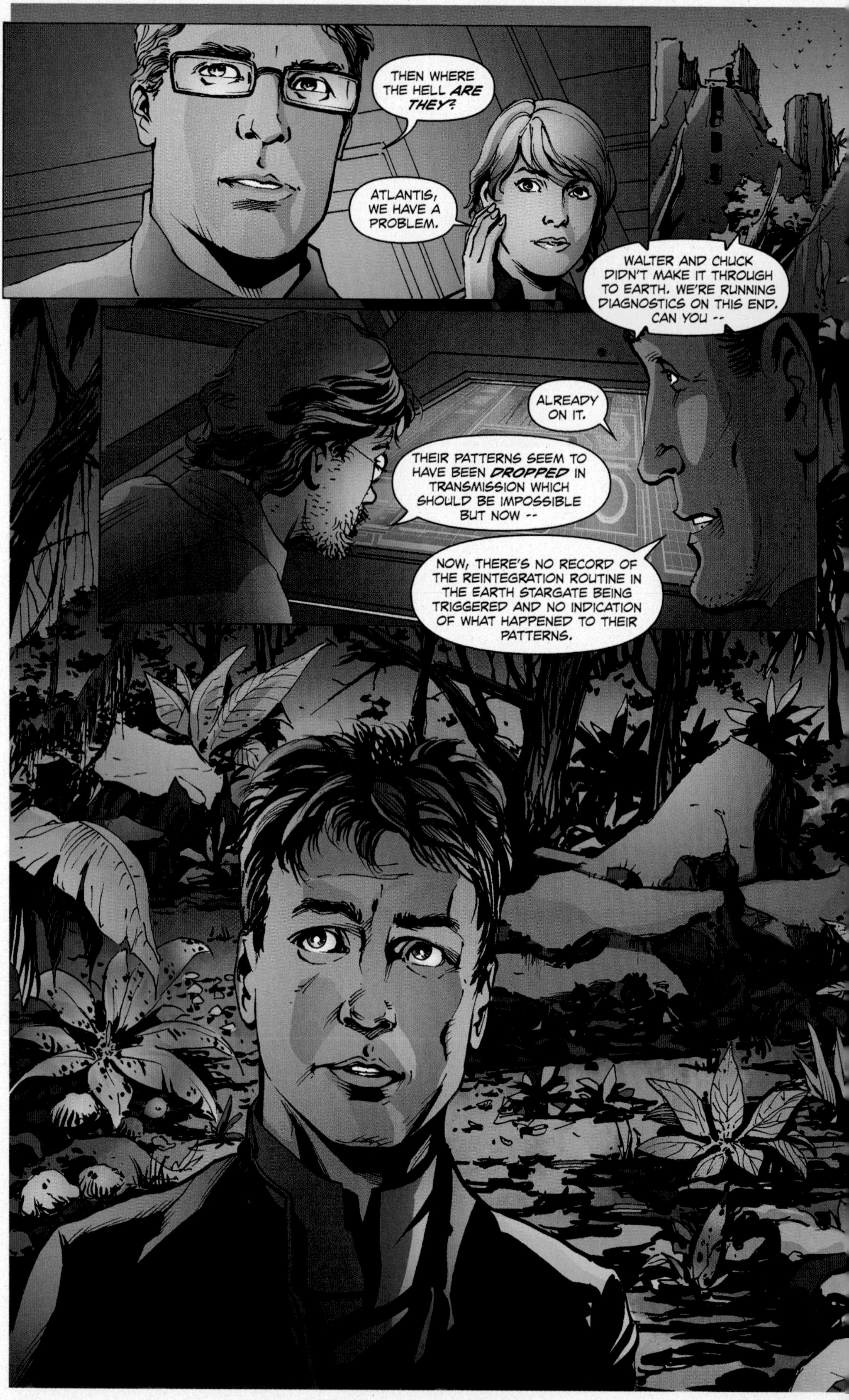

THEN WHERE THE HELL *ARE THEY*?
ATLANTIS, WE HAVE A PROBLEM.
WALTER AND CHUCK DIDN'T MAKE IT THROUGH TO EARTH. WE'RE RUNNING DIAGNOSTICS ON THIS END. CAN YOU --
ALREADY ON IT.
THEIR PATTERNS SEEM TO HAVE BEEN *DROPPED* IN TRANSMISSION WHICH SHOULD BE IMPOSSIBLE BUT NOW --
NOW, THERE'S NO RECORD OF THE REINTEGRATION ROUTINE IN THE EARTH STARGATE BEING TRIGGERED AND NO INDICATION OF WHAT HAPPENED TO THEIR PATTERNS.

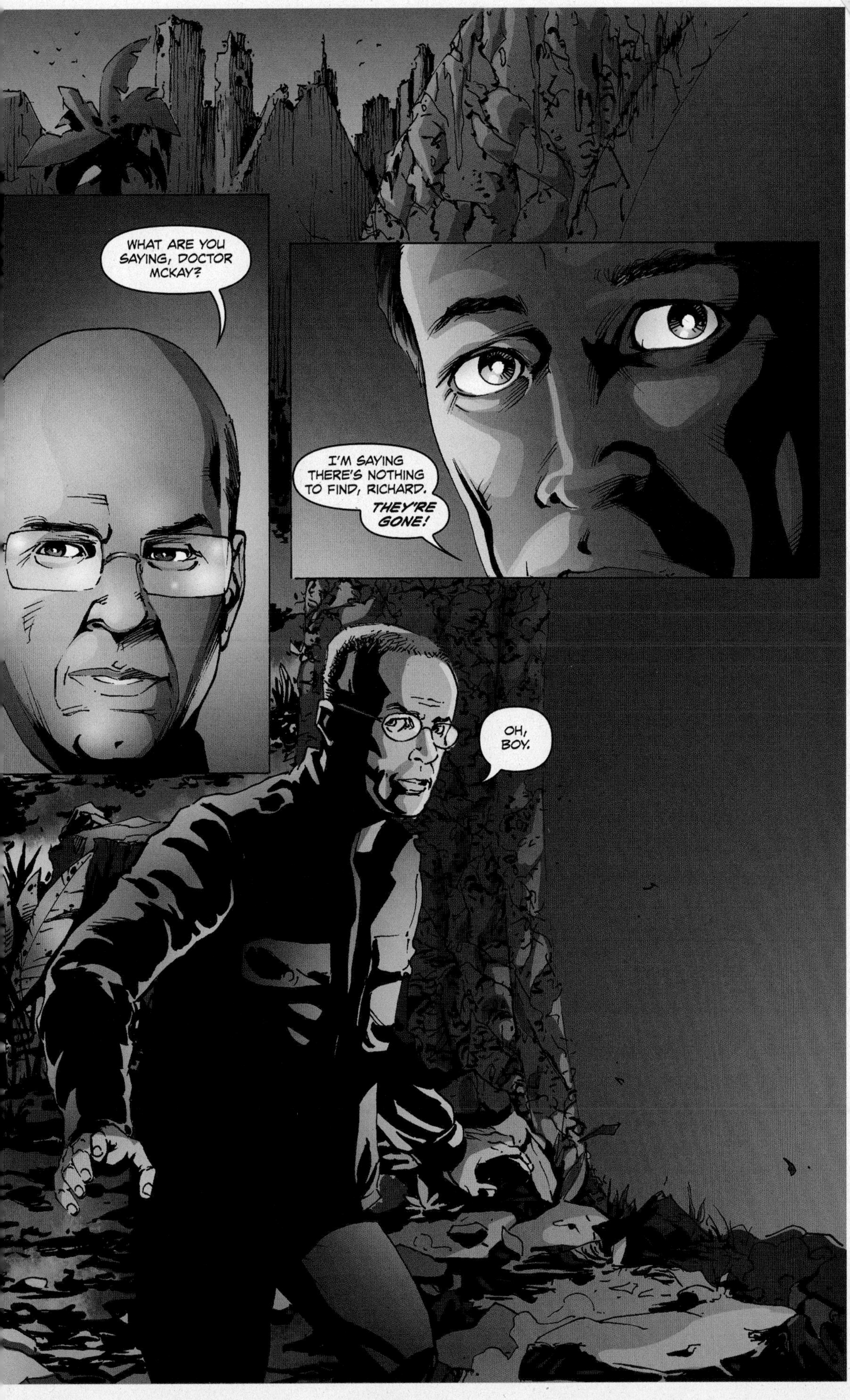
WHAT ARE YOU SAYING, DOCTOR MCKAY?
I'M SAYING THERE'S NOTHING TO FIND, RICHARD. *THEY'RE GONE!*
OH, BOY.

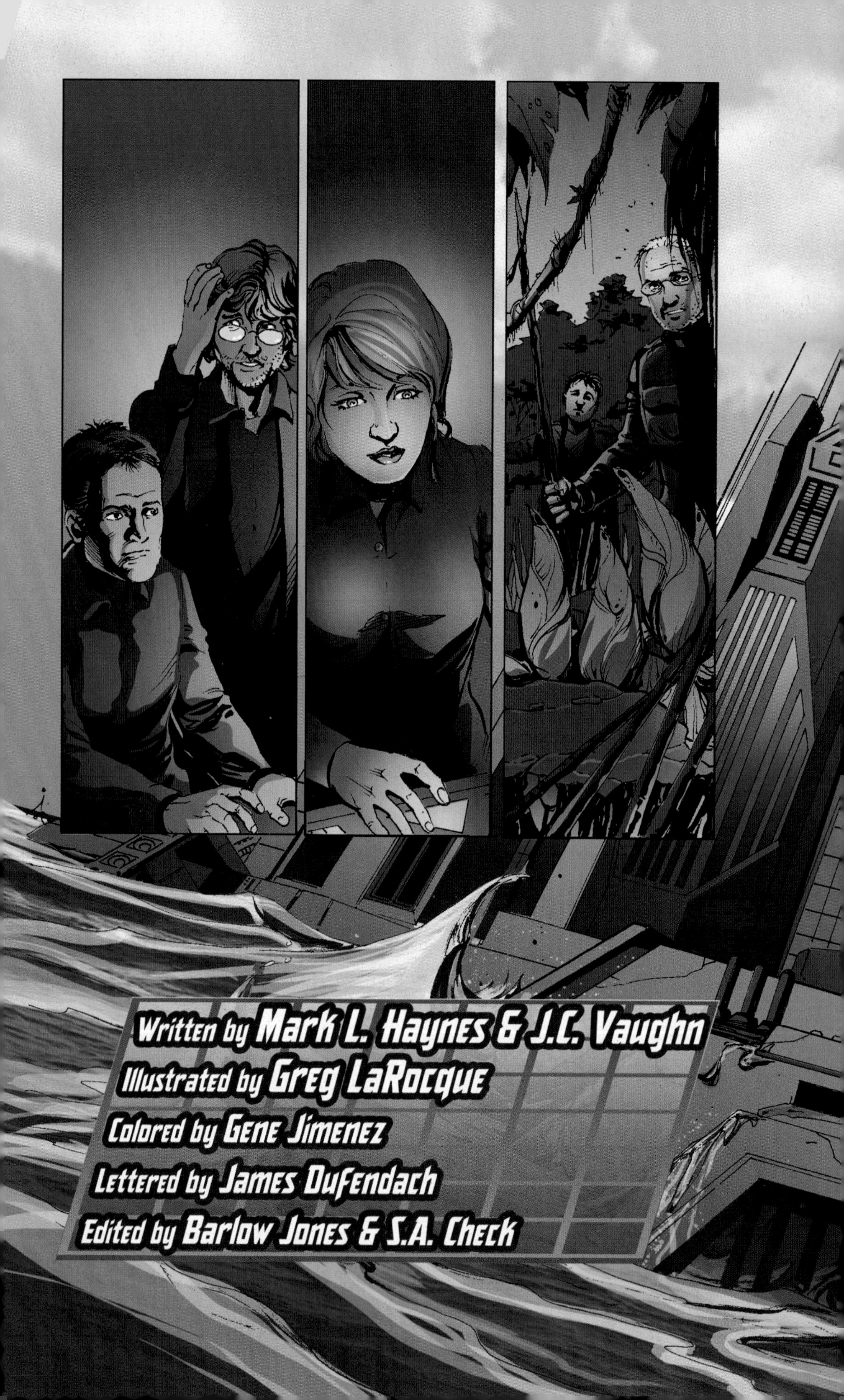
Written by Mark L. Haynes & J.C. Vaughn
Illustrated by Greg LaRocque
Colored by Gene Jimenez
Lettered by James Dufendach
Edited by Barlow Jones & S.A. Check

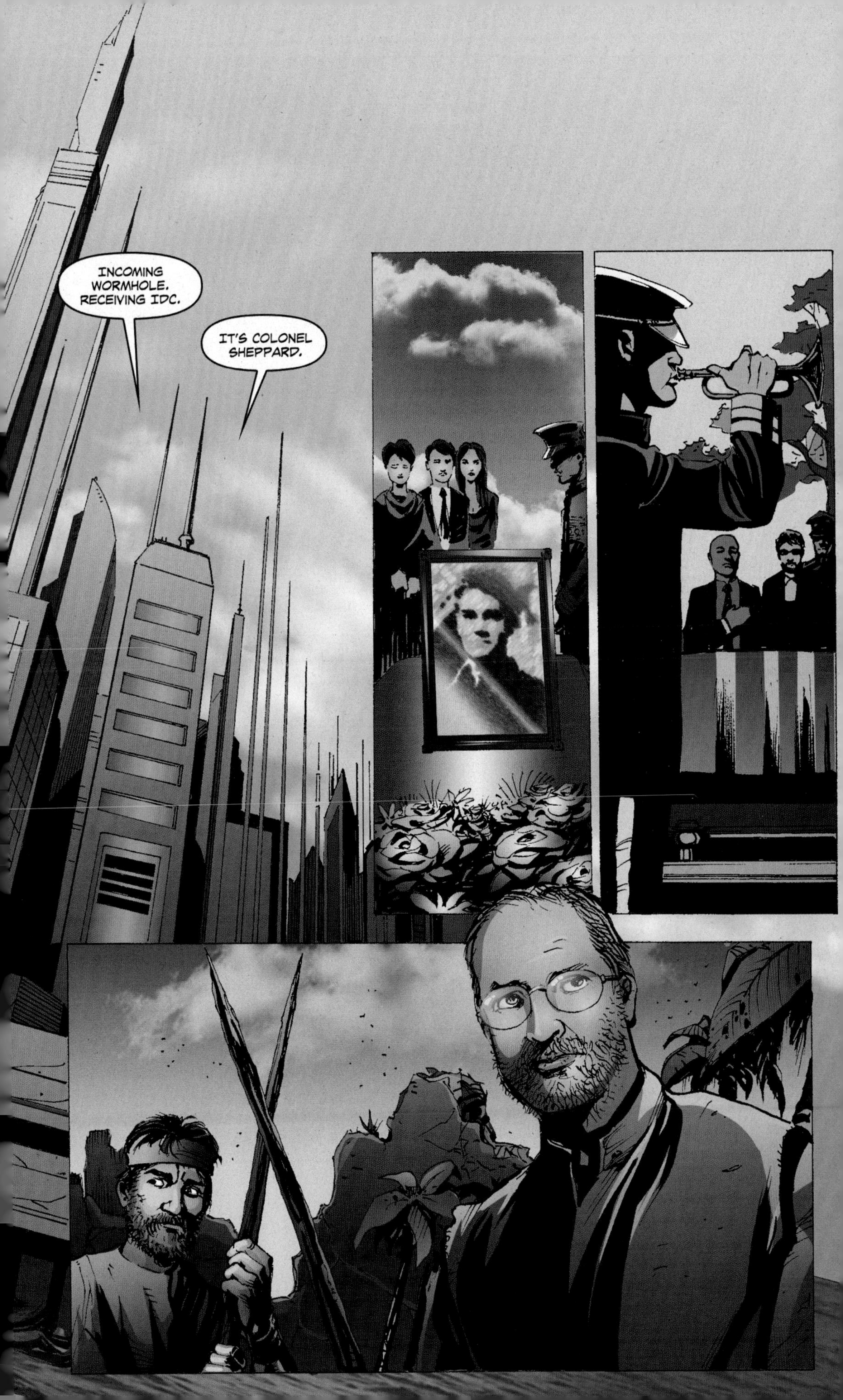
INCOMING WORMHOLE. RECEIVING IDC.
IT'S COLONEL SHEPPARD.

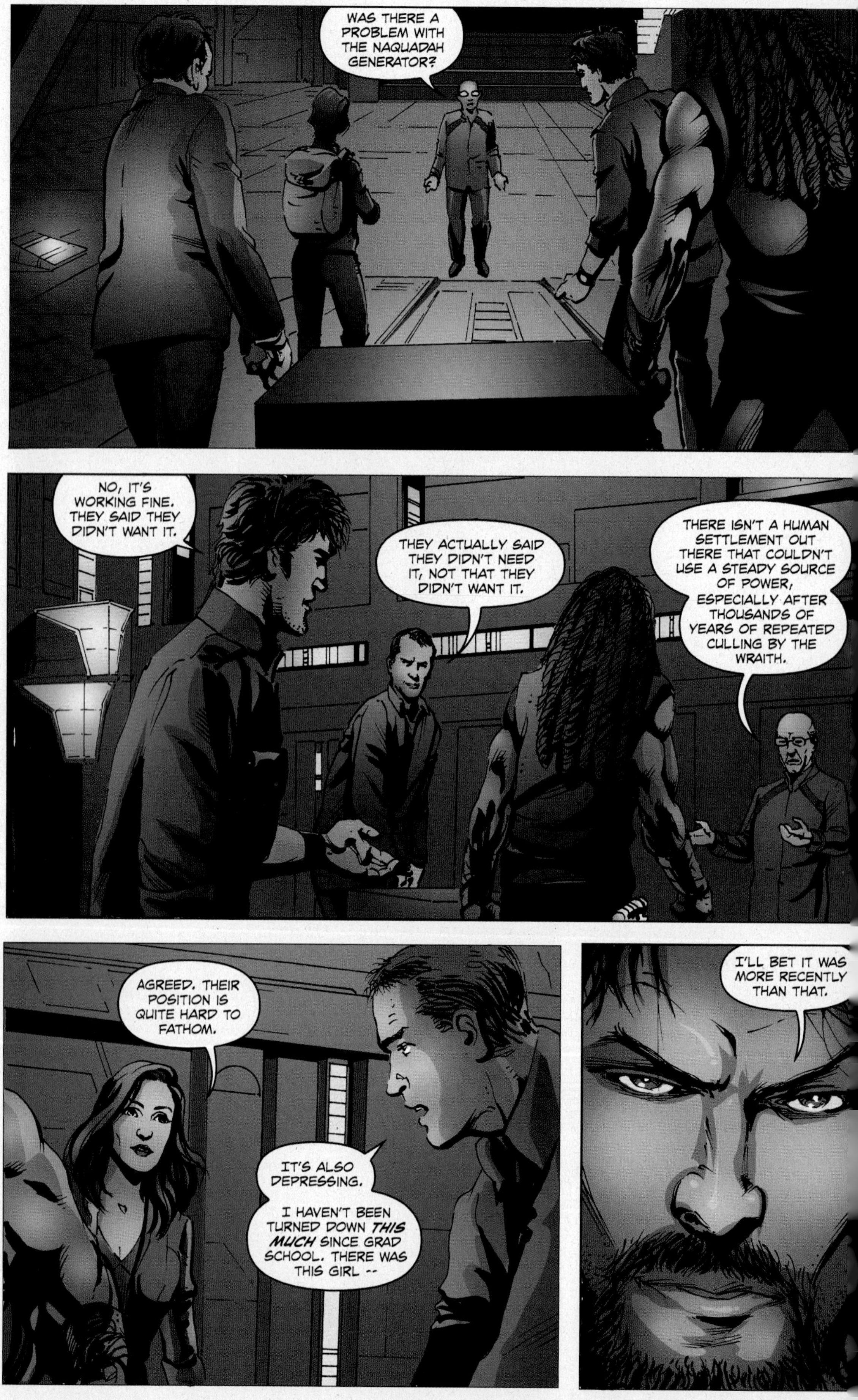
WAS THERE A PROBLEM WITH THE NAQUADAH GENERATOR?
NO, IT'S WORKING FINE. THEY SAID THEY DIDN'T WANT IT.
THEY ACTUALLY SAID THEY DIDN'T NEED IT, NOT THAT THEY DIDN'T WANT IT.
THERE ISN'T A HUMAN SETTLEMENT OUT THERE THAT COULDN'T USE A STEADY SOURCE OF POWER, ESPECIALLY AFTER THOUSANDS OF YEARS OF REPEATED CULLING BY THE WRAITH.
AGREED. THEIR POSITION IS QUITE HARD TO FATHOM.
IT'S ALSO DEPRESSING.
I HAVEN'T BEEN TURNED DOWN *THIS MUCH* SINCE GRAD SCHOOL. THERE WAS THIS GIRL --
I'LL BET IT WAS MORE RECENTLY THAN THAT.

THIS IS GETTING *SERIOUS.*

THIS IS THE FOURTH DEAL WE'VE HAD GO SOUTH IN AS MANY WEEKS.

DID THEY SAY WITH *WHOM* THEY WERE TRADING?

NO, BUT YOU KNOW WHAT I THINK.

BUT WHAT WOULD *JANUS* ACHIEVE BY SUPPLYING OUR ALLIES?

HE MARGINALIZES US. FOR M8G-753, IT WAS POWER GENERATION. FOR THE KUHORIANS, IT WAS ANCIENT *SHIELD TECHNOLOGY.*

AM I ALONE IN WONDERING WHY THIS IS EVEN A *PROBLEM?* WHEN DID WE BECOME THE HOME DEPOT OF THE PEGASUS GALAXY?

WHAT CAN A BUNCH OF THATCH-ROOFED, CLAY-HOUSE MEDIEVAL TYPES DO FOR US ANYWAY?

NO OFFENSE, TEYLA.

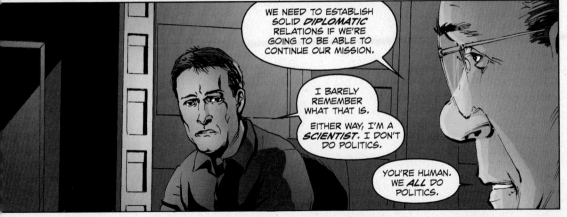

WE NEED TO ESTABLISH SOLID *DIPLOMATIC* RELATIONS IF WE'RE GOING TO BE ABLE TO CONTINUE OUR MISSION.

I BARELY REMEMBER WHAT THAT IS.

EITHER WAY, I'M A *SCIENTIST.* I DON'T DO POLITICS.

YOU'RE HUMAN. WE *ALL* DO POLITICS.

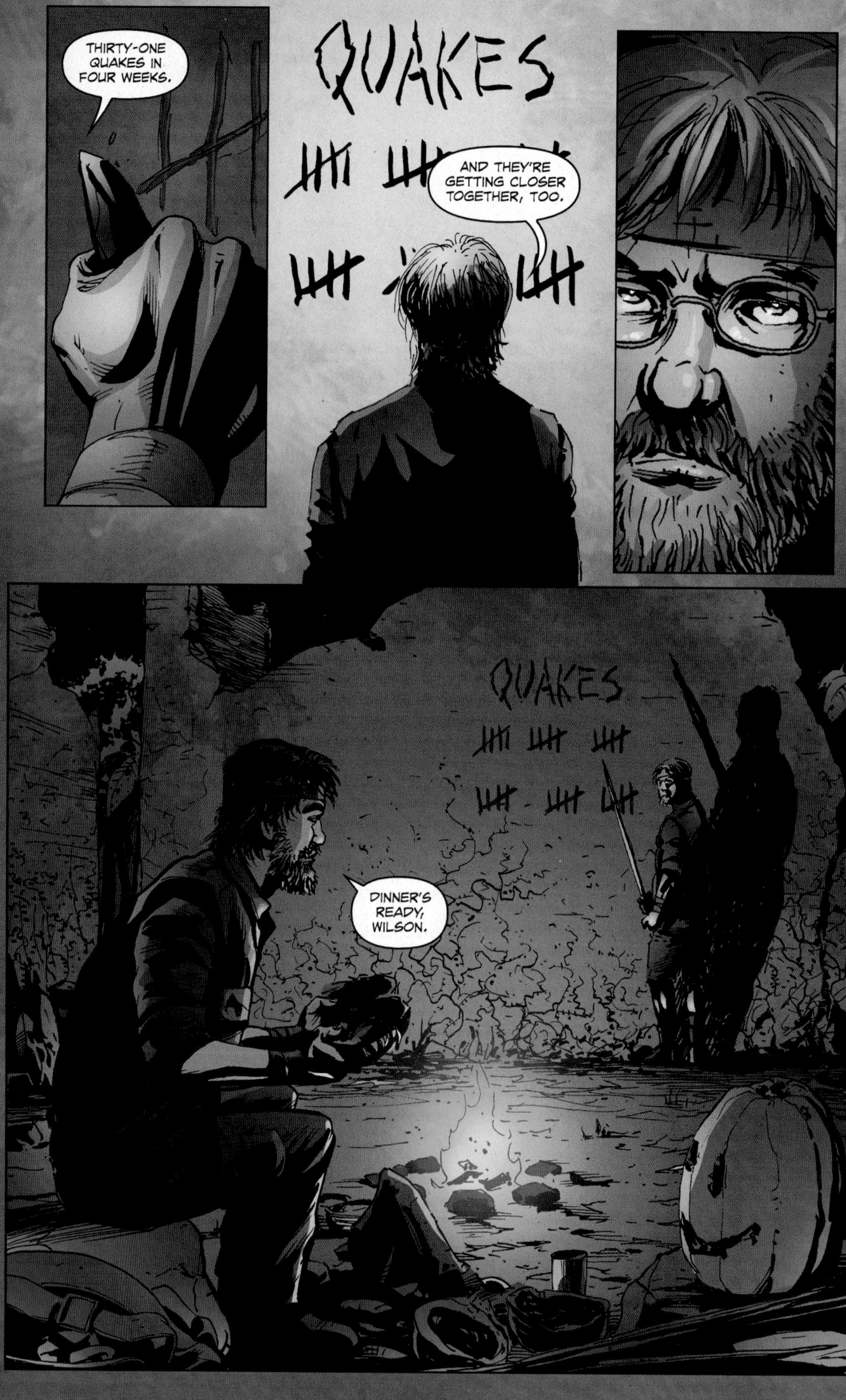

THIRTY-ONE QUAKES IN FOUR WEEKS.
QUAKES
AND THEY'RE GETTING CLOSER TOGETHER, TOO.
QUAKES
DINNER'S READY, WILSON.

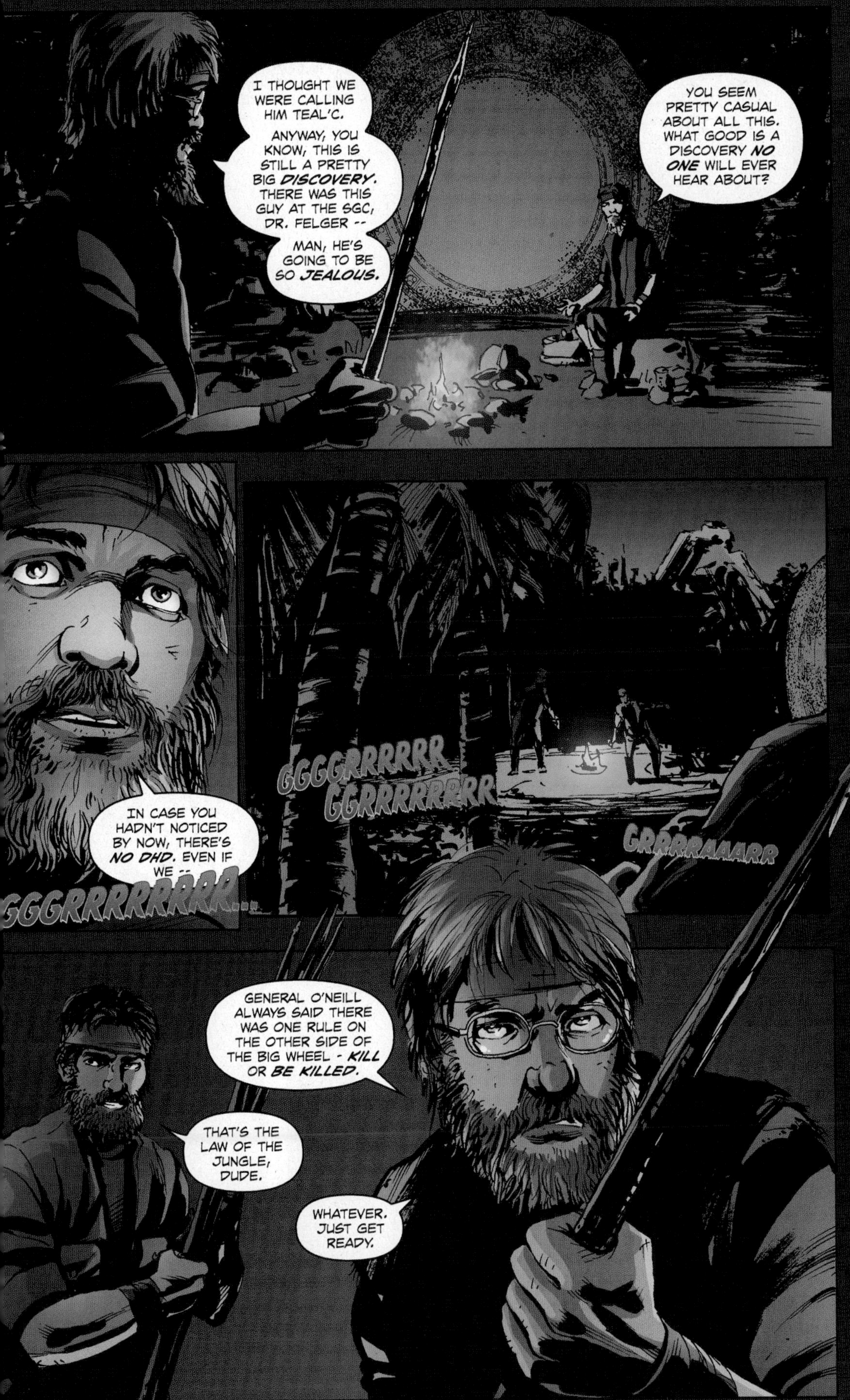
I THOUGHT WE WERE CALLING HIM TEAL'C.
ANYWAY, YOU KNOW, THIS IS STILL A PRETTY BIG *DISCOVERY*. THERE WAS THIS GUY AT THE SGC, DR. FELGER --
MAN, HE'S GOING TO BE SO *JEALOUS*.
YOU SEEM PRETTY CASUAL ABOUT ALL THIS. WHAT GOOD IS A DISCOVERY *NO ONE* WILL EVER HEAR ABOUT?
IN CASE YOU HADN'T NOTICED BY NOW, THERE'S *NO DHD*. EVEN IF WE --
GGGRRRRRRRRR...
GGGGRRRRRR
GGRRRRRRRR
GRRRRAAARR
GENERAL O'NEILL ALWAYS SAID THERE WAS ONE RULE ON THE OTHER SIDE OF THE BIG WHEEL - *KILL* OR *BE KILLED*.
THAT'S THE LAW OF THE JUNGLE, DUDE.
WHATEVER. JUST GET READY.

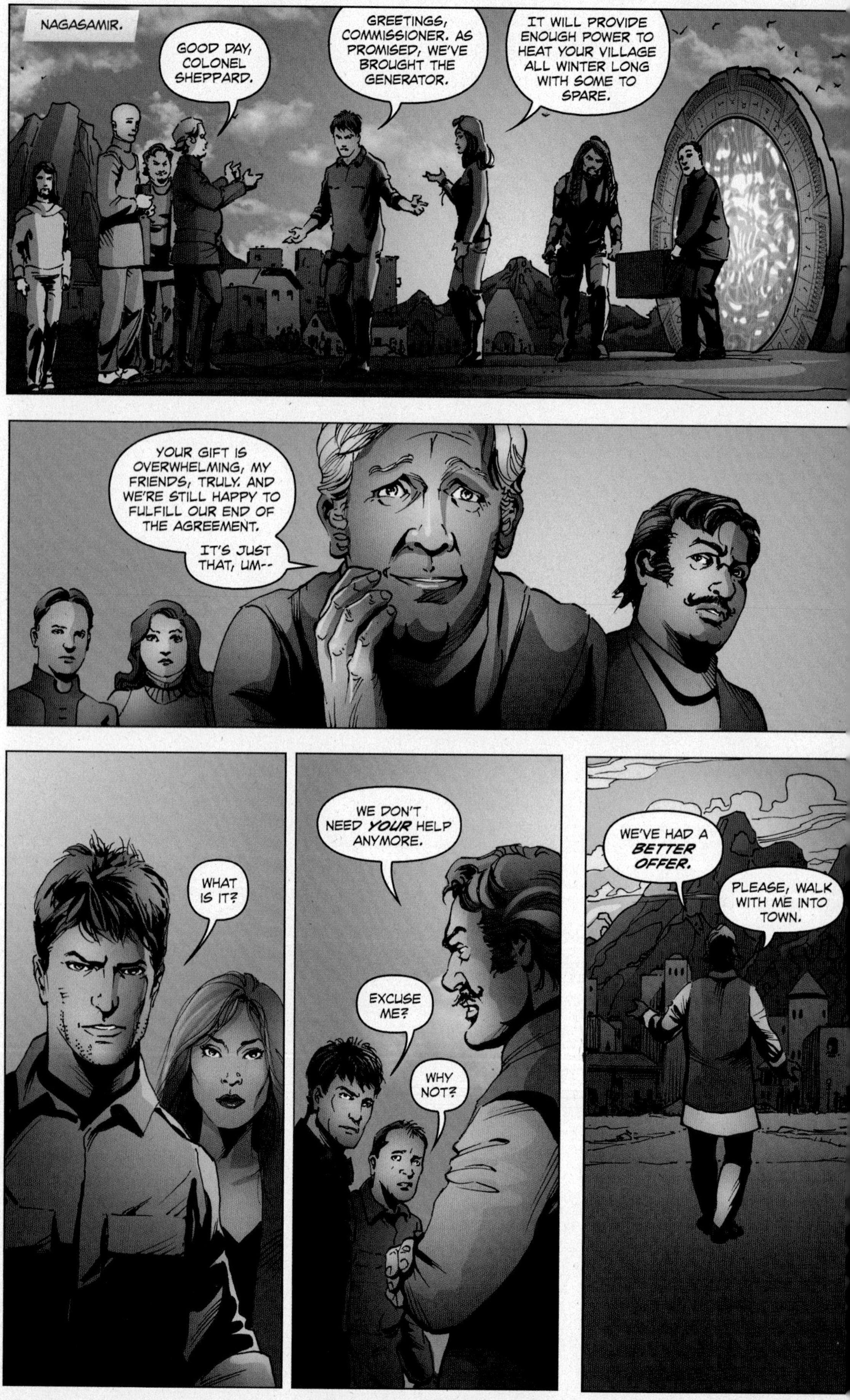
NAGASAMIR.
GOOD DAY, COLONEL SHEPPARD.
GREETINGS, COMMISSIONER. AS PROMISED, WE'VE BROUGHT THE GENERATOR.
IT WILL PROVIDE ENOUGH POWER TO HEAT YOUR VILLAGE ALL WINTER LONG WITH SOME TO SPARE.
YOUR GIFT IS OVERWHELMING, MY FRIENDS, TRULY. AND WE'RE STILL HAPPY TO FULFILL OUR END OF THE AGREEMENT.
IT'S JUST THAT, UM--
WHAT IS IT?
WE DON'T NEED *YOUR* HELP ANYMORE.
EXCUSE ME?
WHY NOT?
WE'VE HAD A ***BETTER OFFER.***
PLEASE, WALK WITH ME INTO TOWN.

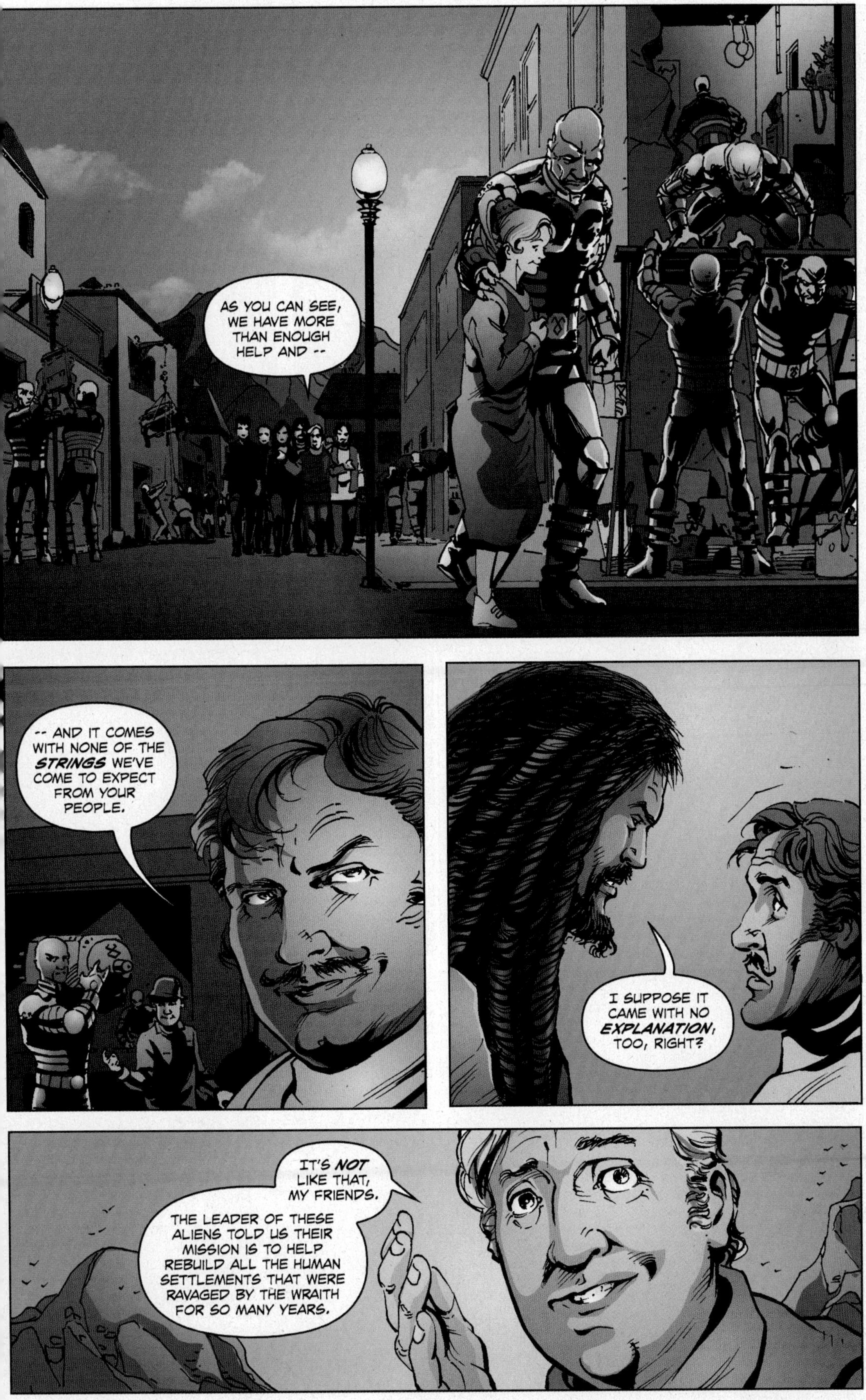
AS YOU CAN SEE, WE HAVE MORE THAN ENOUGH HELP AND --
-- AND IT COMES WITH NONE OF THE STRINGS WE'VE COME TO EXPECT FROM YOUR PEOPLE.
I SUPPOSE IT CAME WITH NO EXPLANATION, TOO, RIGHT?
IT'S NOT LIKE THAT, MY FRIENDS.
THE LEADER OF THESE ALIENS TOLD US THEIR MISSION IS TO HELP REBUILD ALL THE HUMAN SETTLEMENTS THAT WERE RAVAGED BY THE WRAITH FOR SO MANY YEARS.

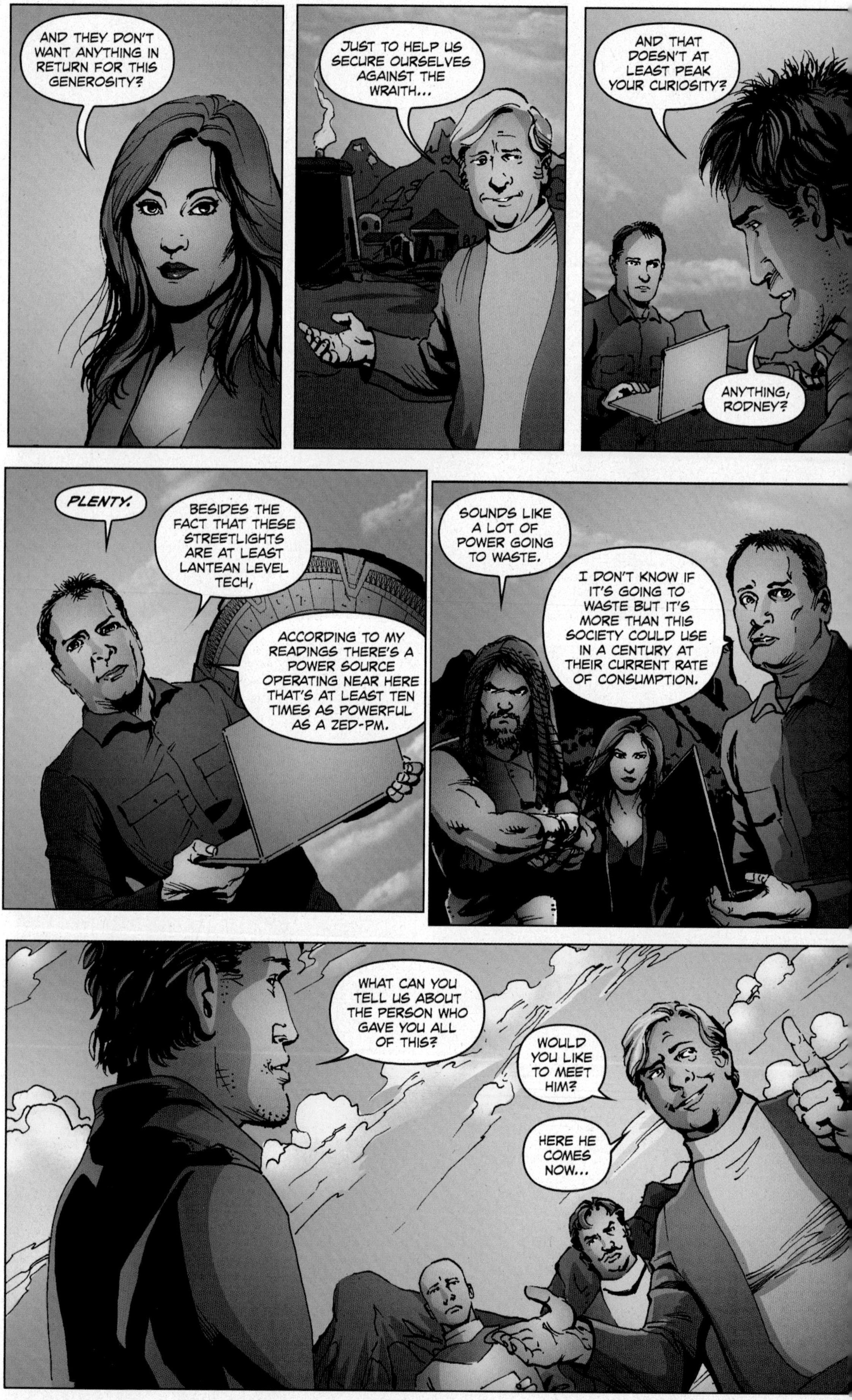
AND THEY DON'T WANT ANYTHING IN RETURN FOR THIS GENEROSITY?
JUST TO HELP US SECURE OURSELVES AGAINST THE WRAITH...
AND THAT DOESN'T AT LEAST PEAK YOUR CURIOSITY?
ANYTHING, RODNEY?
PLENTY.
BESIDES THE FACT THAT THESE STREETLIGHTS ARE AT LEAST LANTEAN LEVEL TECH,
ACCORDING TO MY READINGS THERE'S A POWER SOURCE OPERATING NEAR HERE THAT'S AT LEAST TEN TIMES AS POWERFUL AS A ZED-PM.
SOUNDS LIKE A LOT OF POWER GOING TO WASTE.
I DON'T KNOW IF IT'S GOING TO WASTE BUT IT'S MORE THAN THIS SOCIETY COULD USE IN A CENTURY AT THEIR CURRENT RATE OF CONSUMPTION.
WHAT CAN YOU TELL US ABOUT THE PERSON WHO GAVE YOU ALL OF THIS?
WOULD YOU LIKE TO MEET HIM?
HERE HE COMES NOW...

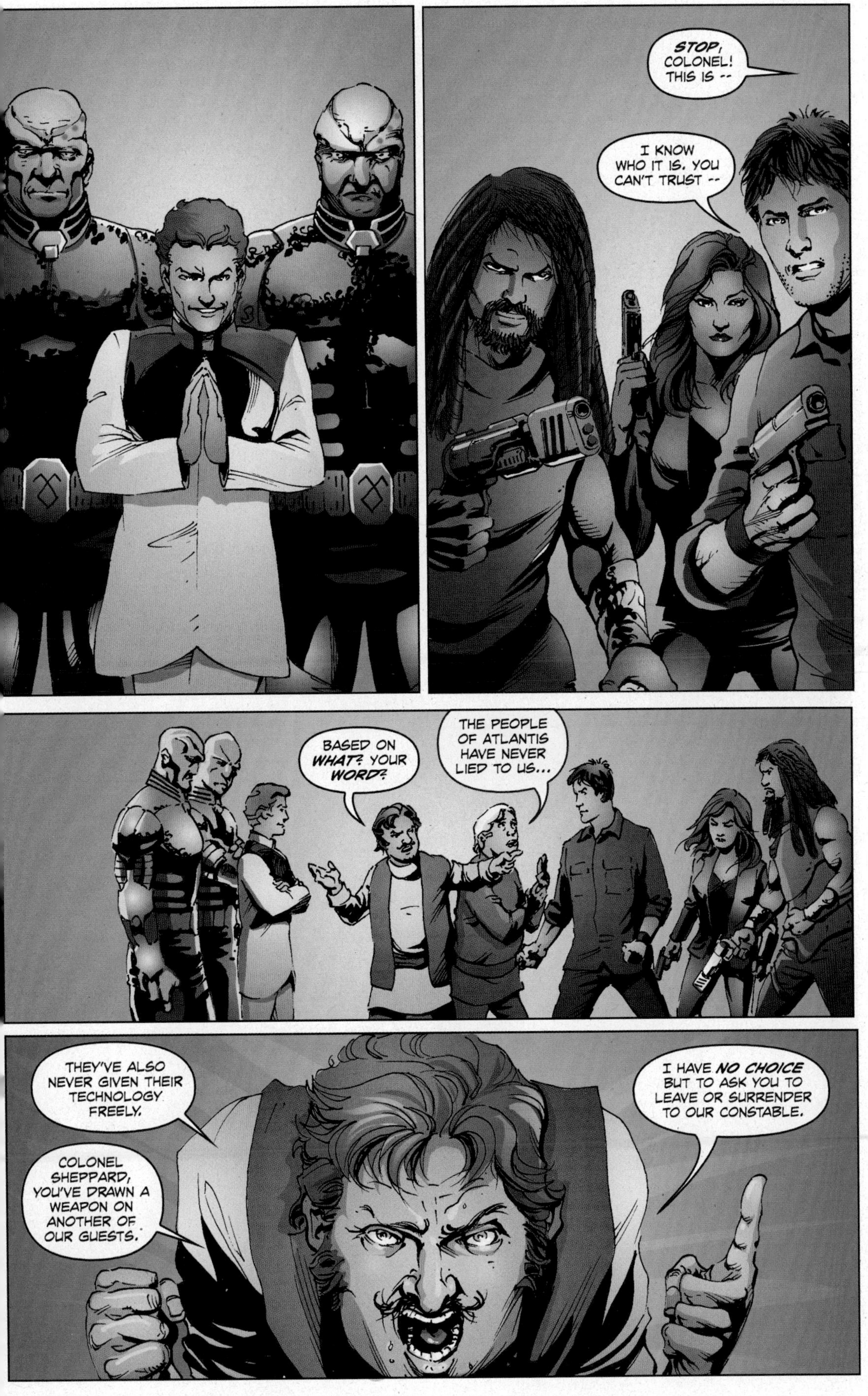
STOP, COLONEL! THIS IS --
I KNOW WHO IT IS. YOU CAN'T TRUST --
BASED ON WHAT? YOUR WORD?
THE PEOPLE OF ATLANTIS HAVE NEVER LIED TO US...
THEY'VE ALSO NEVER GIVEN THEIR TECHNOLOGY FREELY.
COLONEL SHEPPARD, YOU'VE DRAWN A WEAPON ON ANOTHER OF OUR GUESTS.
I HAVE NO CHOICE BUT TO ASK YOU TO LEAVE OR SURRENDER TO OUR CONSTABLE.

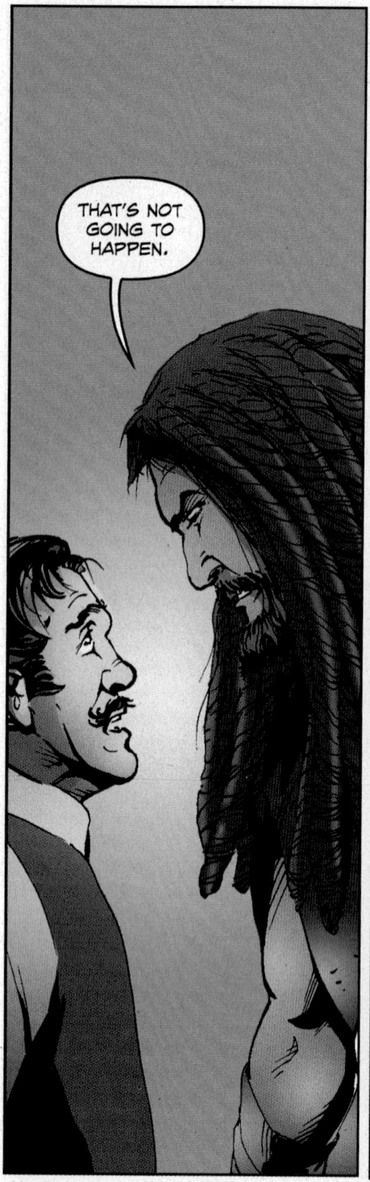
THAT'S NOT GOING TO HAPPEN.

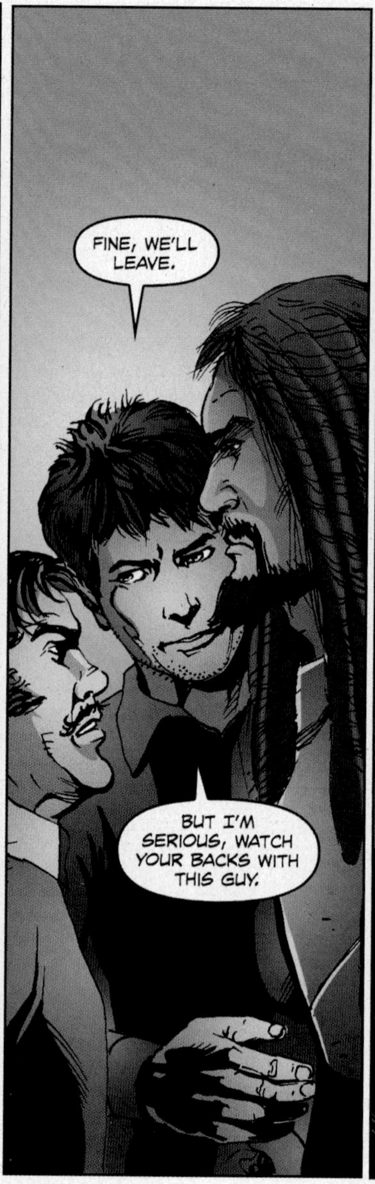
FINE, WE'LL LEAVE.
BUT I'M SERIOUS, WATCH YOUR BACKS WITH THIS GUY.

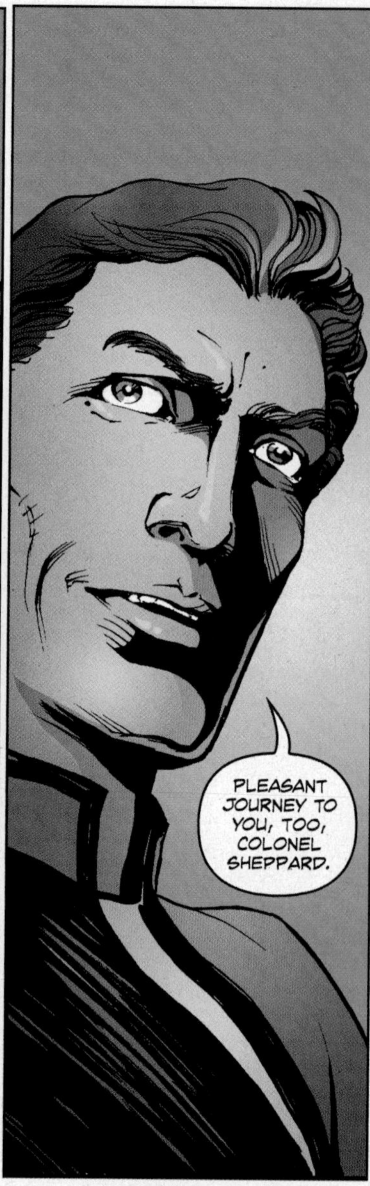
PLEASANT JOURNEY TO YOU, TOO, COLONEL SHEPPARD.

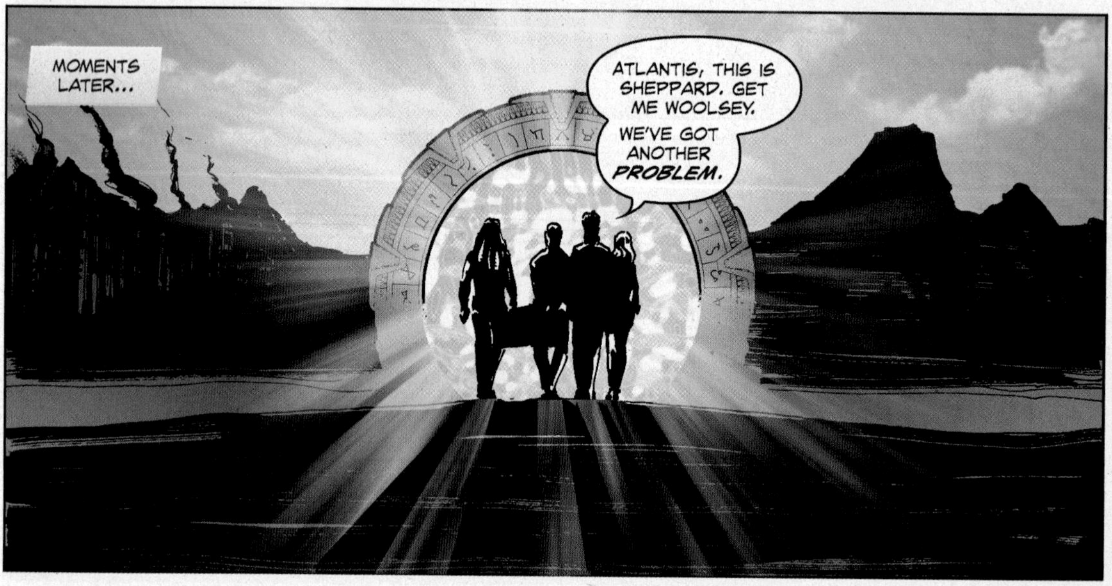
MOMENTS LATER...
ATLANTIS, THIS IS SHEPPARD. GET ME WOOLSEY.
WE'VE GOT ANOTHER *PROBLEM*.

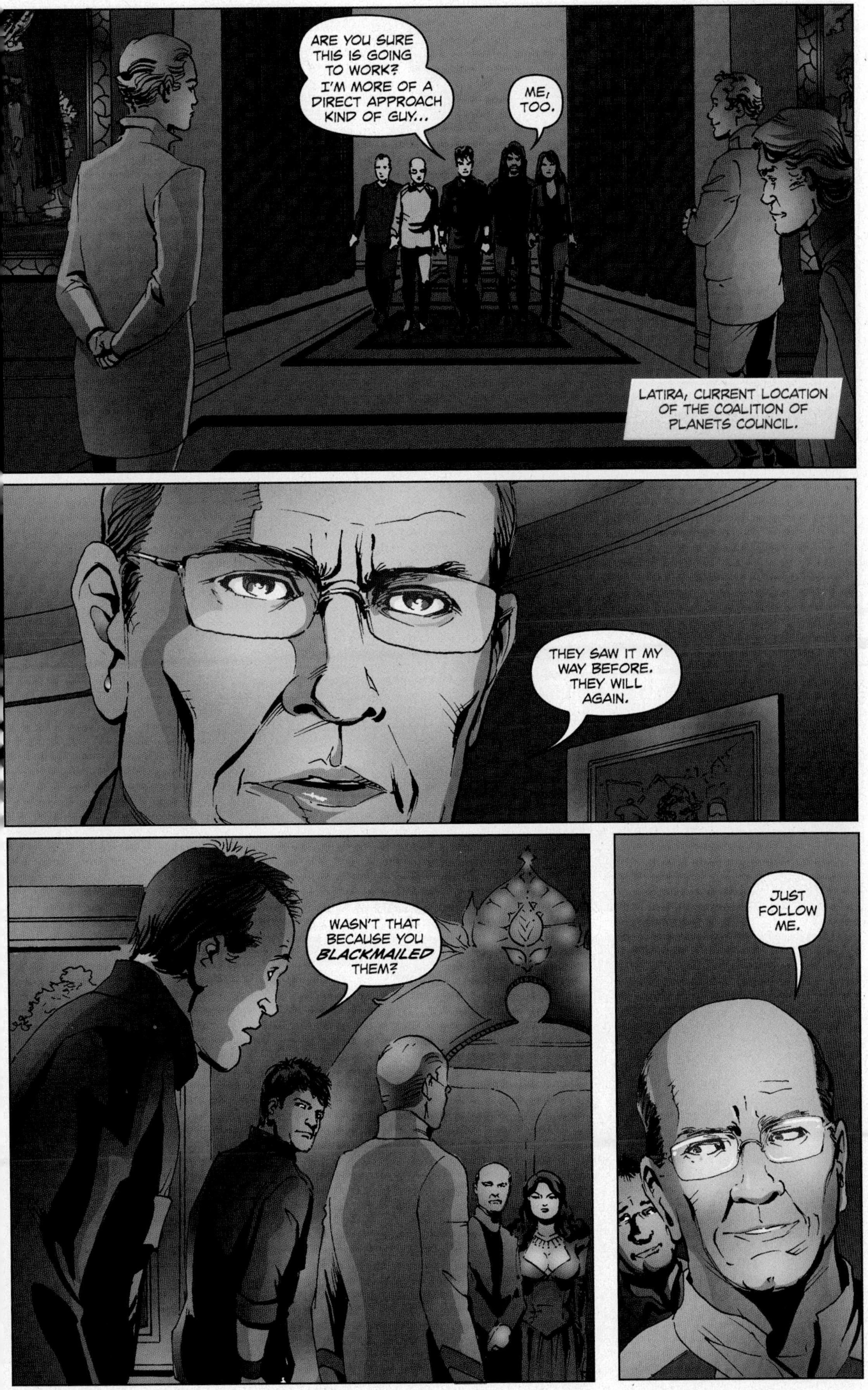

ARE YOU SURE THIS IS GOING TO WORK? I'M MORE OF A DIRECT APPROACH KIND OF GUY...
ME, TOO.
LATIRA, CURRENT LOCATION OF THE COALITION OF PLANETS COUNCIL.
THEY SAW IT MY WAY BEFORE. THEY WILL AGAIN.
WASN'T THAT BECAUSE YOU *BLACKMAILED* THEM?
JUST FOLLOW ME.

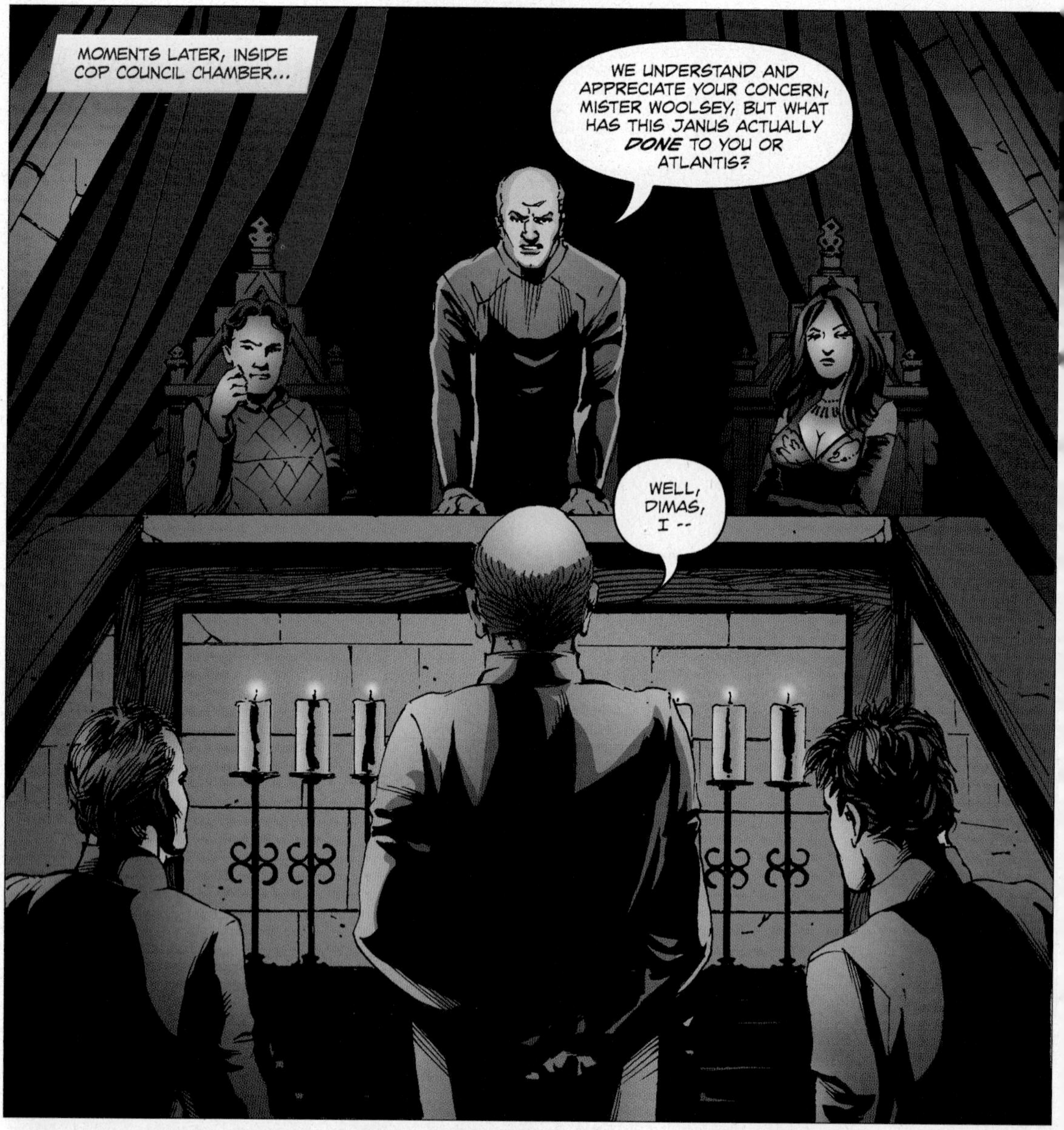
MOMENTS LATER, INSIDE COP COUNCIL CHAMBER...
WE UNDERSTAND AND APPRECIATE YOUR CONCERN, MISTER WOOLSEY, BUT WHAT HAS THIS JANUS ACTUALLY *DONE* TO YOU OR ATLANTIS?
WELL, DIMAS, I --

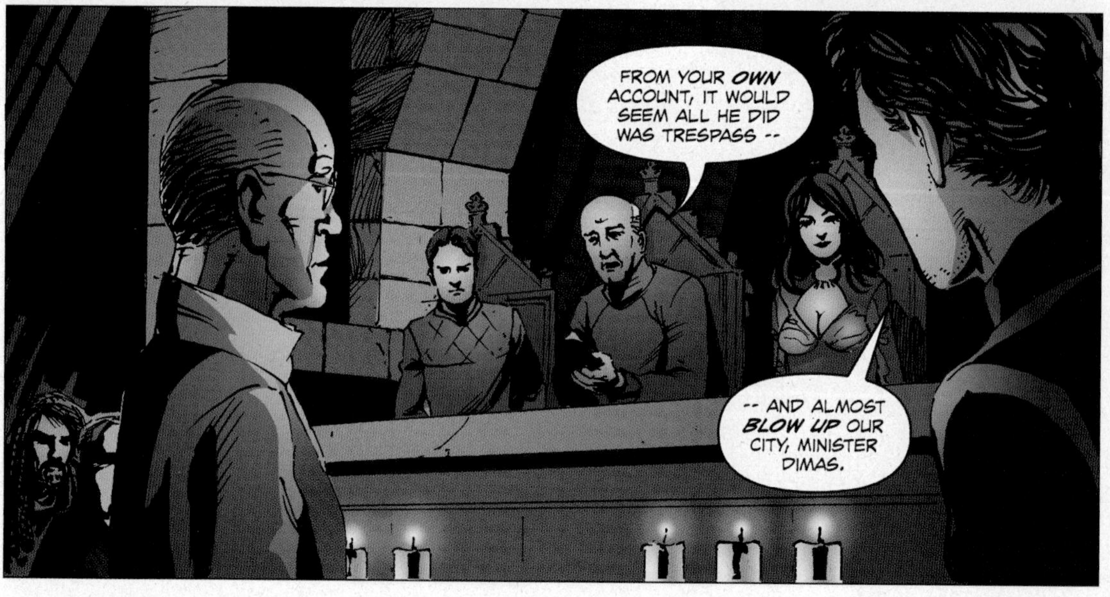
FROM YOUR *OWN* ACCOUNT, IT WOULD SEEM ALL HE DID WAS TRESPASS --
-- AND ALMOST *BLOW UP* OUR CITY, MINISTER DIMAS.

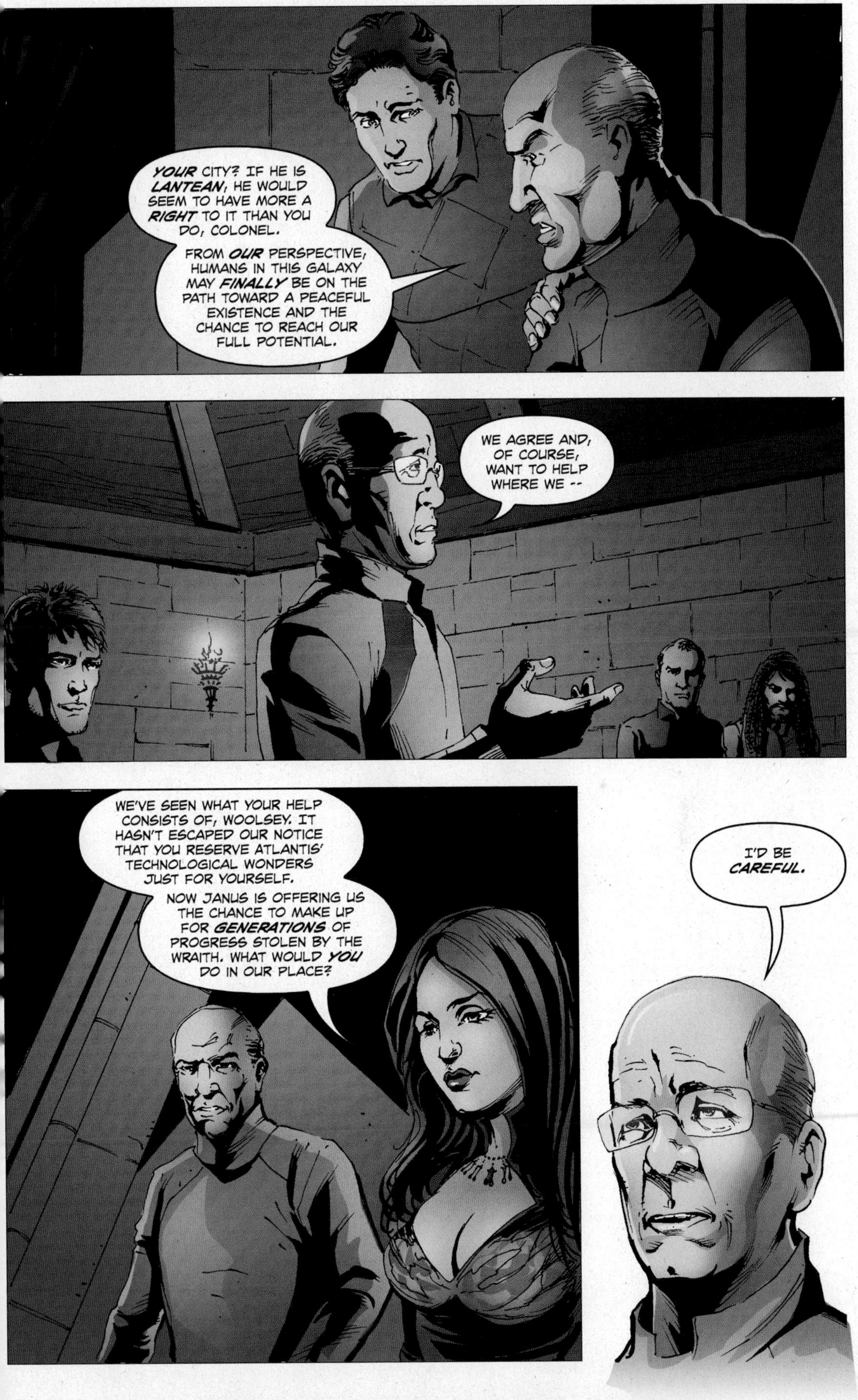
YOUR CITY? IF HE IS LANTEAN, HE WOULD SEEM TO HAVE MORE A RIGHT TO IT THAN YOU DO, COLONEL.
FROM OUR PERSPECTIVE, HUMANS IN THIS GALAXY MAY FINALLY BE ON THE PATH TOWARD A PEACEFUL EXISTENCE AND THE CHANCE TO REACH OUR FULL POTENTIAL.
WE AGREE AND, OF COURSE, WANT TO HELP WHERE WE --
WE'VE SEEN WHAT YOUR HELP CONSISTS OF, WOOLSEY. IT HASN'T ESCAPED OUR NOTICE THAT YOU RESERVE ATLANTIS' TECHNOLOGICAL WONDERS JUST FOR YOURSELF.
NOW JANUS IS OFFERING US THE CHANCE TO MAKE UP FOR GENERATIONS OF PROGRESS STOLEN BY THE WRAITH. WHAT WOULD YOU DO IN OUR PLACE?
I'D BE CAREFUL.

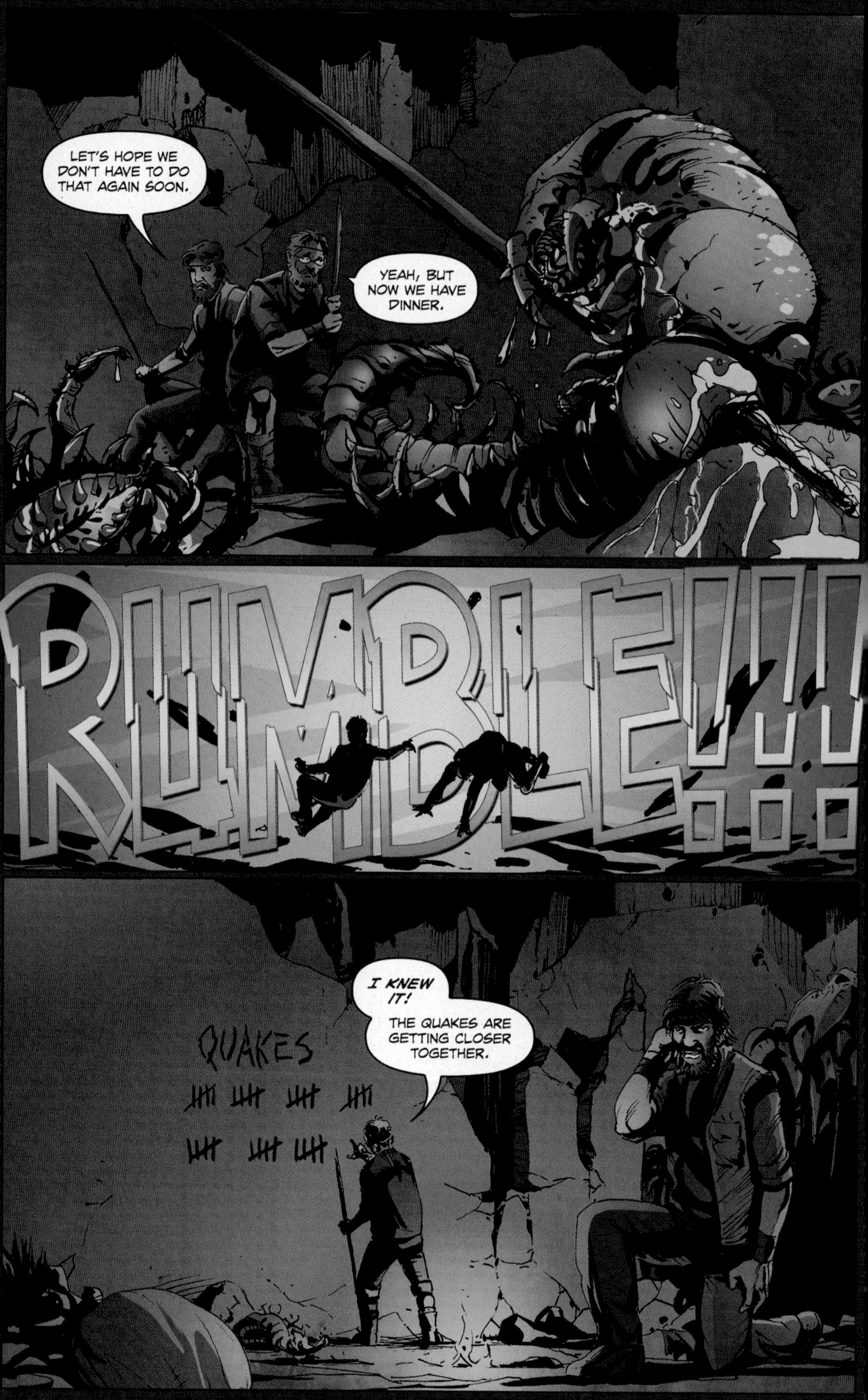
LET'S HOPE WE DON'T HAVE TO DO THAT AGAIN SOON.
YEAH, BUT NOW WE HAVE DINNER.
RUMBLE!!!
RUMBLE...
QUAKES
I KNEW IT!
THE QUAKES ARE GETTING CLOSER TOGETHER.

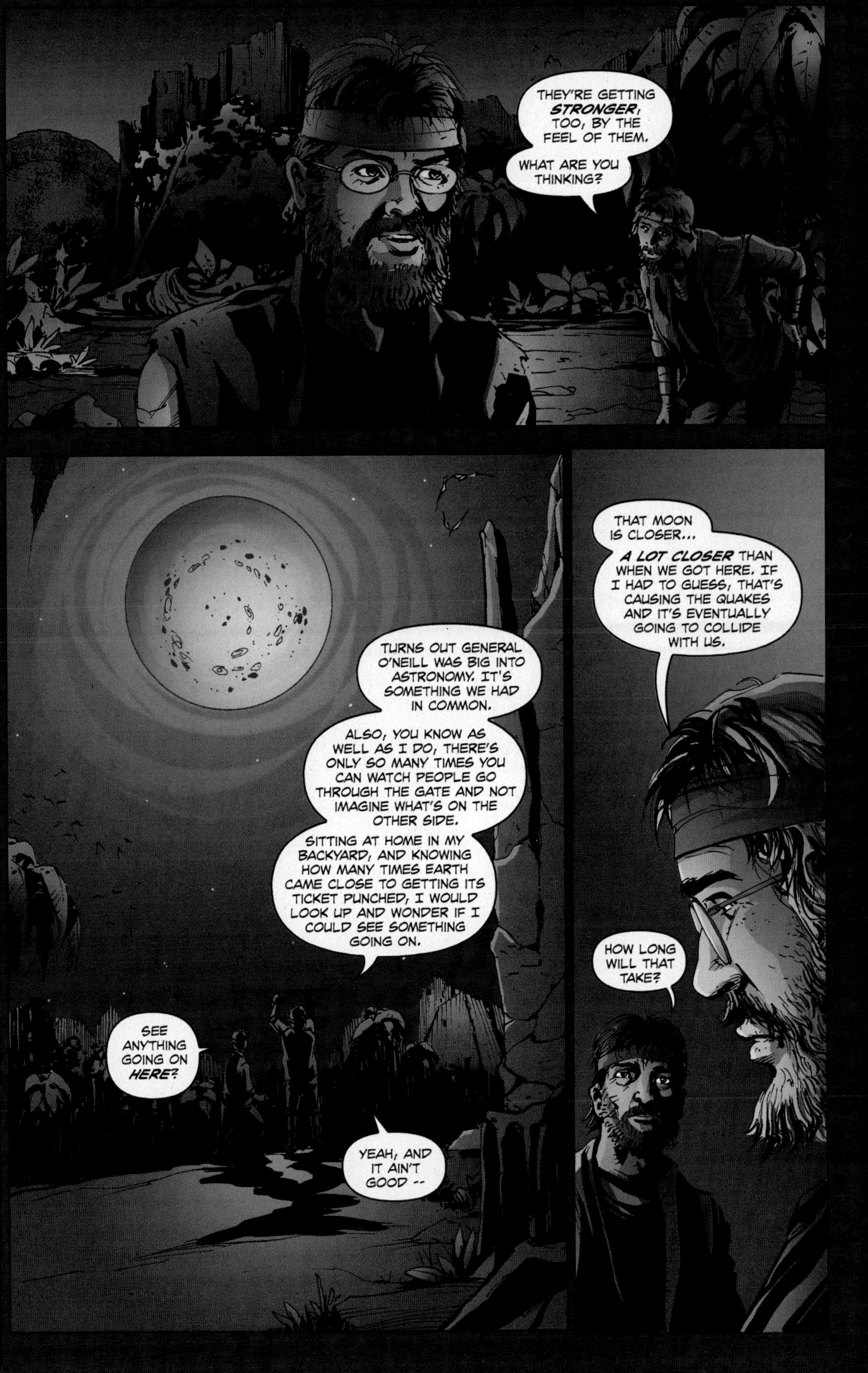

THEY'RE GETTING *STRONGER*, TOO, BY THE FEEL OF THEM.
WHAT ARE YOU THINKING?
TURNS OUT GENERAL O'NEILL WAS BIG INTO ASTRONOMY. IT'S SOMETHING WE HAD IN COMMON.
ALSO, YOU KNOW AS WELL AS I DO, THERE'S ONLY SO MANY TIMES YOU CAN WATCH PEOPLE GO THROUGH THE GATE AND NOT IMAGINE WHAT'S ON THE OTHER SIDE.
SITTING AT HOME IN MY BACKYARD, AND KNOWING HOW MANY TIMES EARTH CAME CLOSE TO GETTING ITS TICKET PUNCHED, I WOULD LOOK UP AND WONDER IF I COULD SEE SOMETHING GOING ON.
SEE ANYTHING GOING ON *HERE*?
YEAH, AND IT AIN'T GOOD --
THAT MOON IS CLOSER... *A LOT CLOSER* THAN WHEN WE GOT HERE. IF I HAD TO GUESS, THAT'S CAUSING THE QUAKES AND IT'S EVENTUALLY GOING TO COLLIDE WITH US.
HOW LONG WILL THAT TAKE?

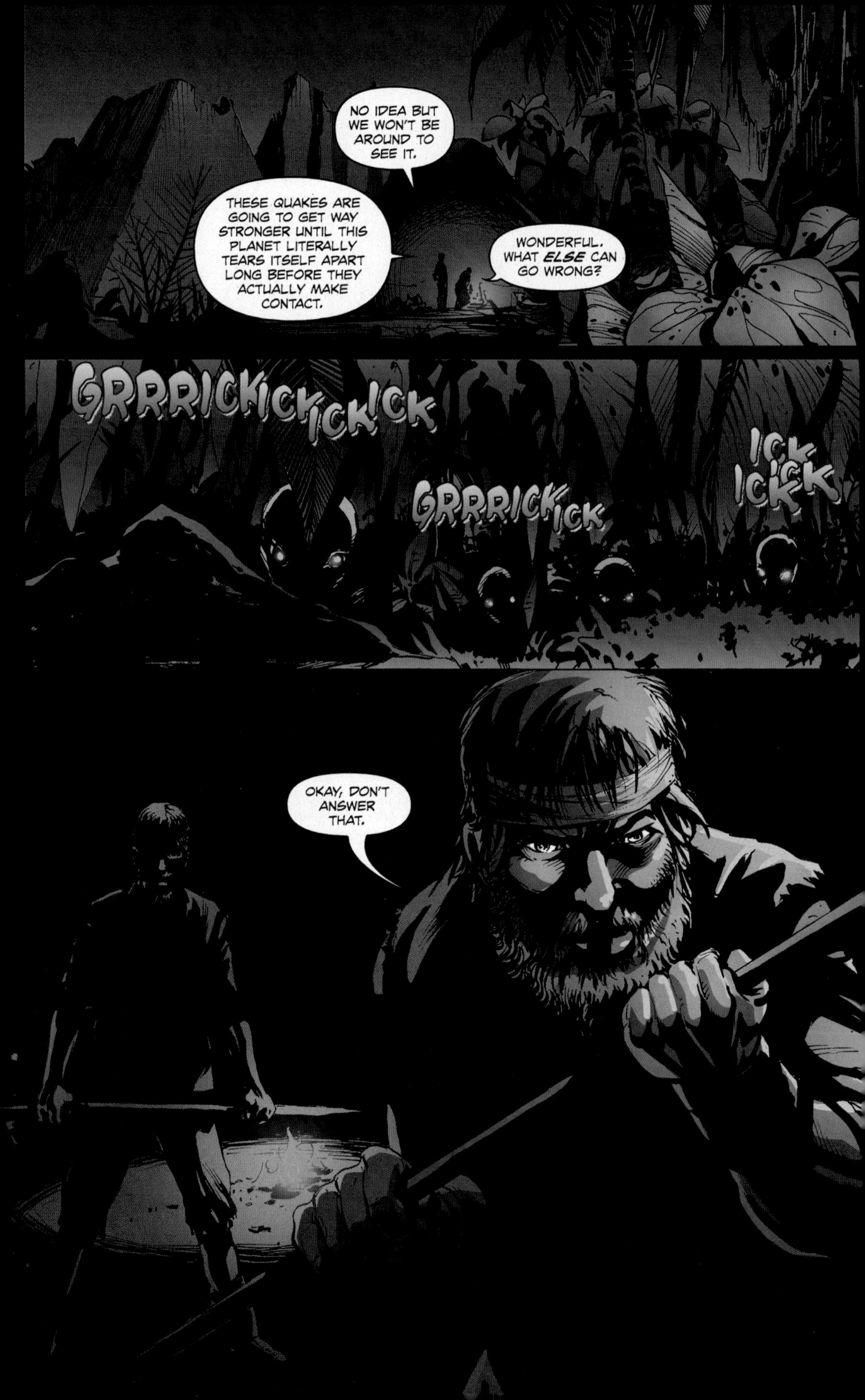
THESE QUAKES ARE GOING TO GET WAY STRONGER UNTIL THIS PLANET LITERALLY TEARS ITSELF APART LONG BEFORE THEY ACTUALLY MAKE CONTACT.
NO IDEA BUT WE WON'T BE AROUND TO SEE IT.
WONDERFUL. WHAT ELSE CAN GO WRONG?
GRRRICKICKICK!CK
GRRRICKICK
ICKICK ICK
OKAY, DON'T ANSWER THAT.

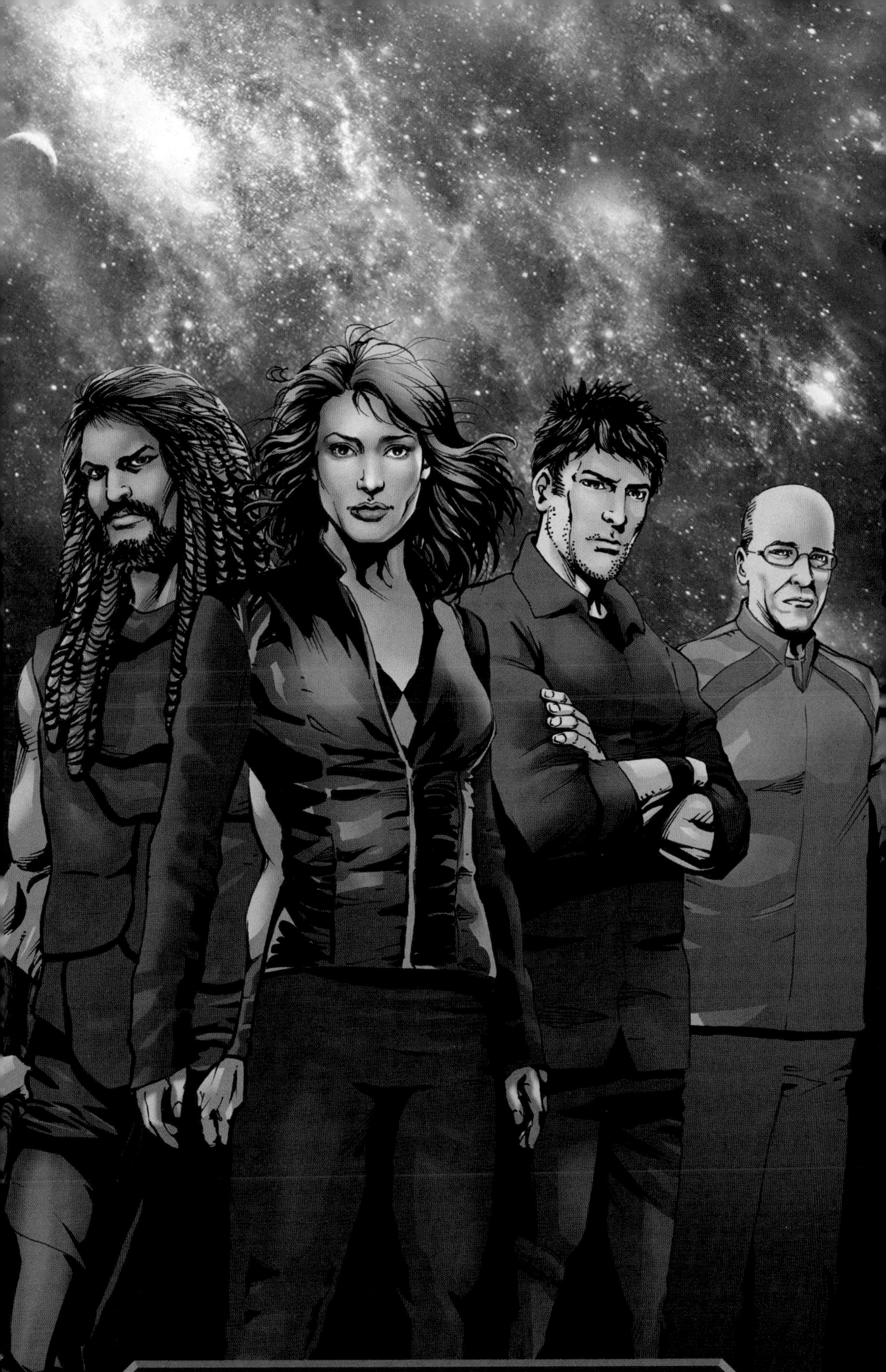

COVER GALLERY

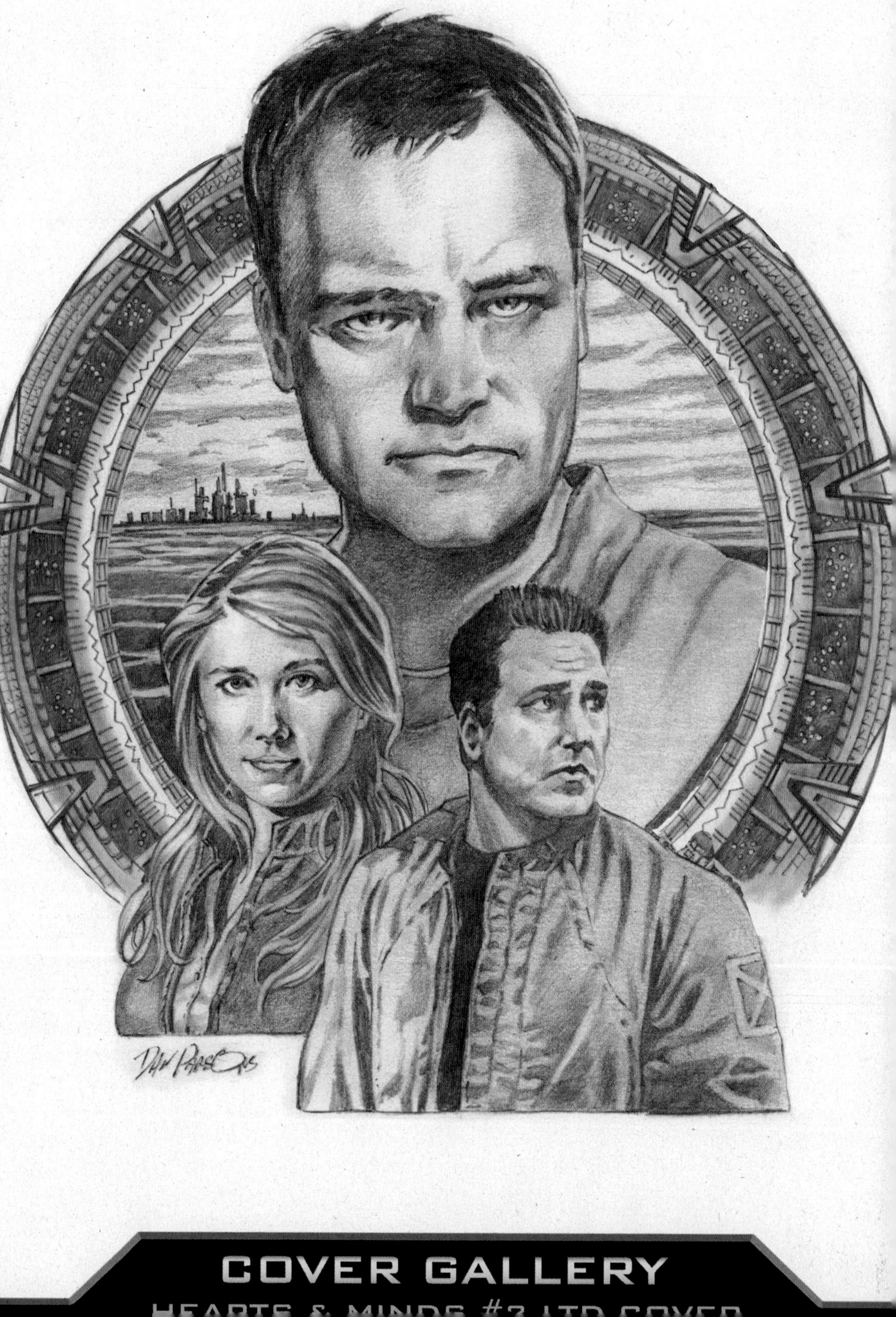

COVER GALLERY

HEARTS & MINDS #3 LTD COVER

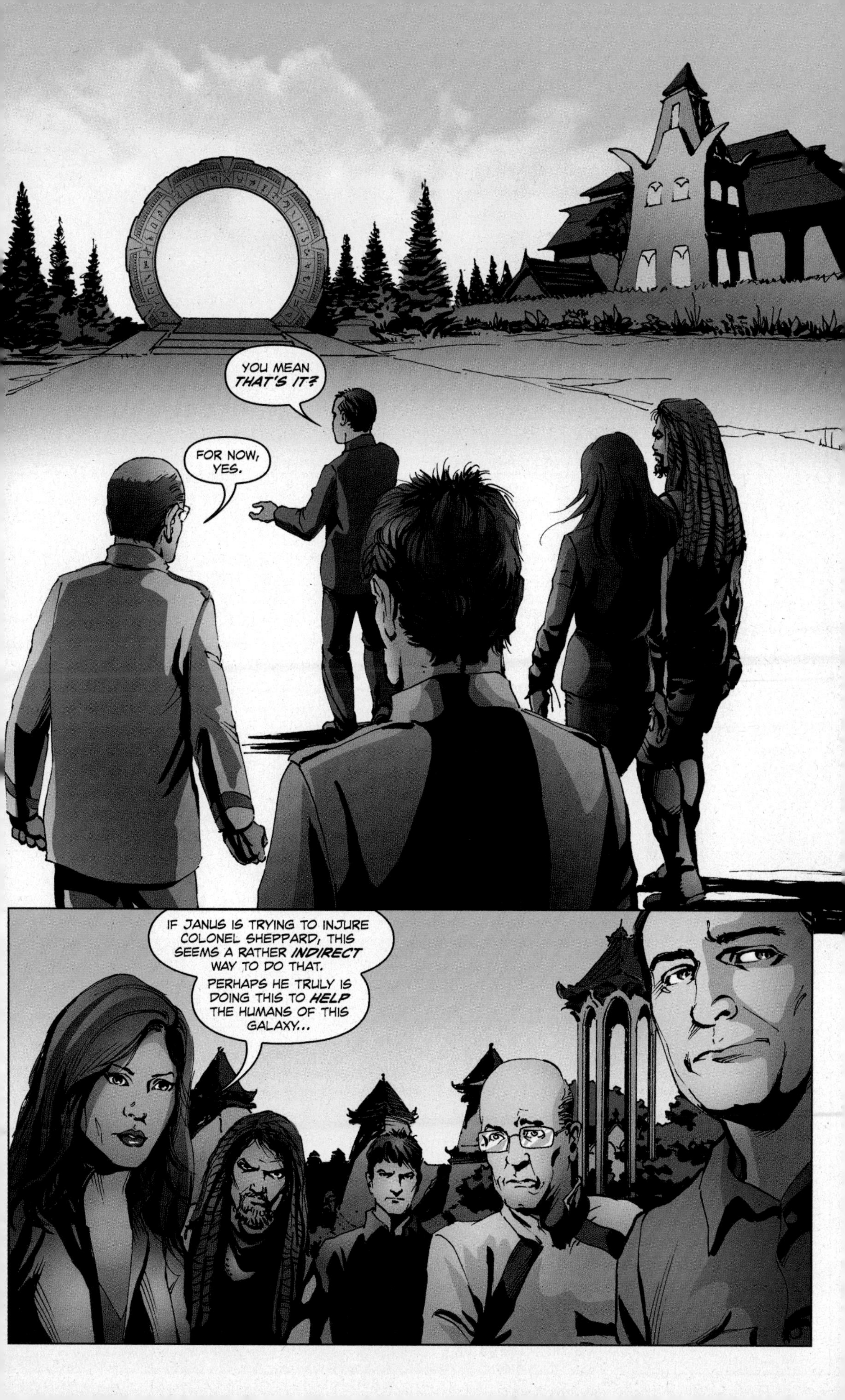
YOU MEAN *THAT'S IT?*
FOR NOW, YES.
IF JANUS IS TRYING TO INJURE COLONEL SHEPPARD, THIS SEEMS A RATHER *INDIRECT* WAY TO DO THAT.
PERHAPS HE TRULY IS DOING THIS TO *HELP* THE HUMANS OF THIS GALAXY...

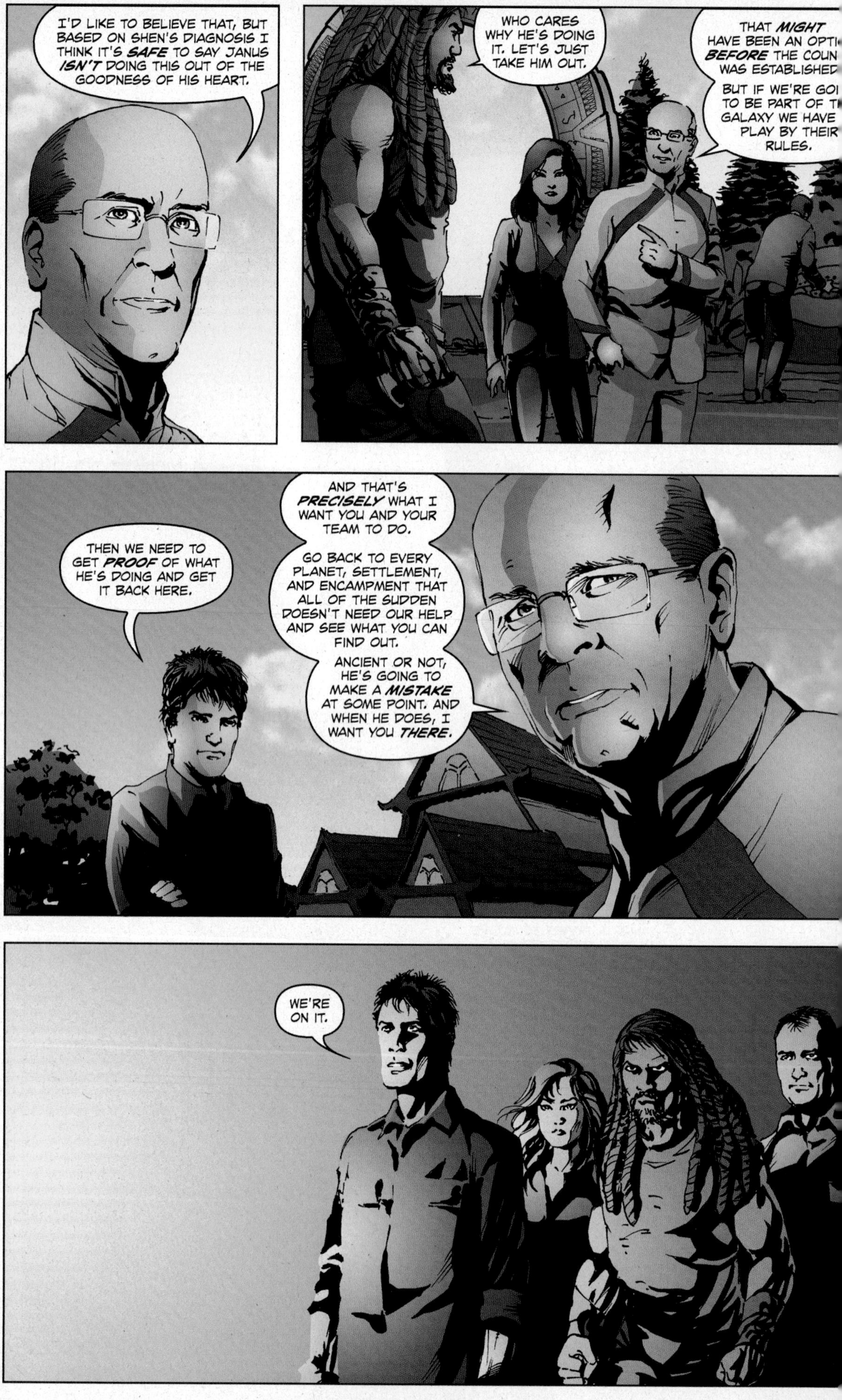
I'D LIKE TO BELIEVE THAT, BUT BASED ON SHEN'S DIAGNOSIS I THINK IT'S SAFE TO SAY JANUS ISN'T DOING THIS OUT OF THE GOODNESS OF HIS HEART.
WHO CARES WHY HE'S DOING IT. LET'S JUST TAKE HIM OUT.
THAT MIGHT HAVE BEEN AN OPTI BEFORE THE COUN WAS ESTABLISHED
BUT IF WE'RE GOI TO BE PART OF T GALAXY WE HAVE PLAY BY THEIR RULES.
THEN WE NEED TO GET PROOF OF WHAT HE'S DOING AND GET IT BACK HERE.
AND THAT'S PRECISELY WHAT I WANT YOU AND YOUR TEAM TO DO.
GO BACK TO EVERY PLANET, SETTLEMENT, AND ENCAMPMENT THAT ALL OF THE SUDDEN DOESN'T NEED OUR HELP AND SEE WHAT YOU CAN FIND OUT.
ANCIENT OR NOT, HE'S GOING TO MAKE A MISTAKE AT SOME POINT. AND WHEN HE DOES, I WANT YOU THERE.
WE'RE ON IT.

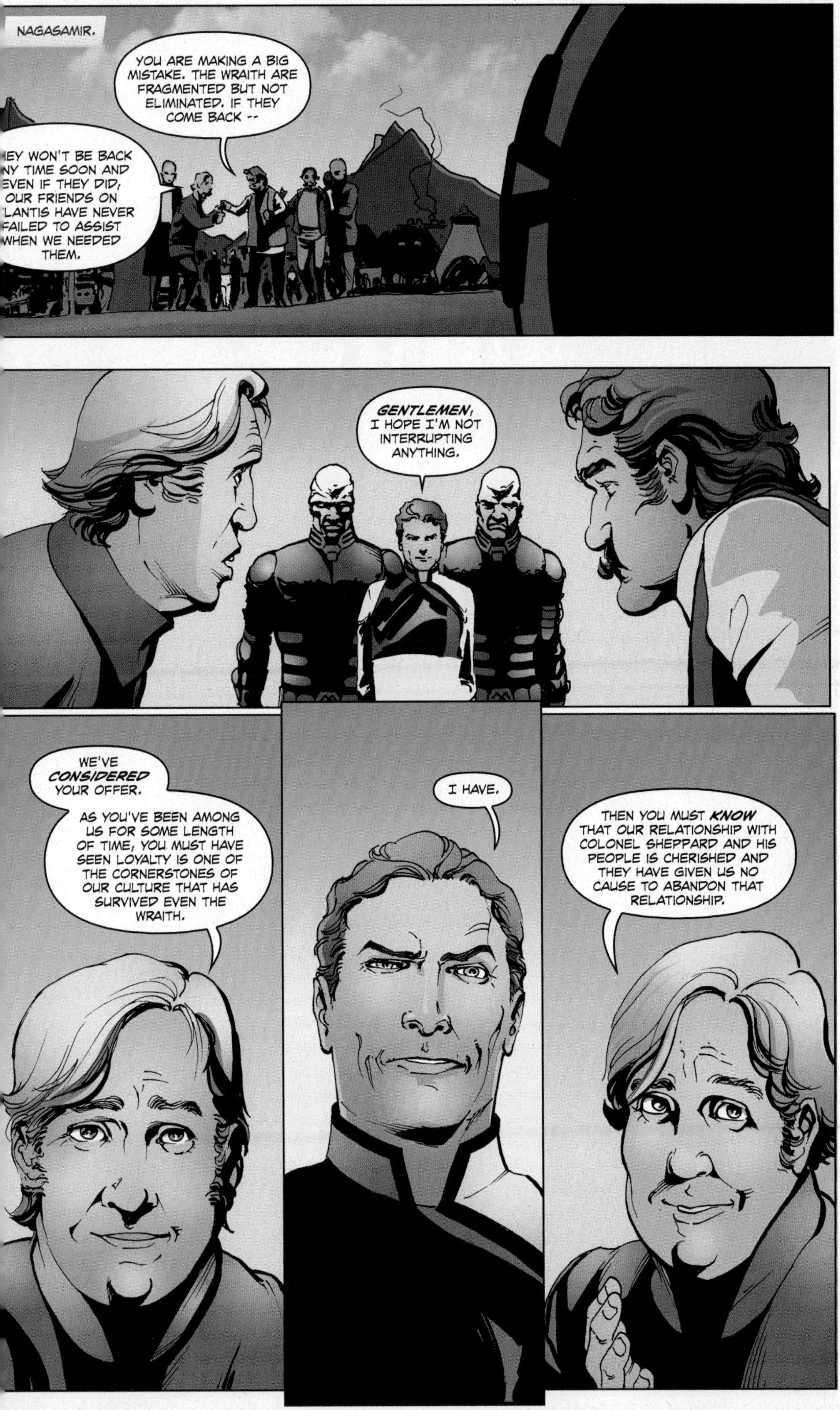

NAGASAMIR.
YOU ARE MAKING A BIG MISTAKE. THE WRAITH ARE FRAGMENTED BUT NOT ELIMINATED. IF THEY COME BACK --
HEY WON'T BE BACK NY TIME SOON AND EVEN IF THEY DID, OUR FRIENDS ON LANTIS HAVE NEVER FAILED TO ASSIST WHEN WE NEEDED THEM.
GENTLEMEN, I HOPE I'M NOT INTERRUPTING ANYTHING.
WE'VE CONSIDERED YOUR OFFER.
AS YOU'VE BEEN AMONG US FOR SOME LENGTH OF TIME, YOU MUST HAVE SEEN LOYALTY IS ONE OF THE CORNERSTONES OF OUR CULTURE THAT HAS SURVIVED EVEN THE WRAITH.
I HAVE.
THEN YOU MUST KNOW THAT OUR RELATIONSHIP WITH COLONEL SHEPPARD AND HIS PEOPLE IS CHERISHED AND THEY HAVE GIVEN US NO CAUSE TO ABANDON THAT RELATIONSHIP.

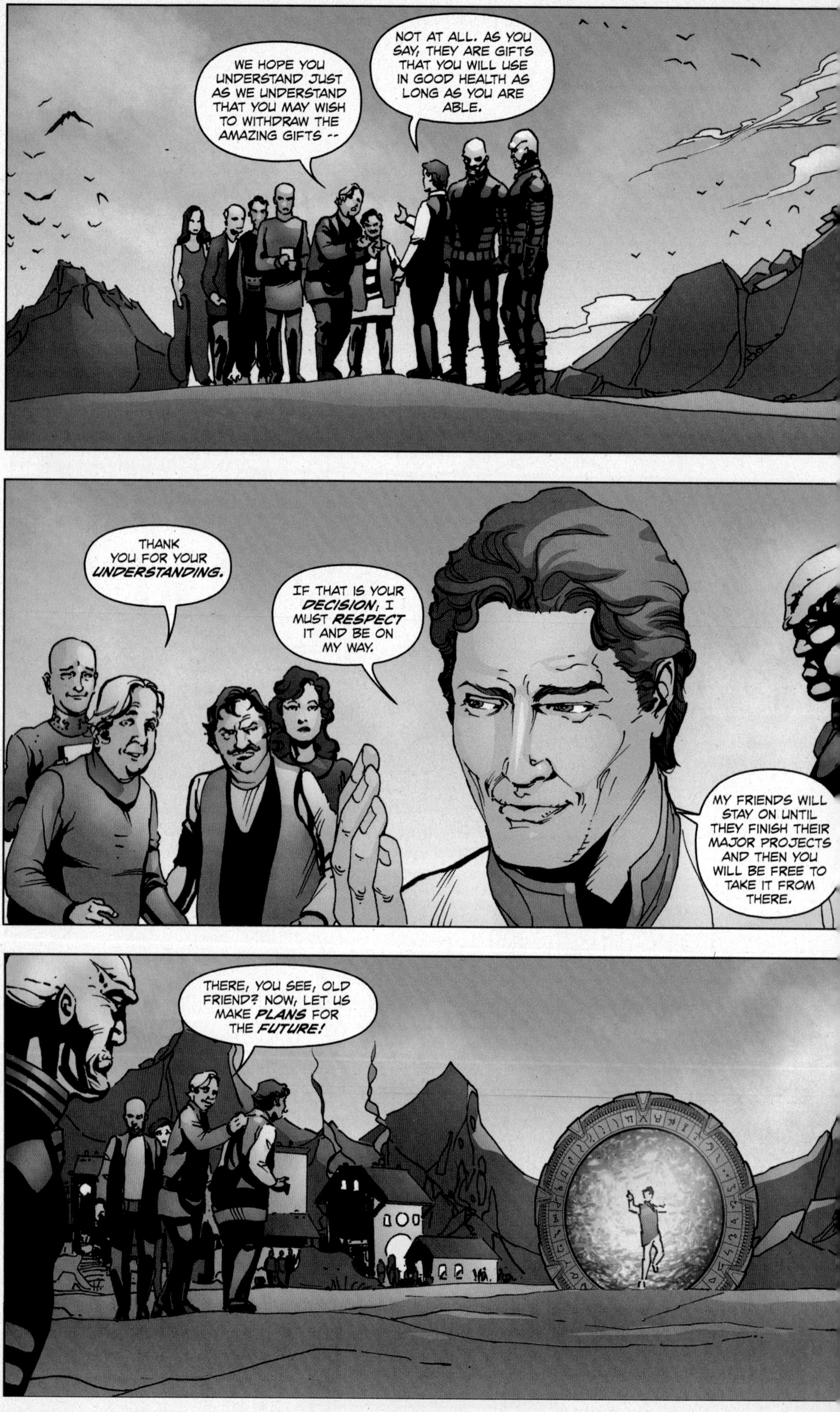

WE HOPE YOU UNDERSTAND JUST AS WE UNDERSTAND THAT YOU MAY WISH TO WITHDRAW THE AMAZING GIFTS --
NOT AT ALL. AS YOU SAY, THEY ARE GIFTS THAT YOU WILL USE IN GOOD HEALTH AS LONG AS YOU ARE ABLE.
THANK YOU FOR YOUR UNDERSTANDING.
IF THAT IS YOUR DECISION, I MUST RESPECT IT AND BE ON MY WAY.
MY FRIENDS WILL STAY ON UNTIL THEY FINISH THEIR MAJOR PROJECTS AND THEN YOU WILL BE FREE TO TAKE IT FROM THERE.
THERE, YOU SEE, OLD FRIEND? NOW, LET US MAKE PLANS FOR THE FUTURE!

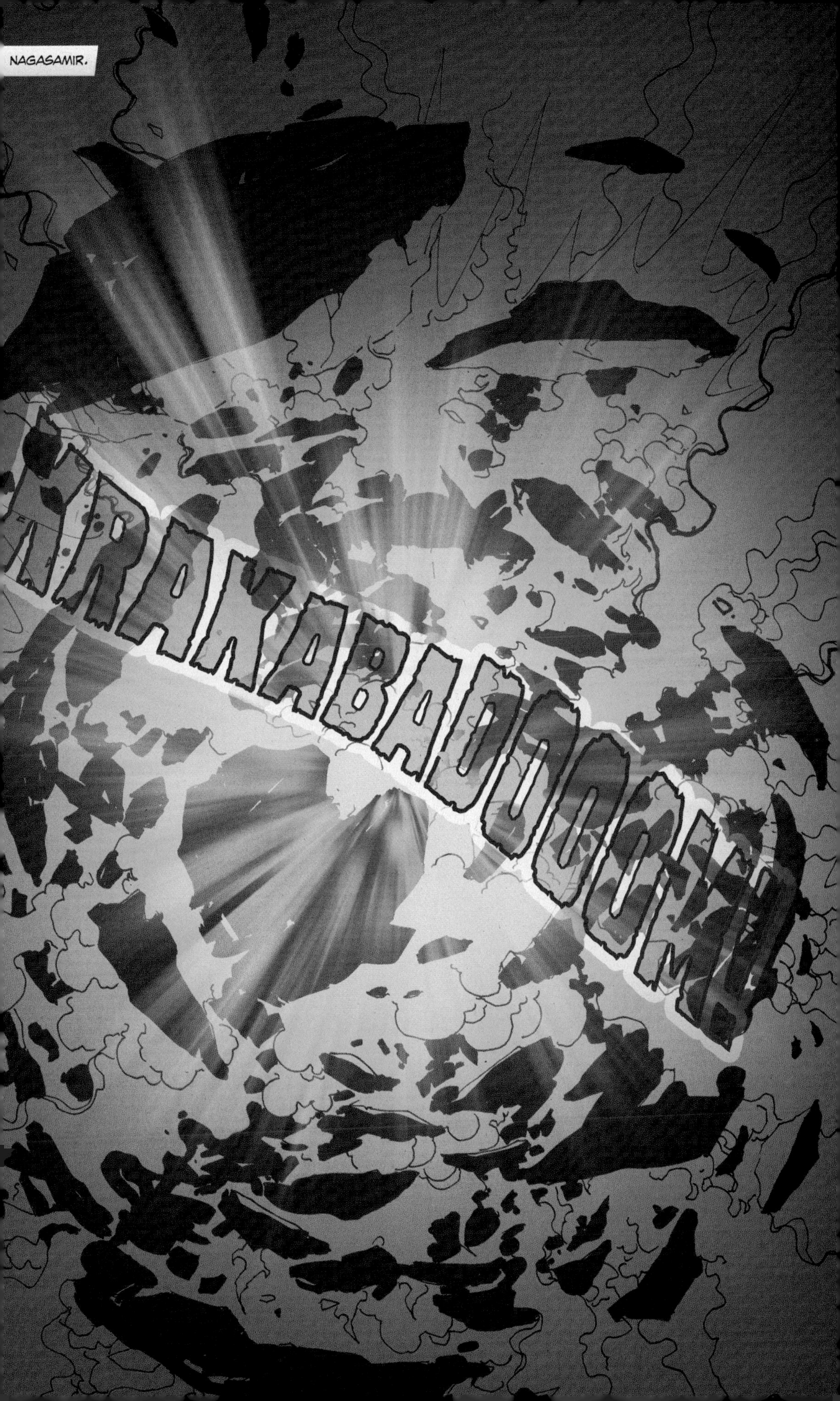
NAGASAMIR.
KRAKABADOOOM!

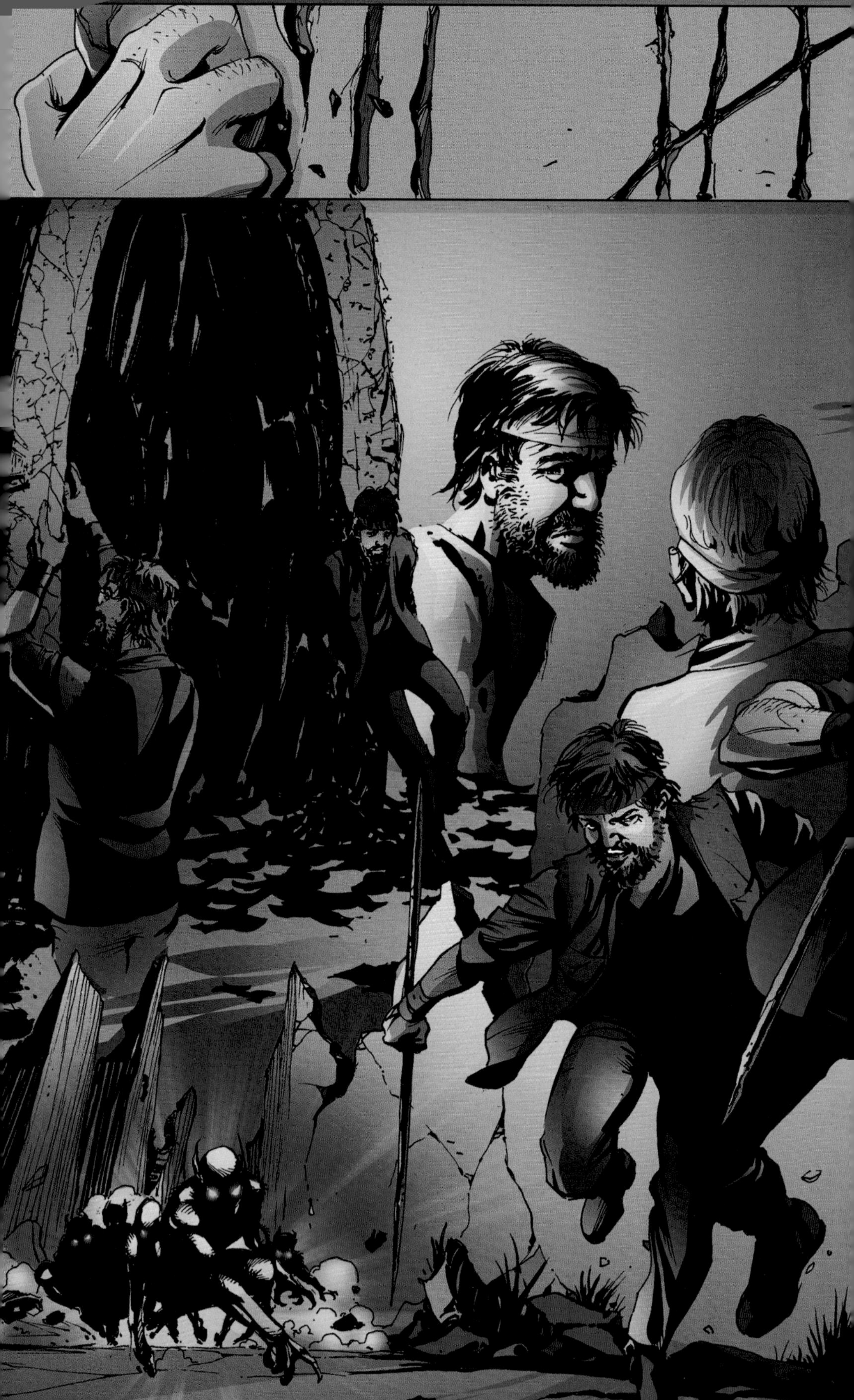

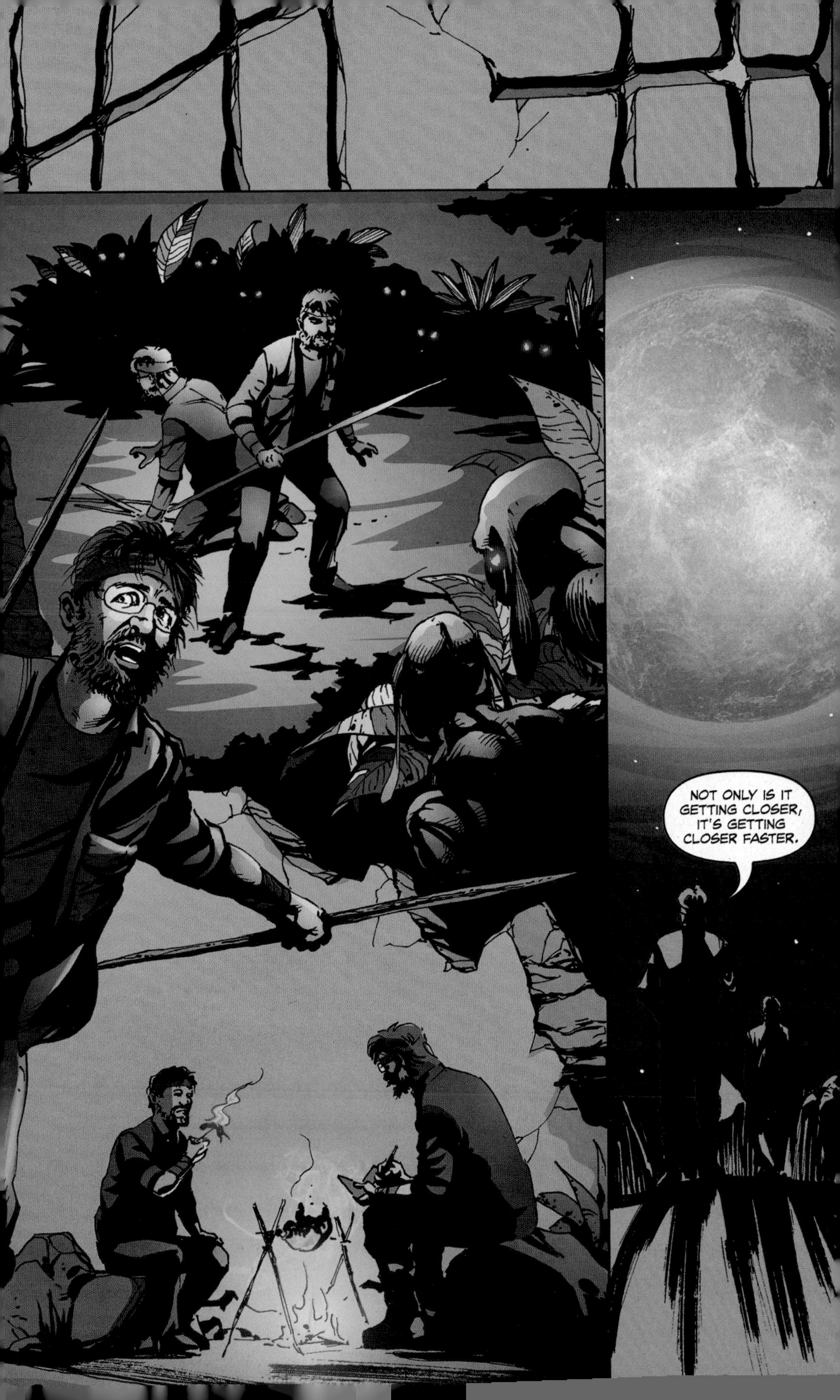
NOT ONLY IS IT GETTING CLOSER, IT'S GETTING CLOSER FASTER.

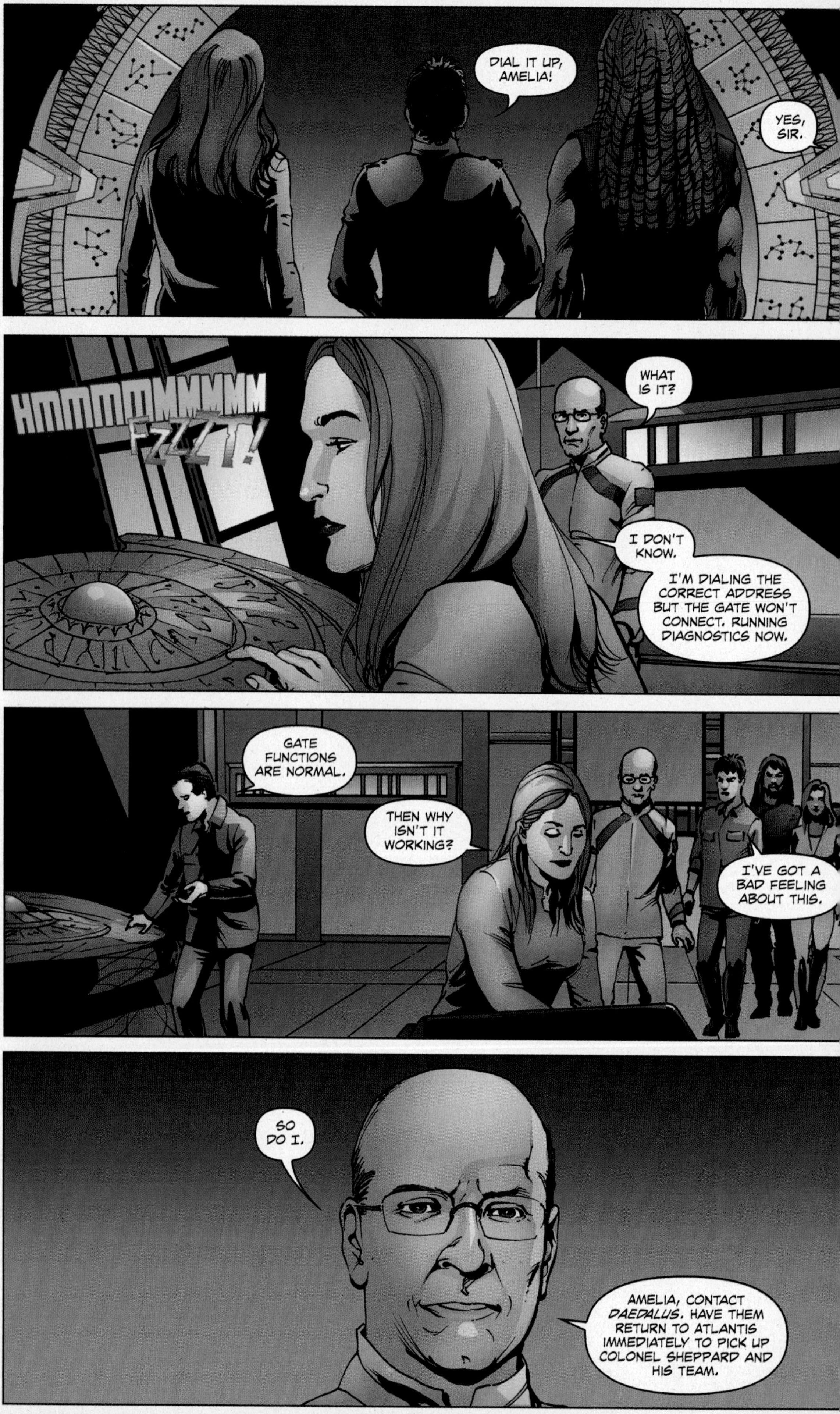
DIAL IT UP, AMELIA!
YES, SIR.
HMMMMMMMMM
FZZZT!
WHAT IS IT?
I DON'T KNOW.
I'M DIALING THE CORRECT ADDRESS BUT THE GATE WON'T CONNECT. RUNNING DIAGNOSTICS NOW.
GATE FUNCTIONS ARE NORMAL.
THEN WHY ISN'T IT WORKING?
I'VE GOT A BAD FEELING ABOUT THIS.
SO DO I.
AMELIA, CONTACT *DAEDALUS*. HAVE THEM RETURN TO ATLANTIS IMMEDIATELY TO PICK UP COLONEL SHEPPARD AND HIS TEAM.

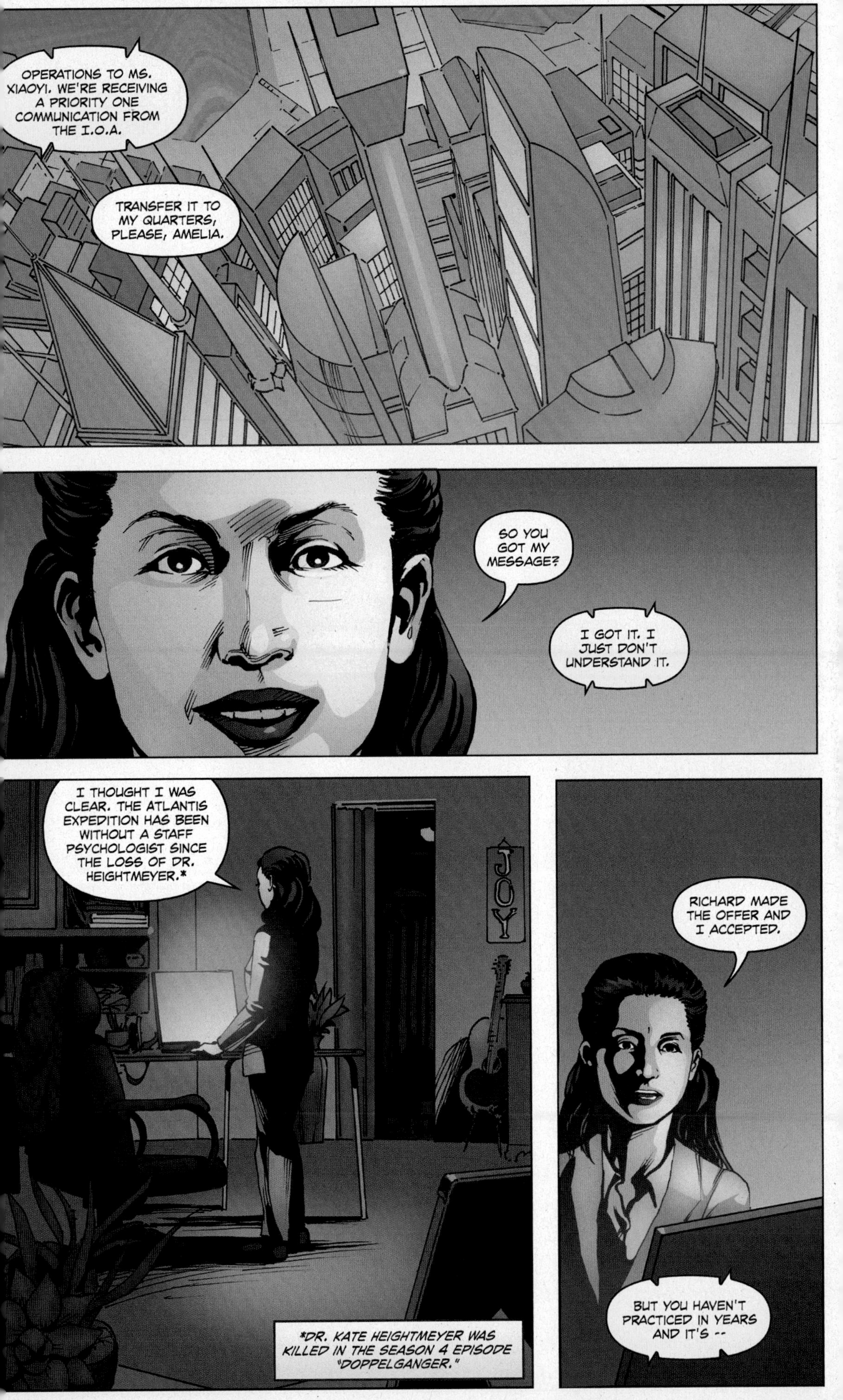

OPERATIONS TO MS. XIAOYI. WE'RE RECEIVING A PRIORITY ONE COMMUNICATION FROM THE I.O.A.
TRANSFER IT TO MY QUARTERS, PLEASE, AMELIA.
SO YOU GOT MY MESSAGE?
I GOT IT. I JUST DON'T UNDERSTAND IT.
I THOUGHT I WAS CLEAR. THE ATLANTIS EXPEDITION HAS BEEN WITHOUT A STAFF PSYCHOLOGIST SINCE THE LOSS OF DR. HEIGHTMEYER.*
JOY
*DR. KATE HEIGHTMEYER WAS KILLED IN THE SEASON 4 EPISODE "DOPPELGANGER."
RICHARD MADE THE OFFER AND I ACCEPTED.
BUT YOU HAVEN'T PRACTICED IN YEARS AND IT'S --

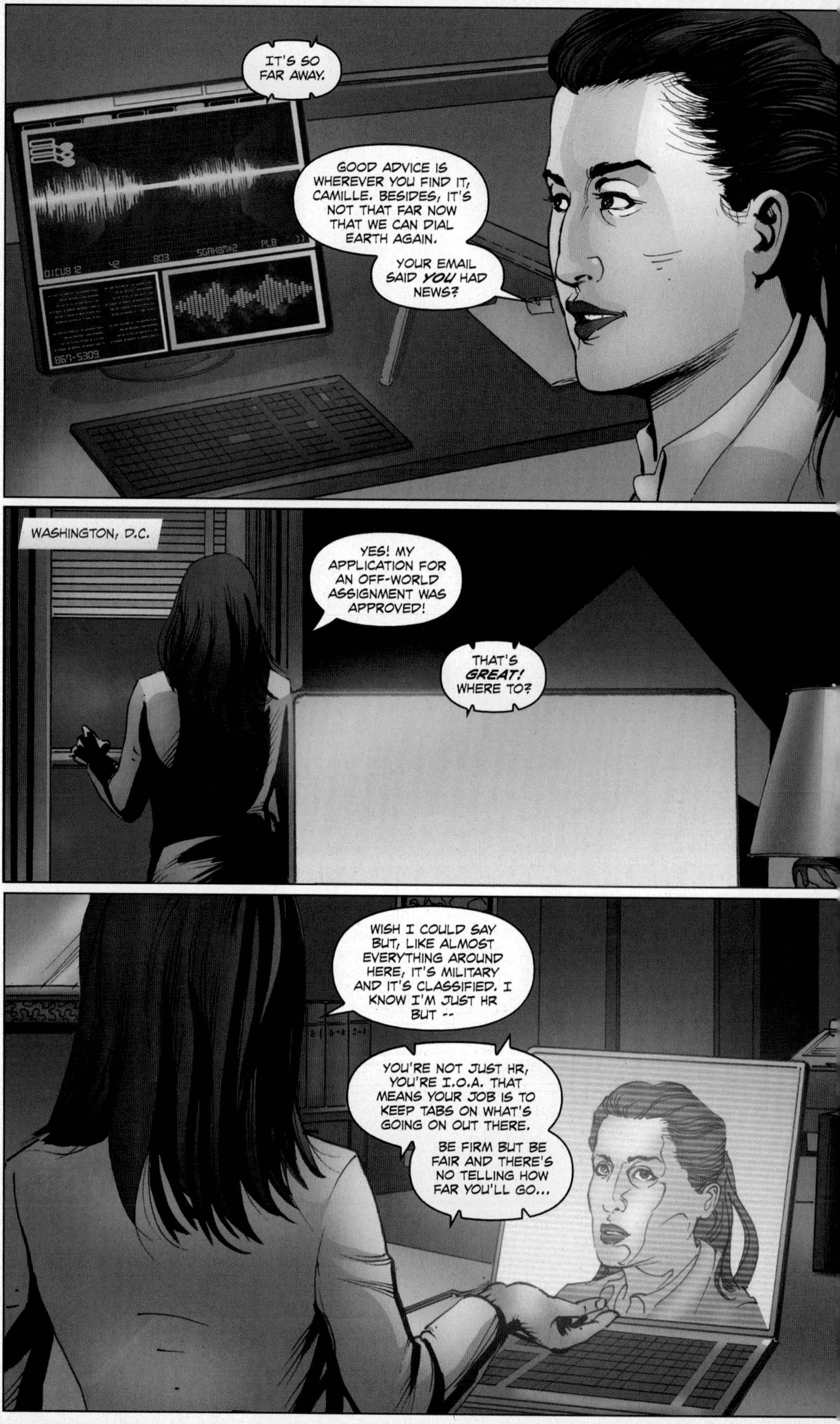
IT'S SO FAR AWAY.
GOOD ADVICE IS WHEREVER YOU FIND IT, CAMILLE. BESIDES, IT'S NOT THAT FAR NOW THAT WE CAN DIAL EARTH AGAIN.
YOUR EMAIL SAID ***YOU*** HAD NEWS?
WASHINGTON, D.C.
YES! MY APPLICATION FOR AN OFF-WORLD ASSIGNMENT WAS APPROVED!
THAT'S ***GREAT!*** WHERE TO?
WISH I COULD SAY BUT, LIKE ALMOST EVERYTHING AROUND HERE, IT'S MILITARY AND IT'S CLASSIFIED. I KNOW I'M JUST HR BUT --
YOU'RE NOT JUST HR, YOU'RE I.O.A. THAT MEANS YOUR JOB IS TO KEEP TABS ON WHAT'S GOING ON OUT THERE.
BE FIRM BUT BE FAIR AND THERE'S NO TELLING HOW FAR YOU'LL GO...

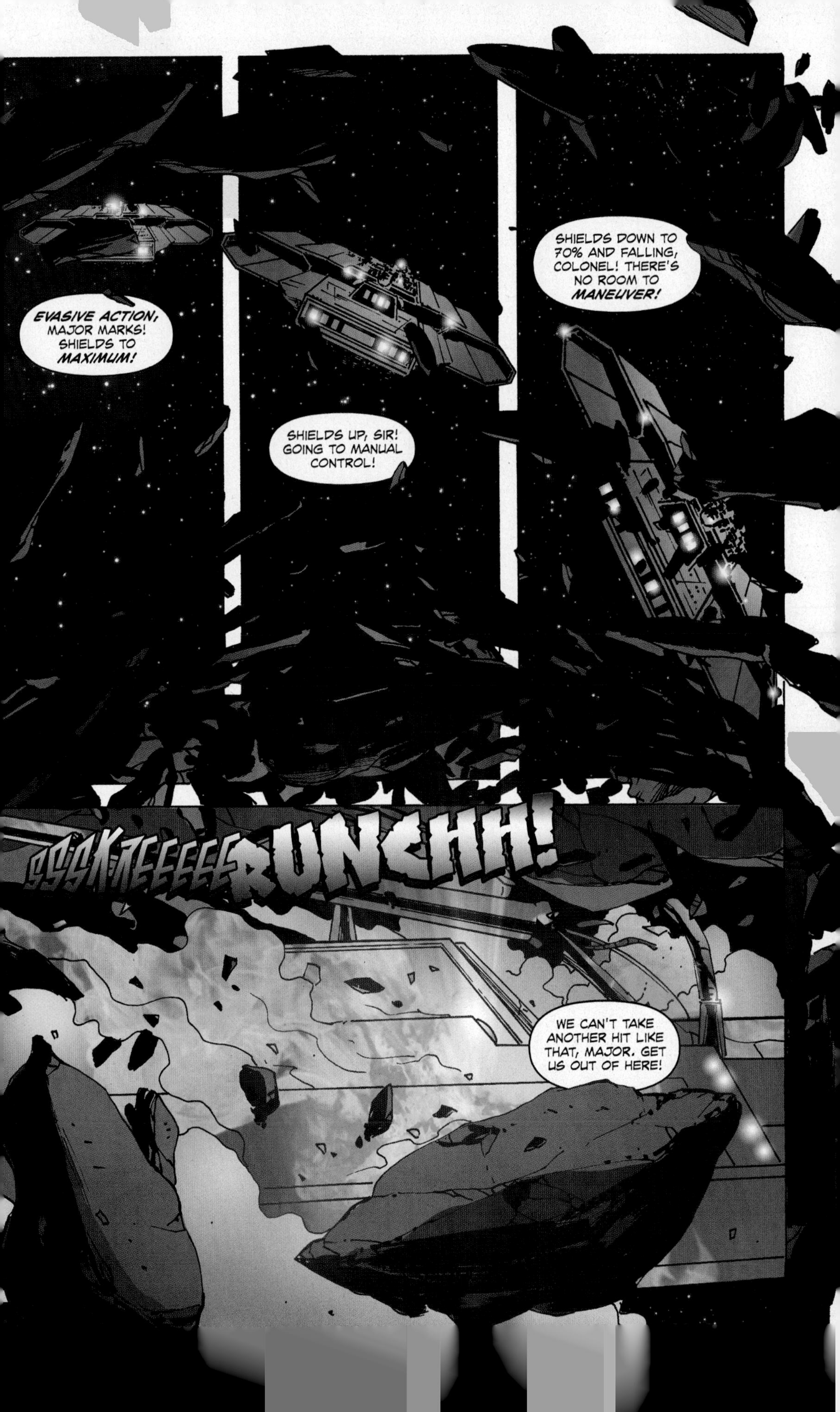
EVASIVE ACTION, MAJOR MARKS! SHIELDS TO MAXIMUM!
SHIELDS UP, SIR! GOING TO MANUAL CONTROL!
SHIELDS DOWN TO 70% AND FALLING, COLONEL! THERE'S NO ROOM TO MANEUVER!
SSSKREEEEECRUNCHH!
WE CAN'T TAKE ANOTHER HIT LIKE THAT, MAJOR. GET US OUT OF HERE!

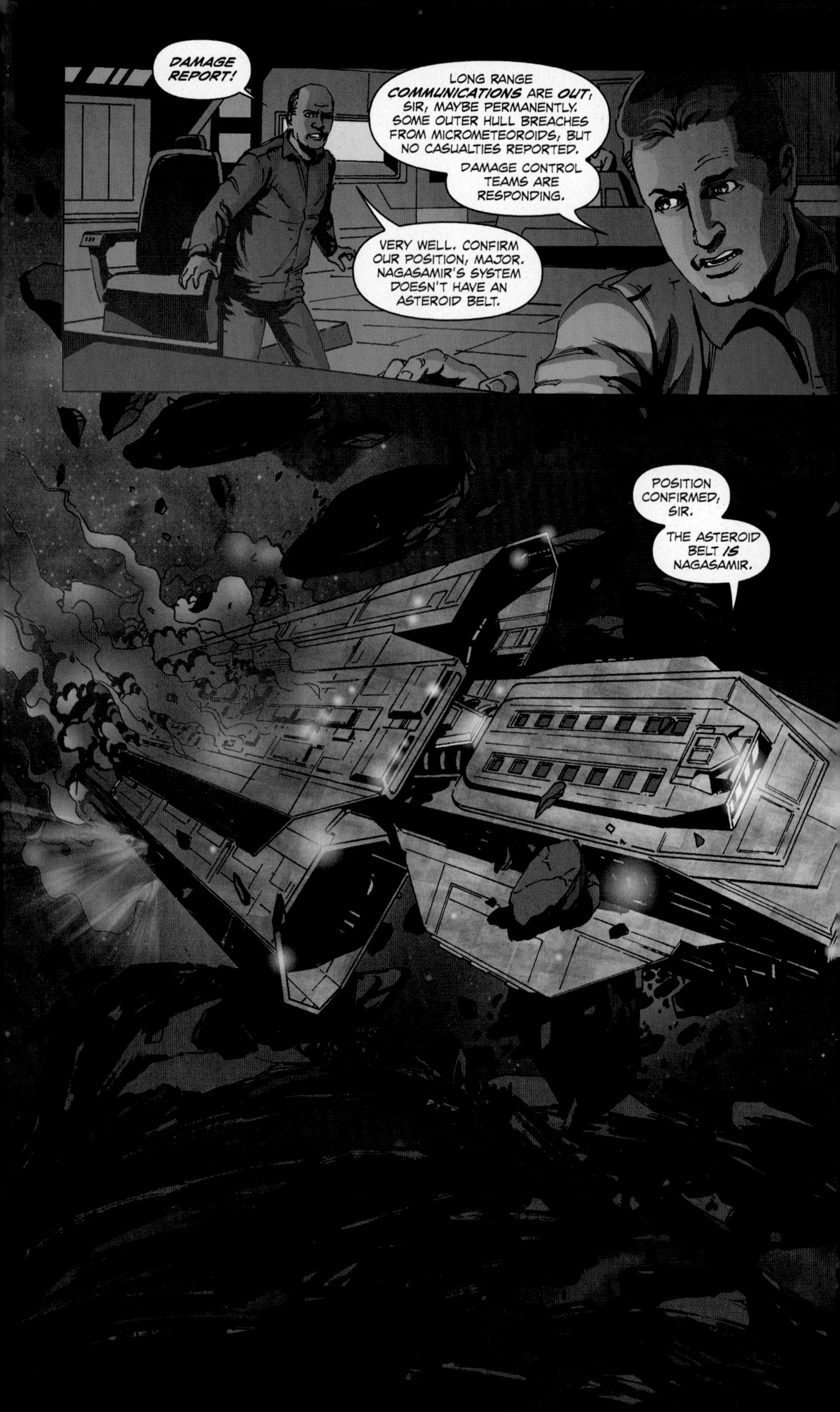
DAMAGE REPORT!
LONG RANGE COMMUNICATIONS ARE OUT, SIR, MAYBE PERMANENTLY. SOME OUTER HULL BREACHES FROM MICROMETEOROIDS, BUT NO CASUALTIES REPORTED.
DAMAGE CONTROL TEAMS ARE RESPONDING.
VERY WELL. CONFIRM OUR POSITION, MAJOR. NAGASAMIR'S SYSTEM DOESN'T HAVE AN ASTEROID BELT.
POSITION CONFIRMED, SIR.
THE ASTEROID BELT IS NAGASAMIR.

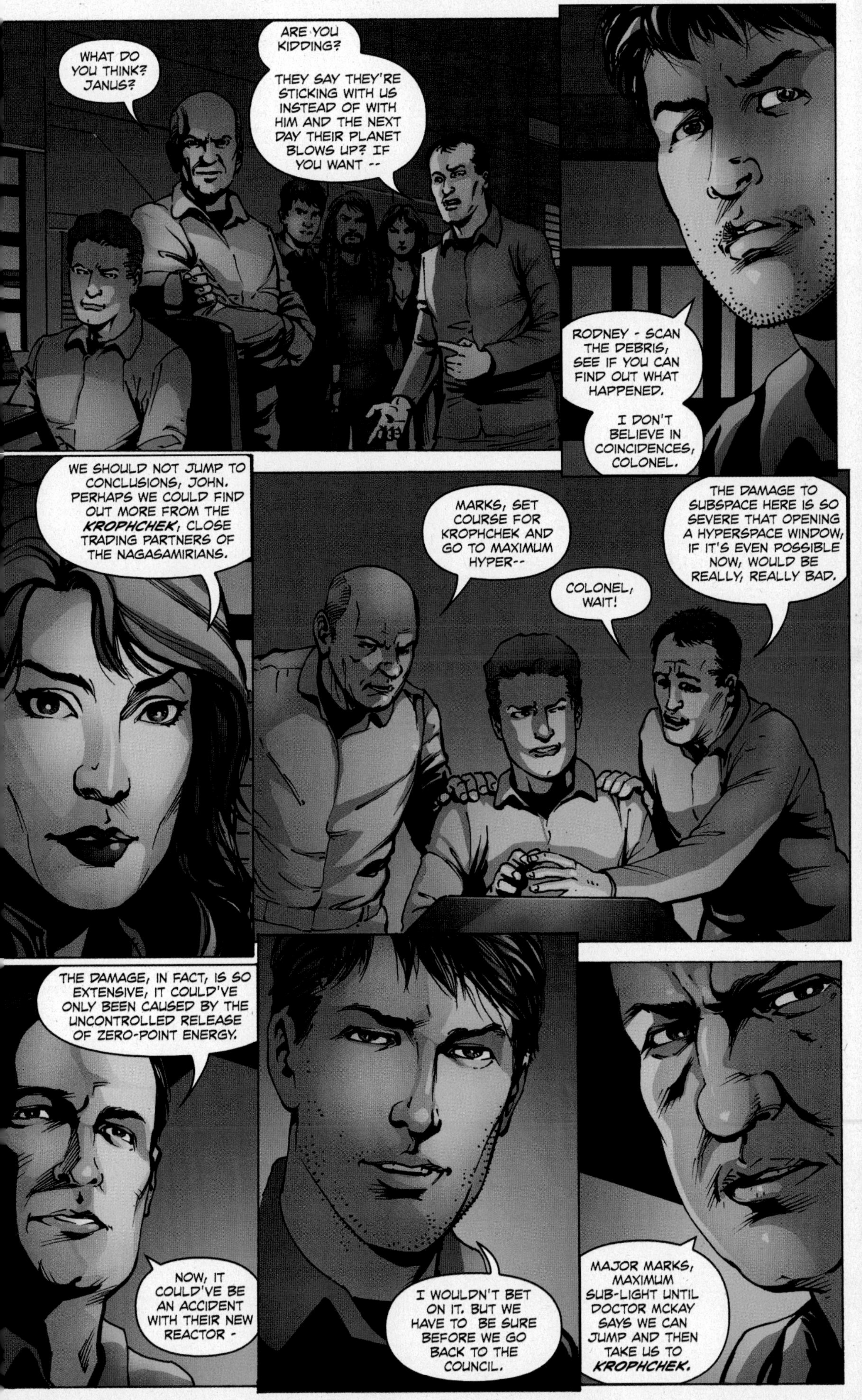
WHAT DO YOU THINK? JANUS?
ARE YOU KIDDING?
THEY SAY THEY'RE STICKING WITH US INSTEAD OF WITH HIM AND THE NEXT DAY THEIR PLANET BLOWS UP? IF YOU WANT --
RODNEY - SCAN THE DEBRIS, SEE IF YOU CAN FIND OUT WHAT HAPPENED.
I DON'T BELIEVE IN COINCIDENCES, COLONEL.
WE SHOULD NOT JUMP TO CONCLUSIONS, JOHN. PERHAPS WE COULD FIND OUT MORE FROM THE ***KROPHCHEK***, CLOSE TRADING PARTNERS OF THE NAGASAMIRIANS.
MARKS, SET COURSE FOR KROPHCHEK AND GO TO MAXIMUM HYPER--
COLONEL, WAIT!
THE DAMAGE TO SUBSPACE HERE IS SO SEVERE THAT OPENING A HYPERSPACE WINDOW, IF IT'S EVEN POSSIBLE NOW, WOULD BE REALLY, REALLY BAD.
THE DAMAGE, IN FACT, IS SO EXTENSIVE, IT COULD'VE ONLY BEEN CAUSED BY THE UNCONTROLLED RELEASE OF ZERO-POINT ENERGY.
NOW, IT COULD'VE BE AN ACCIDENT WITH THEIR NEW REACTOR -
I WOULDN'T BET ON IT. BUT WE HAVE TO BE SURE BEFORE WE GO BACK TO THE COUNCIL.
MAJOR MARKS, MAXIMUM SUB-LIGHT UNTIL DOCTOR MCKAY SAYS WE CAN JUMP AND THEN TAKE US TO ***KROPHCHEK.***

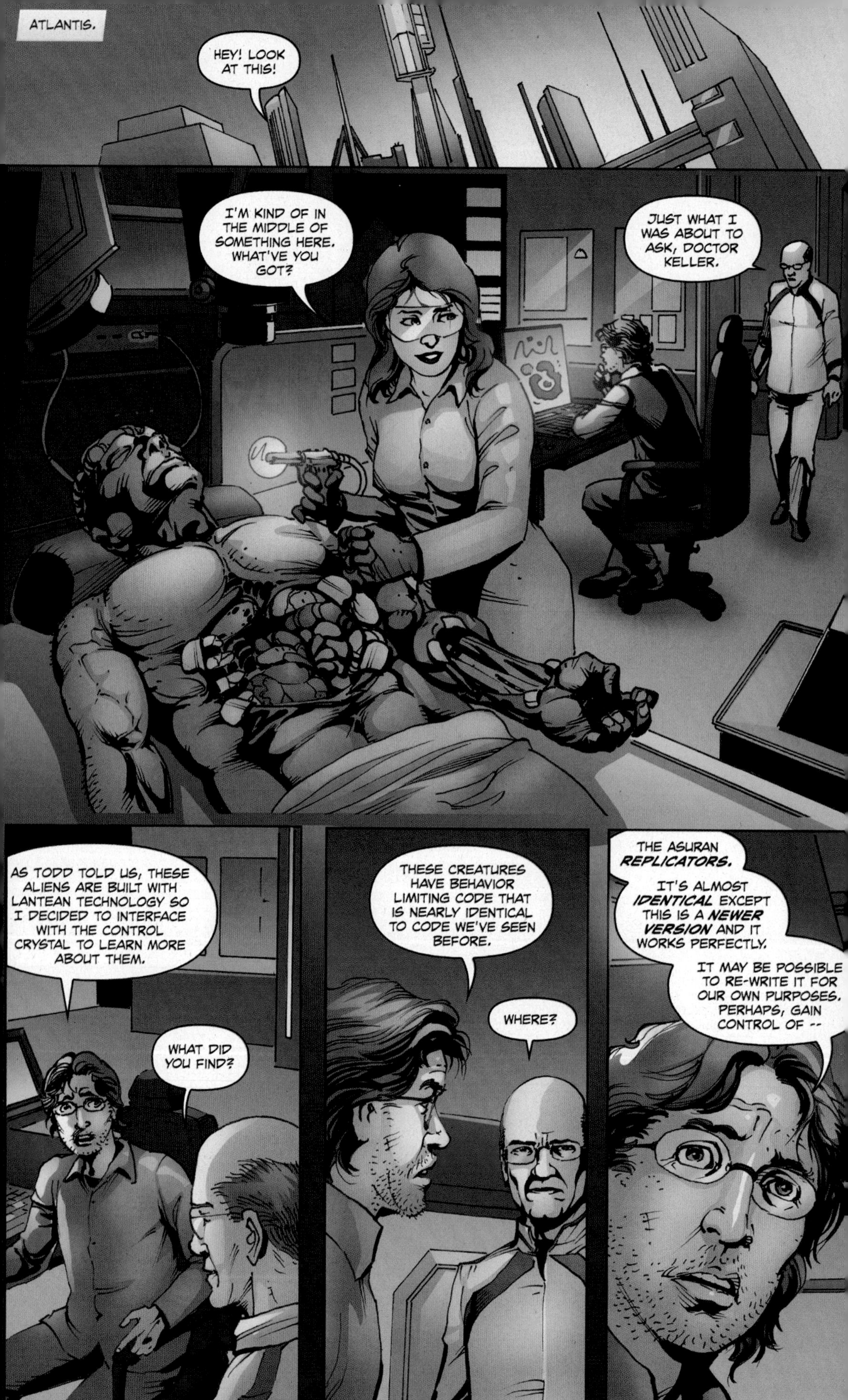
ATLANTIS.
HEY! LOOK AT THIS!
I'M KIND OF IN THE MIDDLE OF SOMETHING HERE. WHAT'VE YOU GOT?
JUST WHAT I WAS ABOUT TO ASK, DOCTOR KELLER.
AS TODD TOLD US, THESE ALIENS ARE BUILT WITH LANTEAN TECHNOLOGY SO I DECIDED TO INTERFACE WITH THE CONTROL CRYSTAL TO LEARN MORE ABOUT THEM.
WHAT DID YOU FIND?
THESE CREATURES HAVE BEHAVIOR LIMITING CODE THAT IS NEARLY IDENTICAL TO CODE WE'VE SEEN BEFORE.
WHERE?
THE ASURAN *REPLICATORS.*
IT'S ALMOST *IDENTICAL* EXCEPT THIS IS A *NEWER VERSION* AND IT WORKS PERFECTLY.
IT MAY BE POSSIBLE TO RE-WRITE IT FOR OUR OWN PURPOSES. PERHAPS, GAIN CONTROL OF --

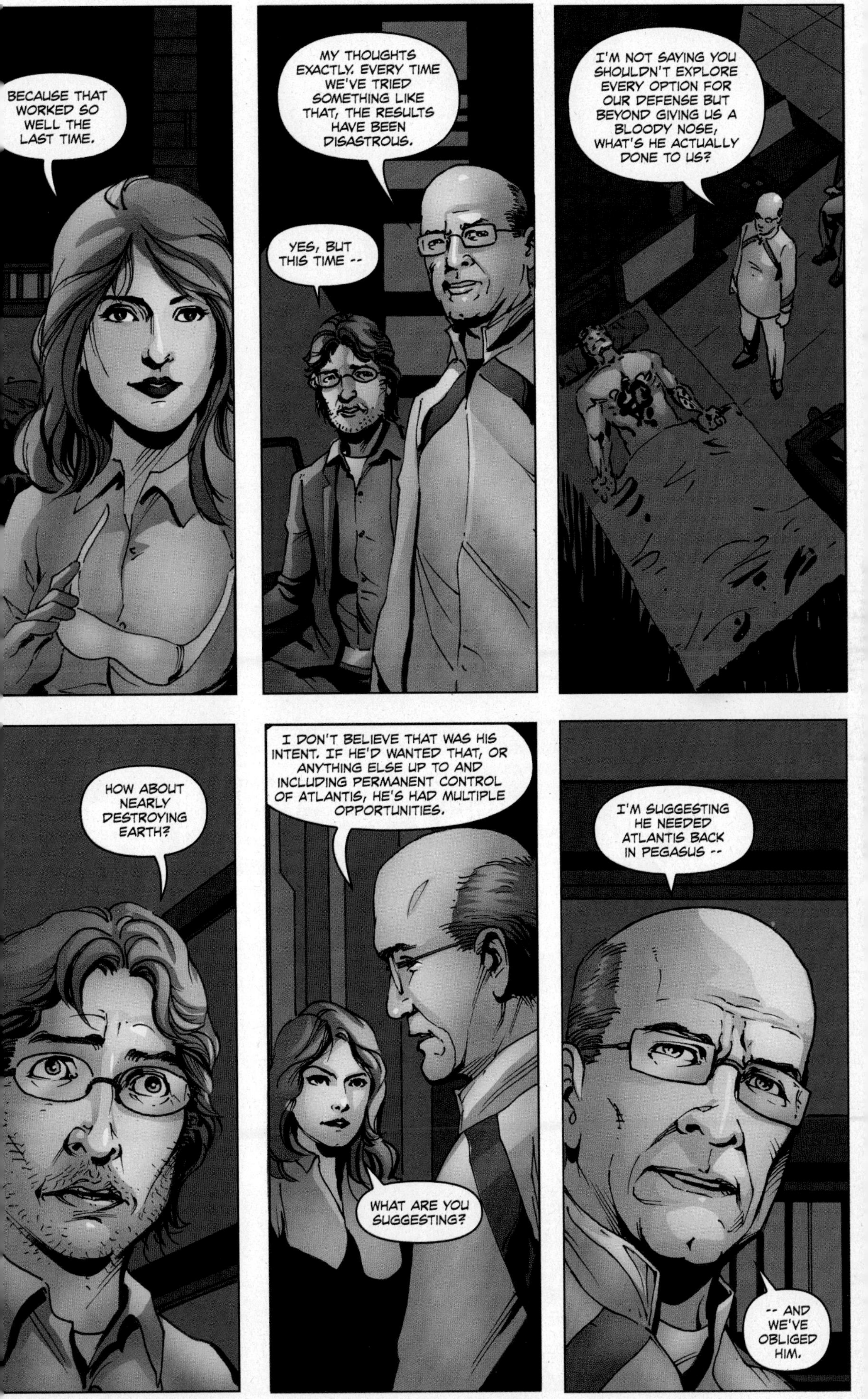

BECAUSE THAT WORKED SO WELL THE LAST TIME.
MY THOUGHTS EXACTLY. EVERY TIME WE'VE TRIED SOMETHING LIKE THAT, THE RESULTS HAVE BEEN DISASTROUS.
YES, BUT THIS TIME --
I'M NOT SAYING YOU SHOULDN'T EXPLORE EVERY OPTION FOR OUR DEFENSE BUT BEYOND GIVING US A BLOODY NOSE, WHAT'S HE ACTUALLY DONE TO US?
HOW ABOUT NEARLY DESTROYING EARTH?
I DON'T BELIEVE THAT WAS HIS INTENT. IF HE'D WANTED THAT, OR ANYTHING ELSE UP TO AND INCLUDING PERMANENT CONTROL OF ATLANTIS, HE'S HAD MULTIPLE OPPORTUNITIES.
WHAT ARE YOU SUGGESTING?
I'M SUGGESTING HE NEEDED ATLANTIS BACK IN PEGASUS --
-- AND WE'VE OBLIGED HIM.

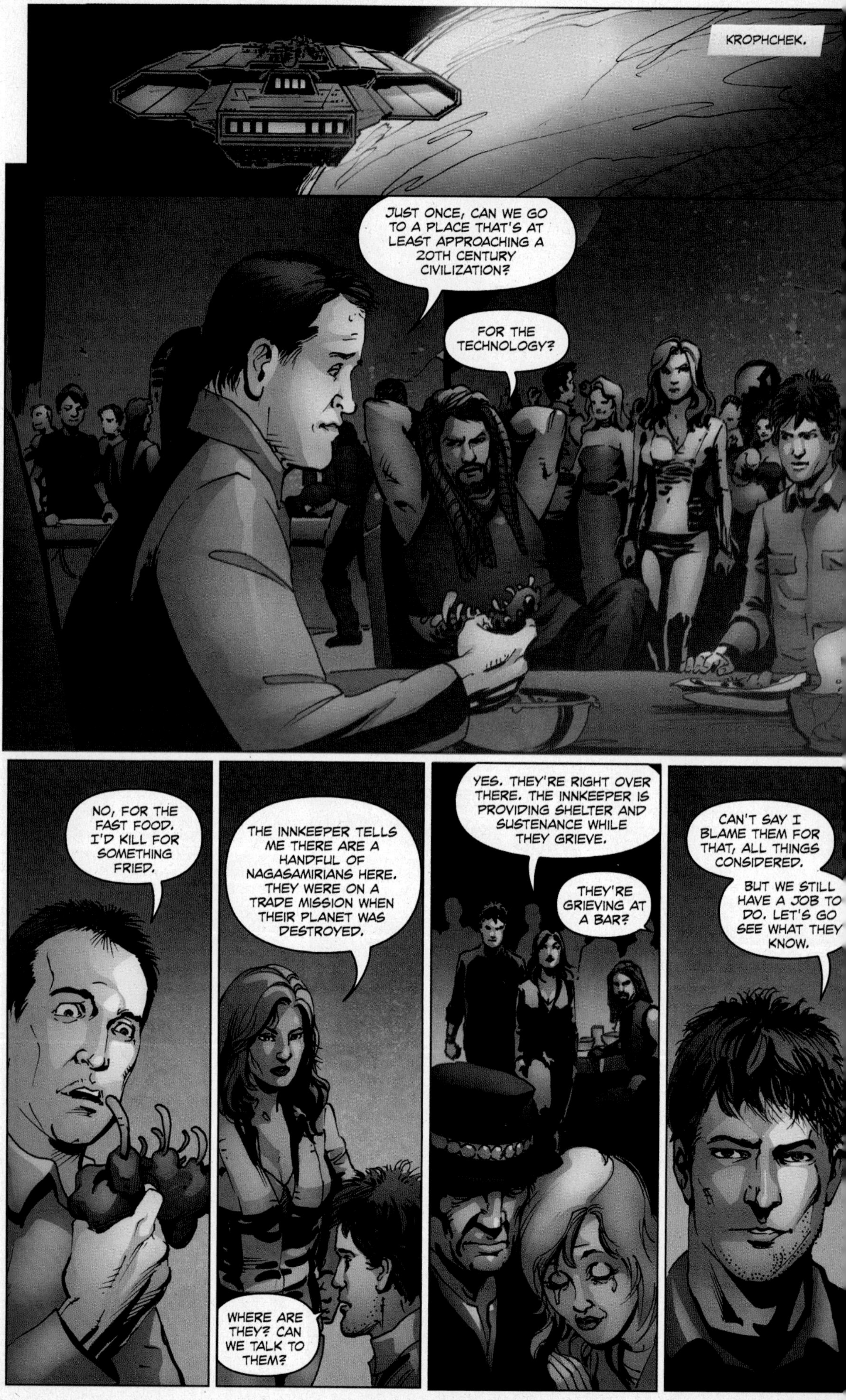
KROPHCHEK.
JUST ONCE, CAN WE GO TO A PLACE THAT'S AT LEAST APPROACHING A 20TH CENTURY CIVILIZATION?
FOR THE TECHNOLOGY?
NO, FOR THE FAST FOOD. I'D KILL FOR SOMETHING FRIED.
THE INNKEEPER TELLS ME THERE ARE A HANDFUL OF NAGASAMIRIANS HERE. THEY WERE ON A TRADE MISSION WHEN THEIR PLANET WAS DESTROYED.
WHERE ARE THEY? CAN WE TALK TO THEM?
YES. THEY'RE RIGHT OVER THERE. THE INNKEEPER IS PROVIDING SHELTER AND SUSTENANCE WHILE THEY GRIEVE.
THEY'RE GRIEVING AT A BAR?
CAN'T SAY I BLAME THEM FOR THAT, ALL THINGS CONSIDERED.
BUT WE STILL HAVE A JOB TO DO. LET'S GO SEE WHAT THEY KNOW.

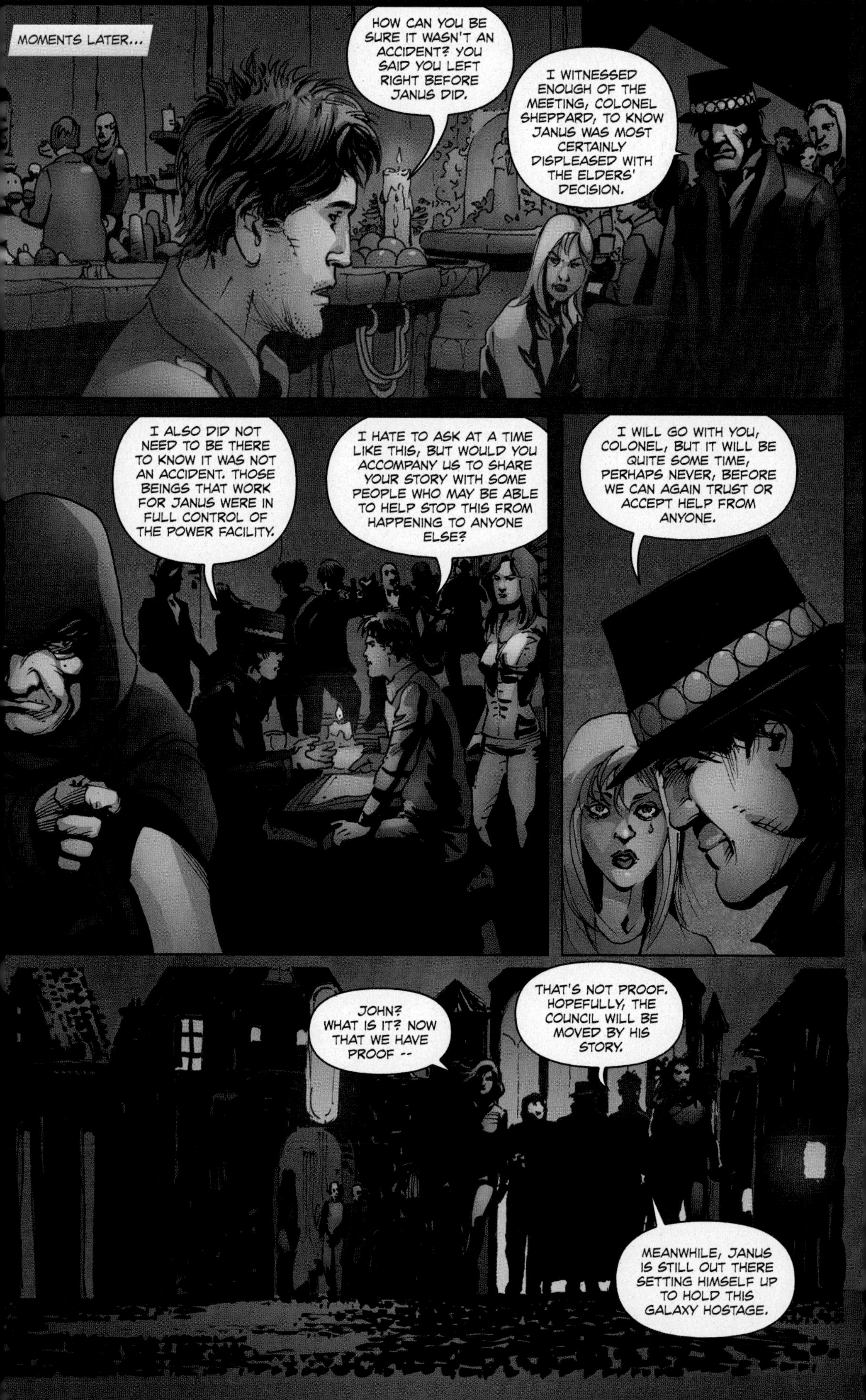
MOMENTS LATER...
HOW CAN YOU BE SURE IT WASN'T AN ACCIDENT? YOU SAID YOU LEFT RIGHT BEFORE JANUS DID.
I WITNESSED ENOUGH OF THE MEETING, COLONEL SHEPPARD, TO KNOW JANUS WAS MOST CERTAINLY DISPLEASED WITH THE ELDERS' DECISION.
I ALSO DID NOT NEED TO BE THERE TO KNOW IT WAS NOT AN ACCIDENT. THOSE BEINGS THAT WORK FOR JANUS WERE IN FULL CONTROL OF THE POWER FACILITY.
I HATE TO ASK AT A TIME LIKE THIS, BUT WOULD YOU ACCOMPANY US TO SHARE YOUR STORY WITH SOME PEOPLE WHO MAY BE ABLE TO HELP STOP THIS FROM HAPPENING TO ANYONE ELSE?
I WILL GO WITH YOU, COLONEL, BUT IT WILL BE QUITE SOME TIME, PERHAPS NEVER, BEFORE WE CAN AGAIN TRUST OR ACCEPT HELP FROM ANYONE.
JOHN? WHAT IS IT? NOW THAT WE HAVE PROOF --
THAT'S NOT PROOF. HOPEFULLY, THE COUNCIL WILL BE MOVED BY HIS STORY.
MEANWHILE, JANUS IS STILL OUT THERE SETTING HIMSELF UP TO HOLD THIS GALAXY HOSTAGE.

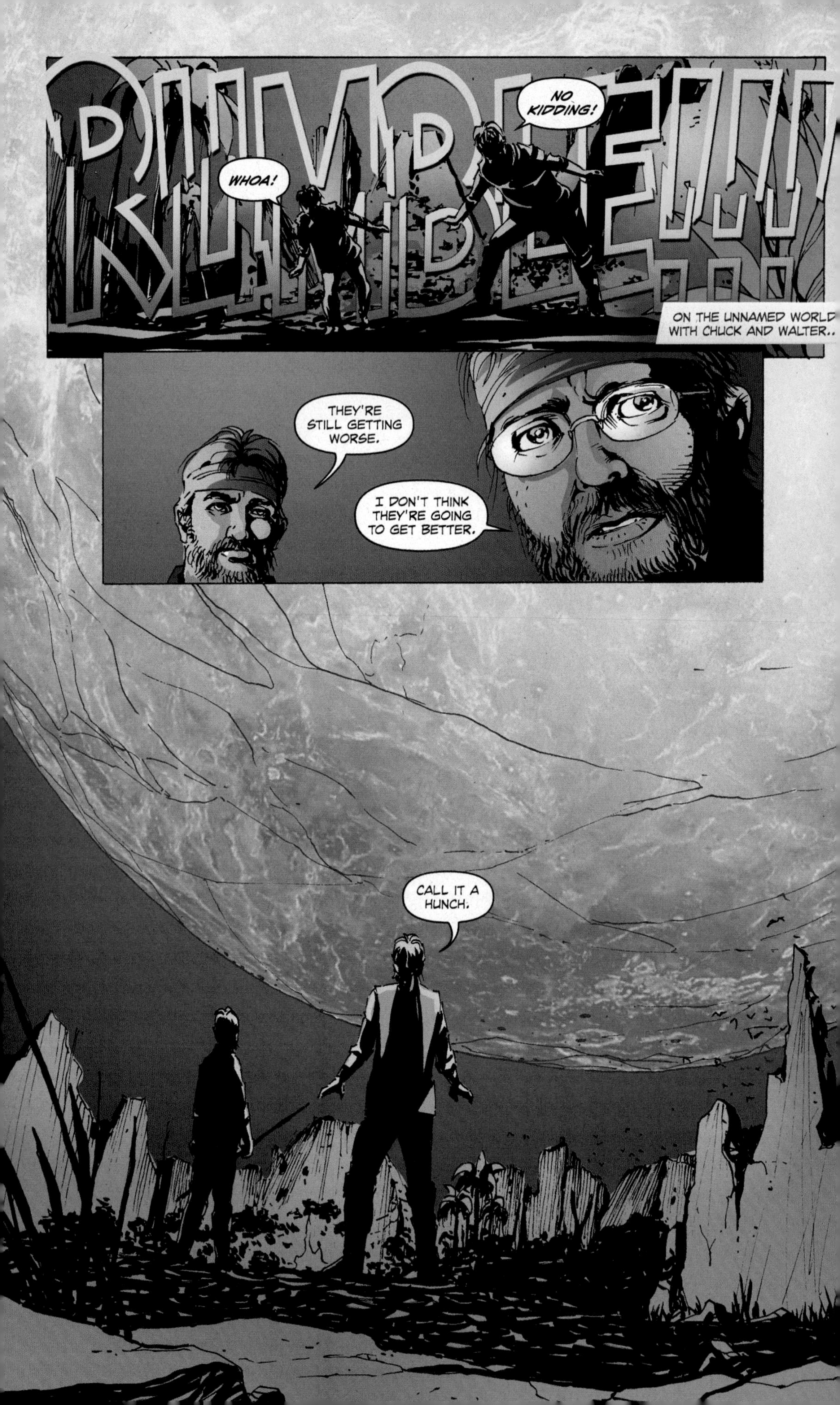
WHOA!
NO KIDDING!
ON THE UNNAMED WORLD WITH CHUCK AND WALTER...
THEY'RE STILL GETTING WORSE.
I DON'T THINK THEY'RE GOING TO GET BETTER.
CALL IT A HUNCH.

DID WE GET WHAT WE NEED, COLONEL?

NOT EXACTLY, SIR, BUT IF LONG-RANGE COMMS ARE BACK ONLINE, WE SHOULD CONTACT ATLANTIS AND --

BA-WHOOM!

MARKS, WHAT WAS THAT?!?

WE'RE UNDER ATTACK, SIR! MULTIPLE FIGHTERS INBOUND. SHIELDS ARE UP BUT WEAPONS AND HYPERDRIVE SYSTEMS ARE OFF-LINE.

GET US OUT OF ORBIT SO WE CAN MANEUVER! MAXIMUM SUB-LIGHT!

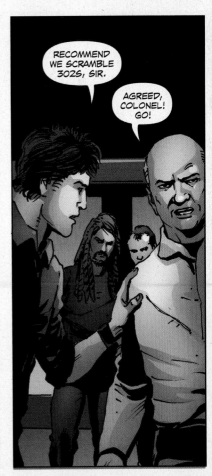

RECOMMEND WE SCRAMBLE 302S, SIR.

AGREED, COLONEL! GO!

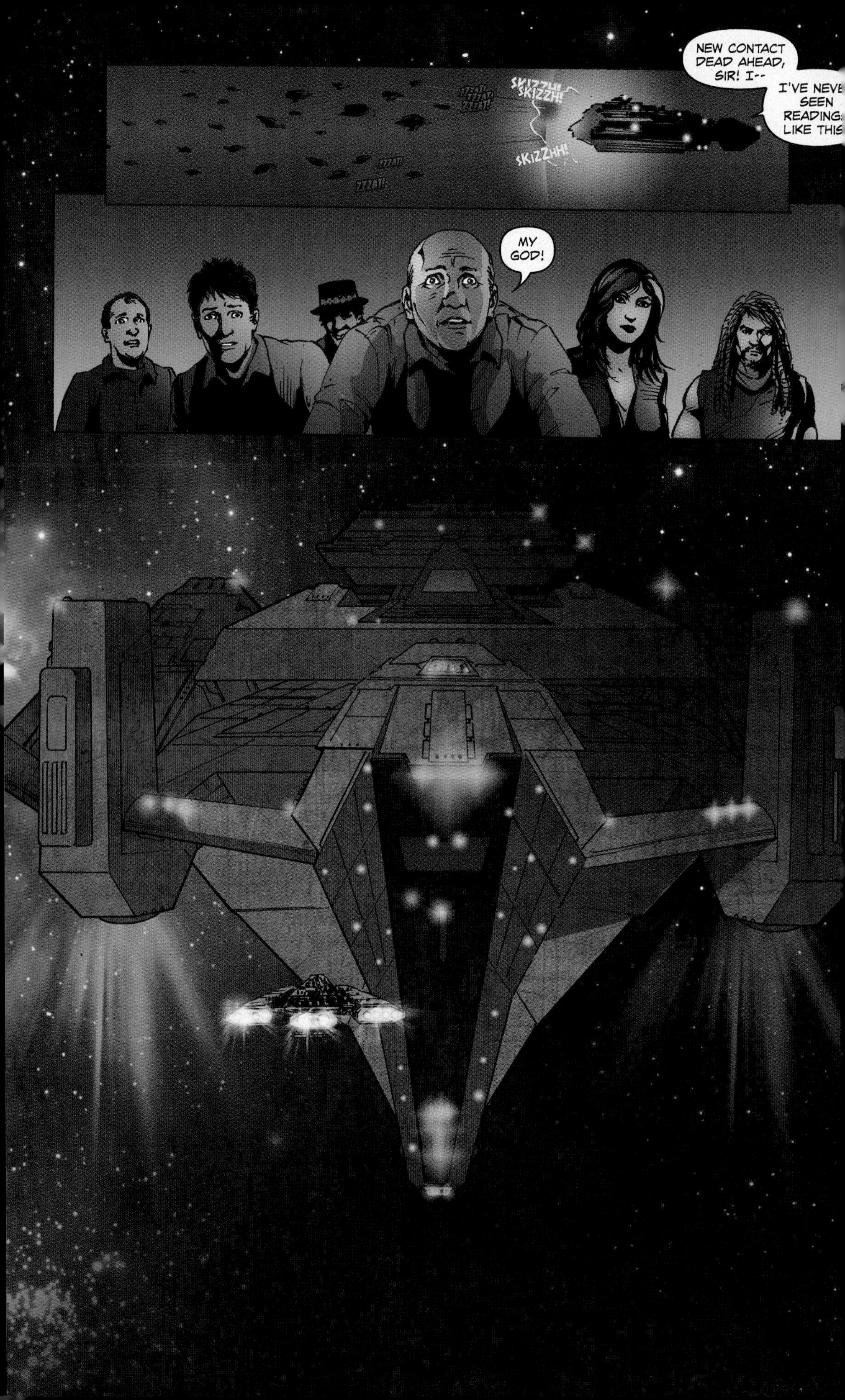
NEW CONTACT DEAD AHEAD, SIR! I--
I'VE NEVE SEEN READING LIKE THIS
SKIZZH!
SKIZZHH!
ZZZAT!
ZZZAT!
MY GOD!

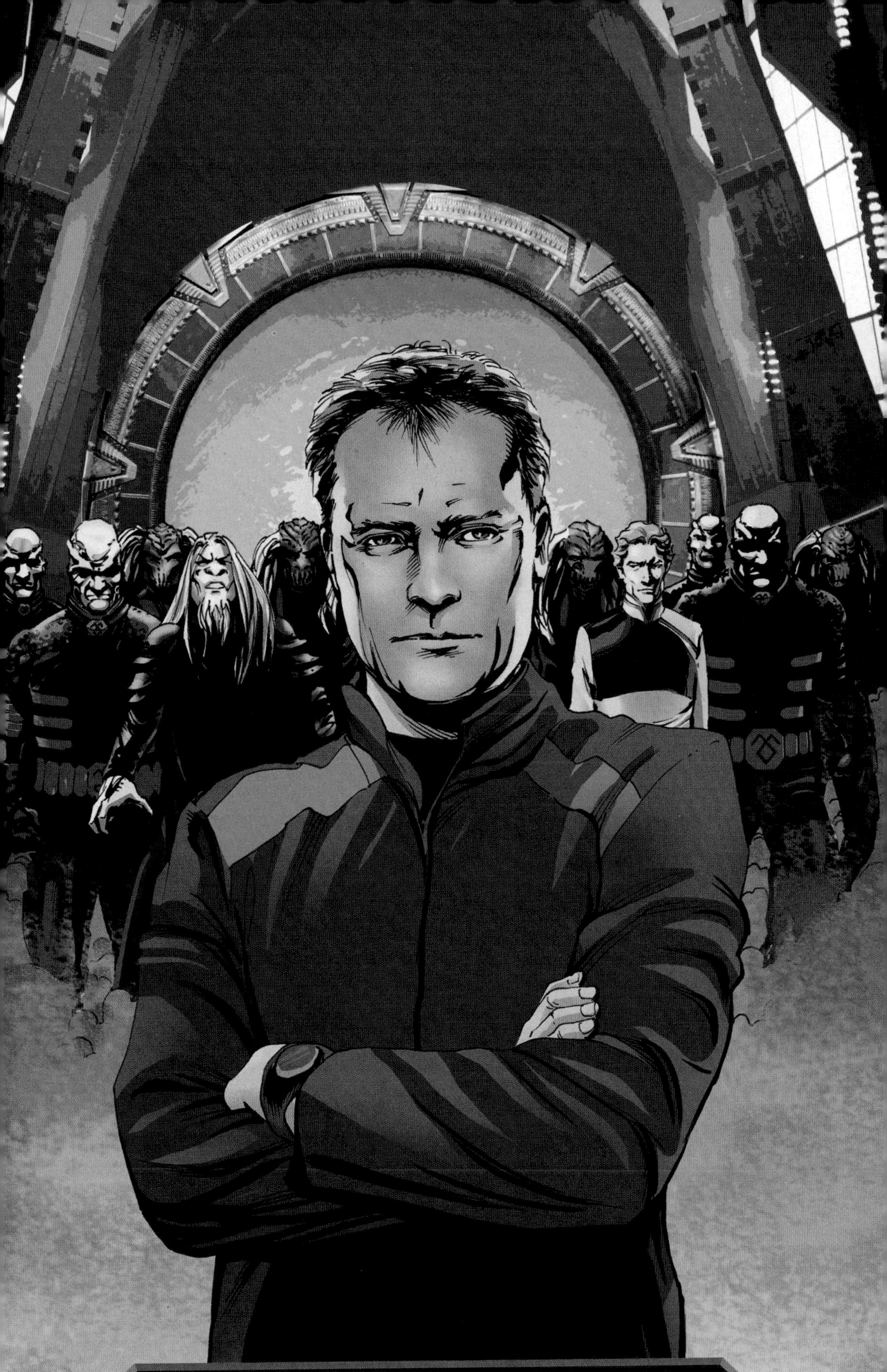

COVER GALLERY

HEARTS & MINDS #3 MAIN COVER

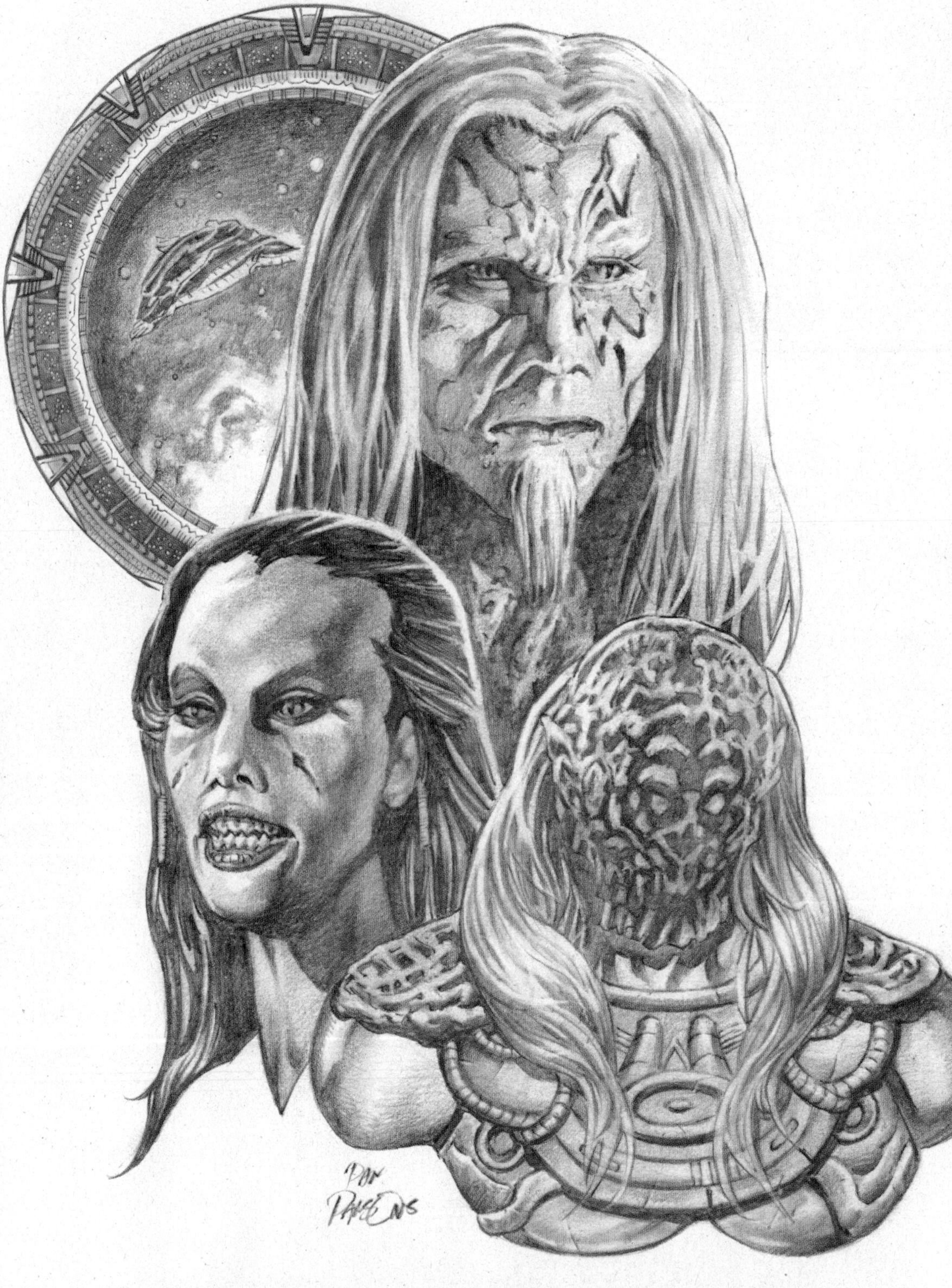

COVER GALLERY

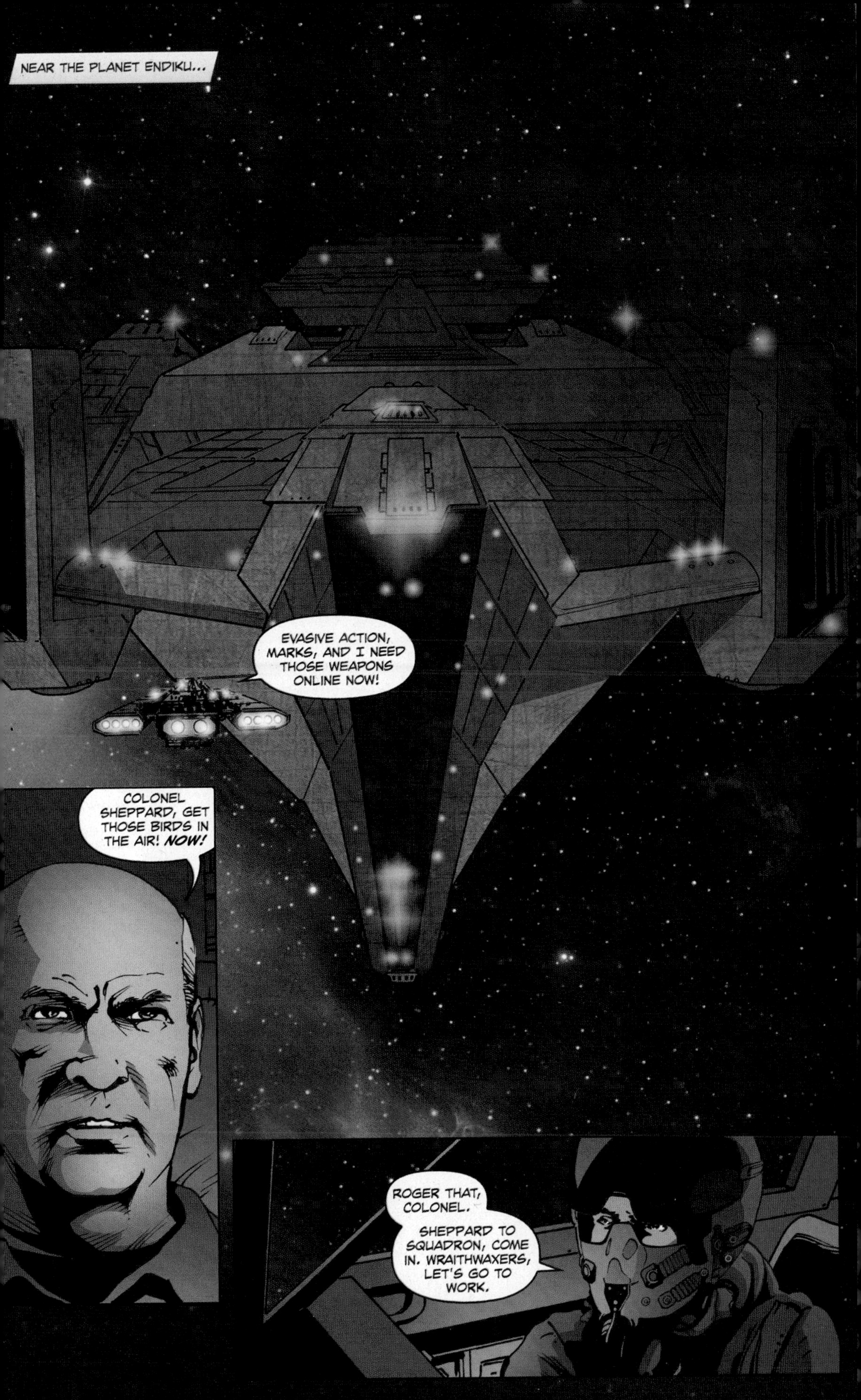
NEAR THE PLANET ENDIKU...
EVASIVE ACTION, MARKS, AND I NEED THOSE WEAPONS ONLINE NOW!
COLONEL SHEPPARD, GET THOSE BIRDS IN THE AIR! *NOW!*
ROGER THAT, COLONEL.
SHEPPARD TO SQUADRON, COME IN. WRAITHWAXERS, LET'S GO TO WORK.

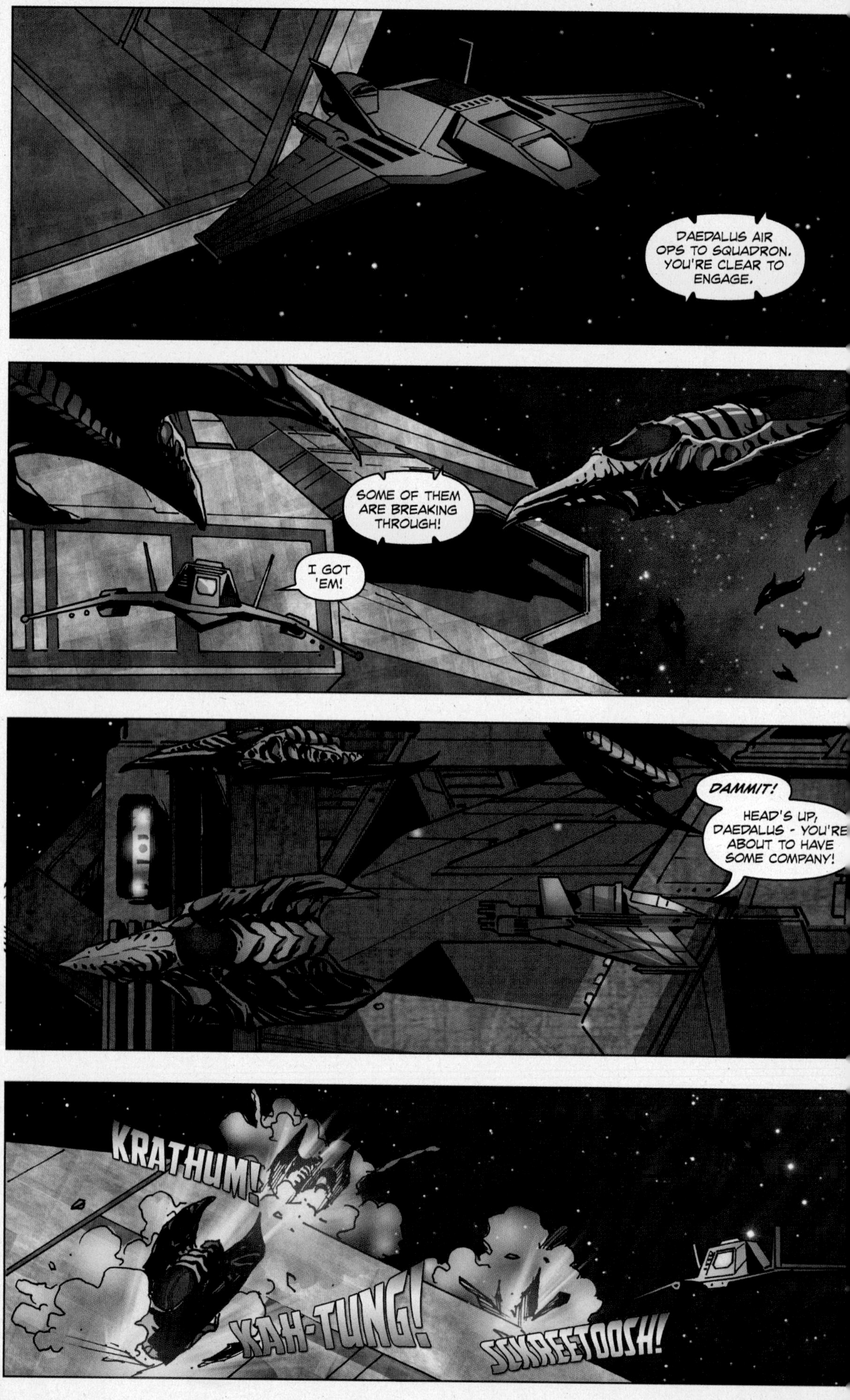
DAEDALUS AIR OPS TO SQUADRON. YOU'RE CLEAR TO ENGAGE.
SOME OF THEM ARE BREAKING THROUGH!
I GOT 'EM!
DAMMIT!
HEAD'S UP, DAEDALUS - YOU'RE ABOUT TO HAVE SOME COMPANY!
KRATHUM!
KAH-TUNG!
SCKREETOOSH!

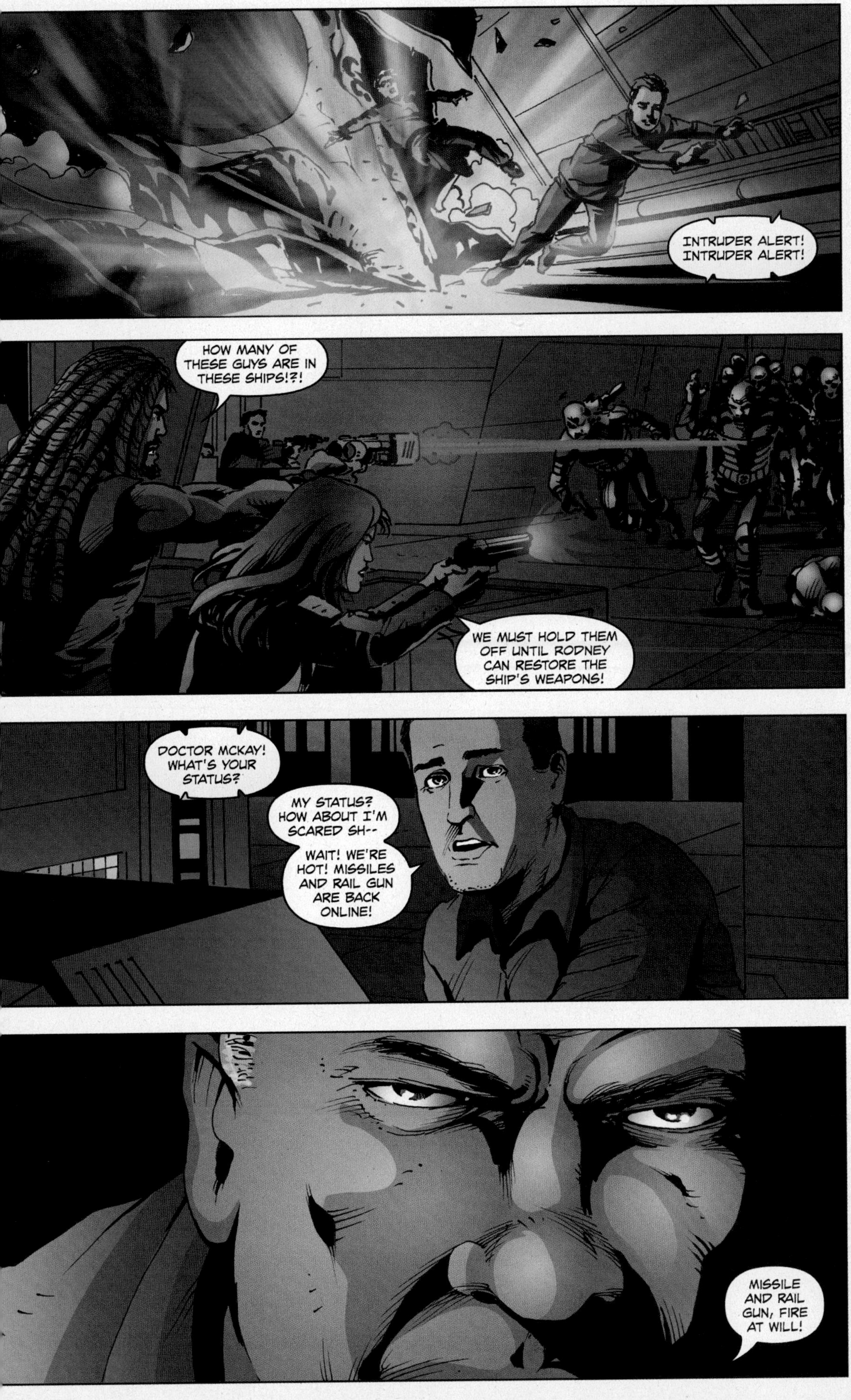
INTRUDER ALERT! INTRUDER ALERT!
HOW MANY OF THESE GUYS ARE IN THESE SHIPS!?!
WE MUST HOLD THEM OFF UNTIL RODNEY CAN RESTORE THE SHIP'S WEAPONS!
DOCTOR MCKAY! WHAT'S YOUR STATUS?
MY STATUS? HOW ABOUT I'M SCARED SH--
WAIT! WE'RE HOT! MISSILES AND RAIL GUN ARE BACK ONLINE!
MISSILE AND RAIL GUN, FIRE AT WILL!

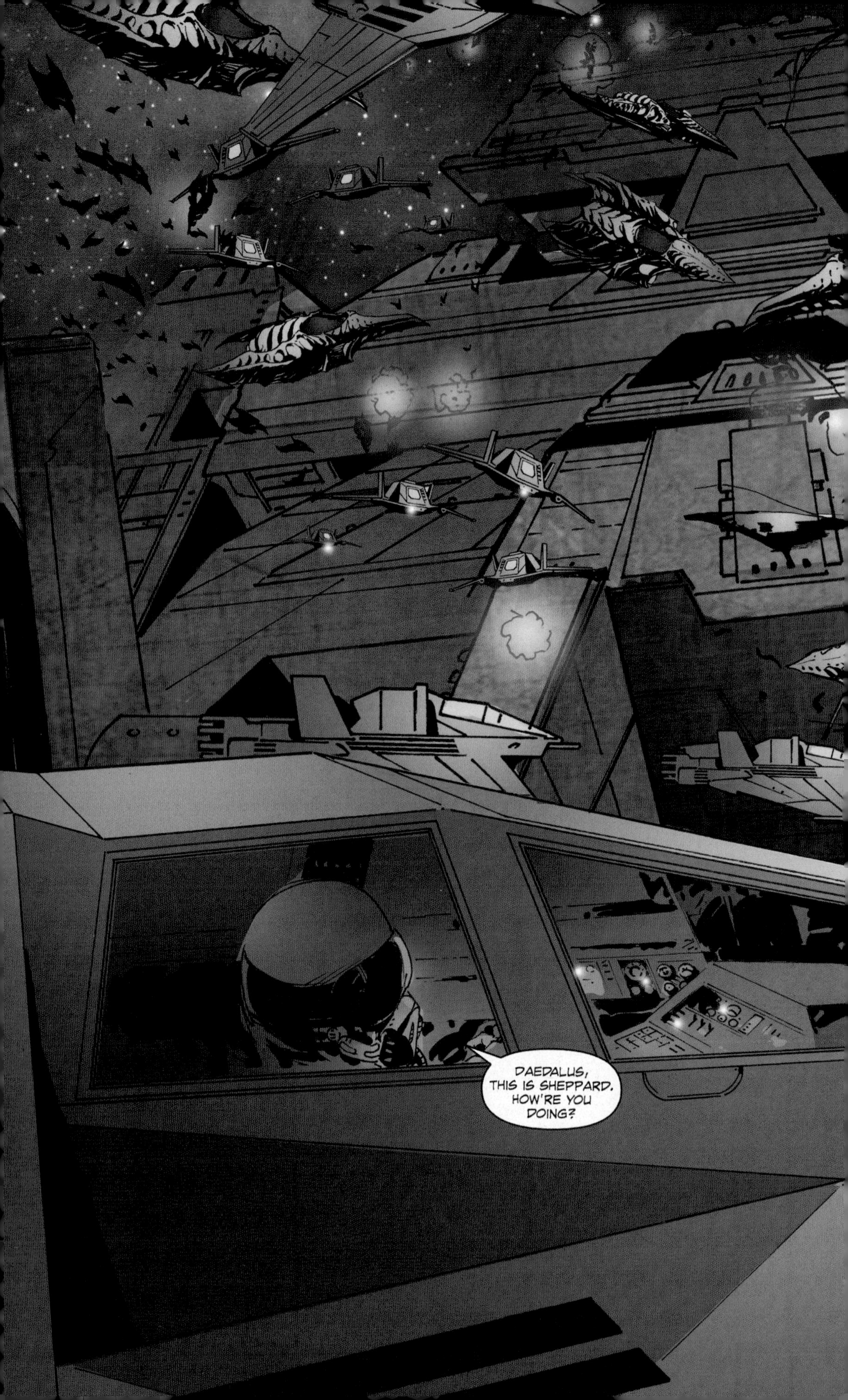
DAEDALUS, THIS IS SHEPPARD. HOW'RE YOU DOING?

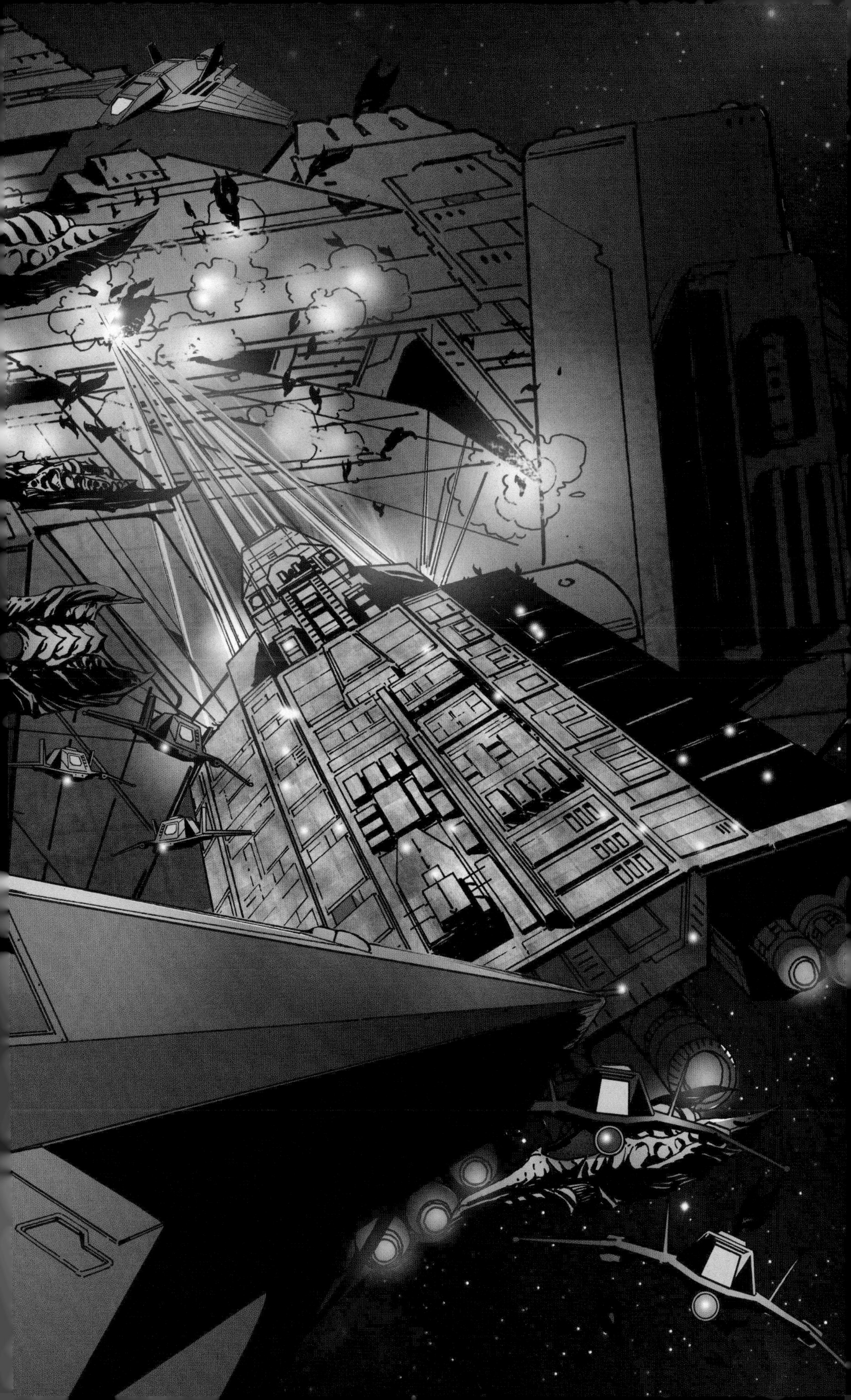

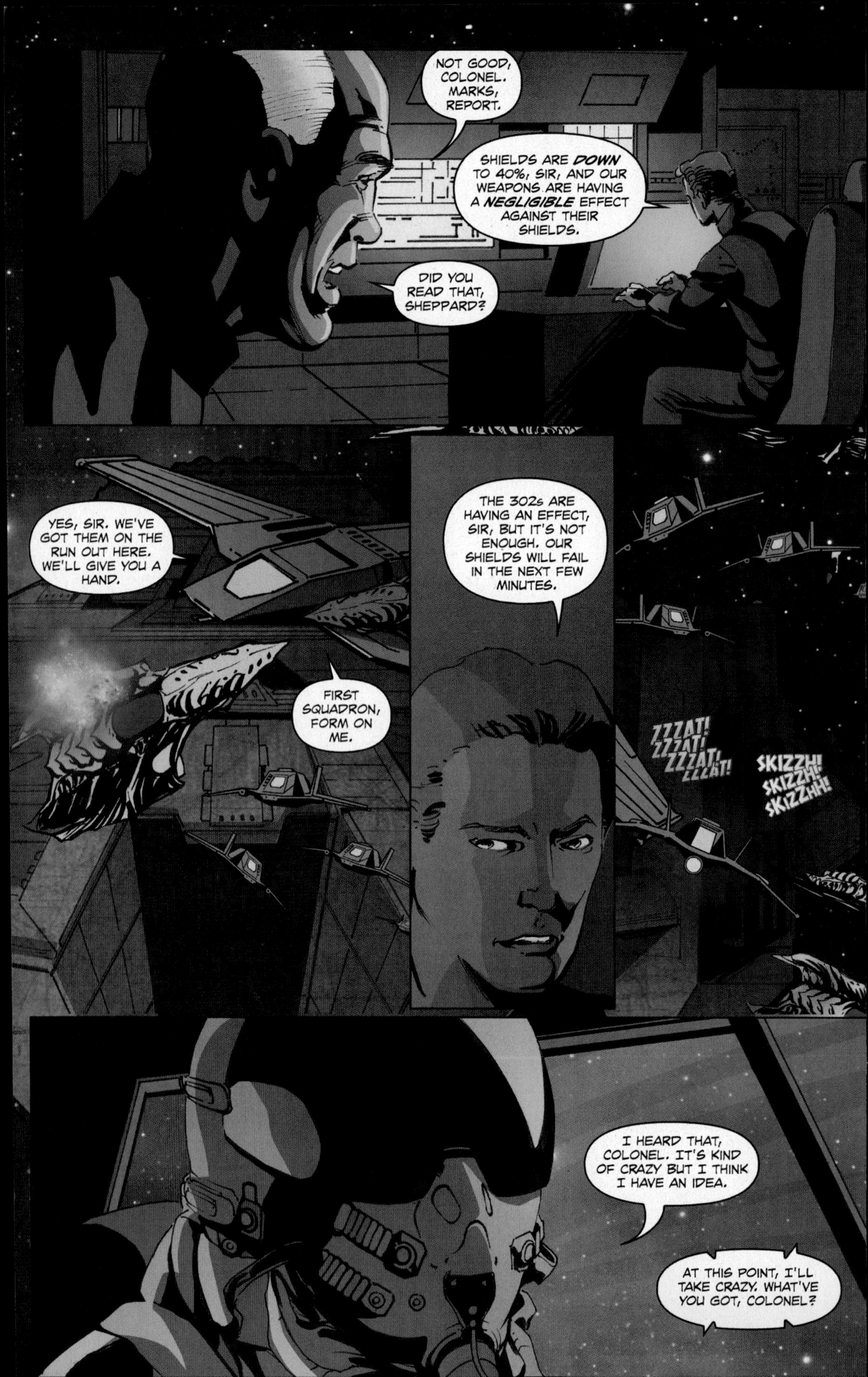
NOT GOOD, COLONEL. MARKS, REPORT.
SHIELDS ARE *DOWN* TO 40%, SIR, AND OUR WEAPONS ARE HAVING A *NEGLIGIBLE* EFFECT AGAINST THEIR SHIELDS.
DID YOU READ THAT, SHEPPARD?
YES, SIR. WE'VE GOT THEM ON THE RUN OUT HERE. WE'LL GIVE YOU A HAND.
FIRST SQUADRON, FORM ON ME.
THE 302s ARE HAVING AN EFFECT, SIR, BUT IT'S NOT ENOUGH. OUR SHIELDS WILL FAIL IN THE NEXT FEW MINUTES.
ZZZAT! ZZZAT! ZZZAT! ZZZAT!
SKIZZH! SKIZZH! SKIZZHH!
I HEARD THAT, COLONEL. IT'S KIND OF CRAZY BUT I THINK I HAVE AN IDEA.
AT THIS POINT, I'LL TAKE CRAZY. WHAT'VE YOU GOT, COLONEL?

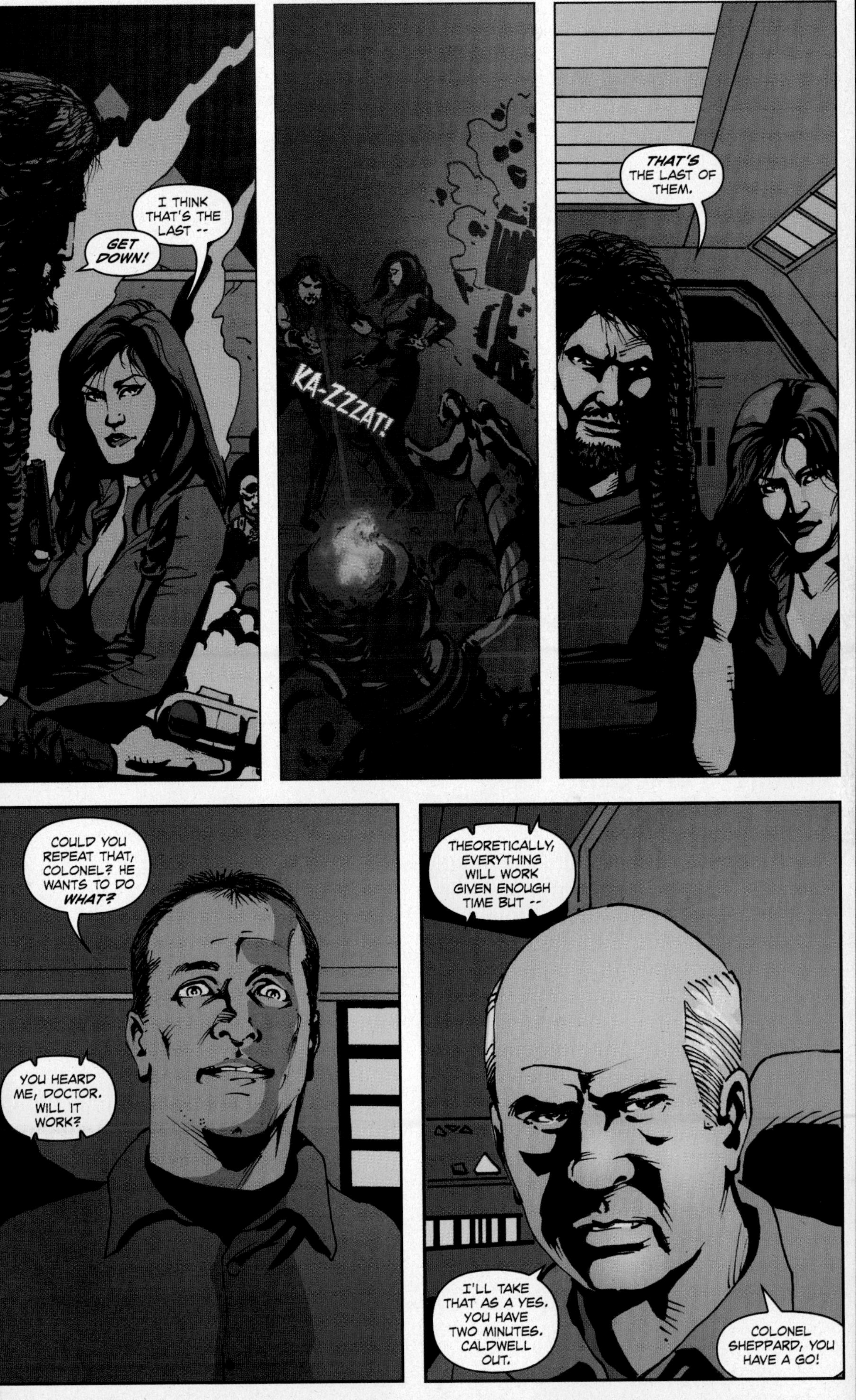
I THINK THAT'S THE LAST --
GET DOWN!
KA-ZZZAT!
THAT'S THE LAST OF THEM.
COULD YOU REPEAT THAT, COLONEL? HE WANTS TO DO WHAT?
YOU HEARD ME, DOCTOR. WILL IT WORK?
THEORETICALLY, EVERYTHING WILL WORK GIVEN ENOUGH TIME BUT --
I'LL TAKE THAT AS A YES. YOU HAVE TWO MINUTES. CALDWELL OUT.
COLONEL SHEPPARD, YOU HAVE A GO!

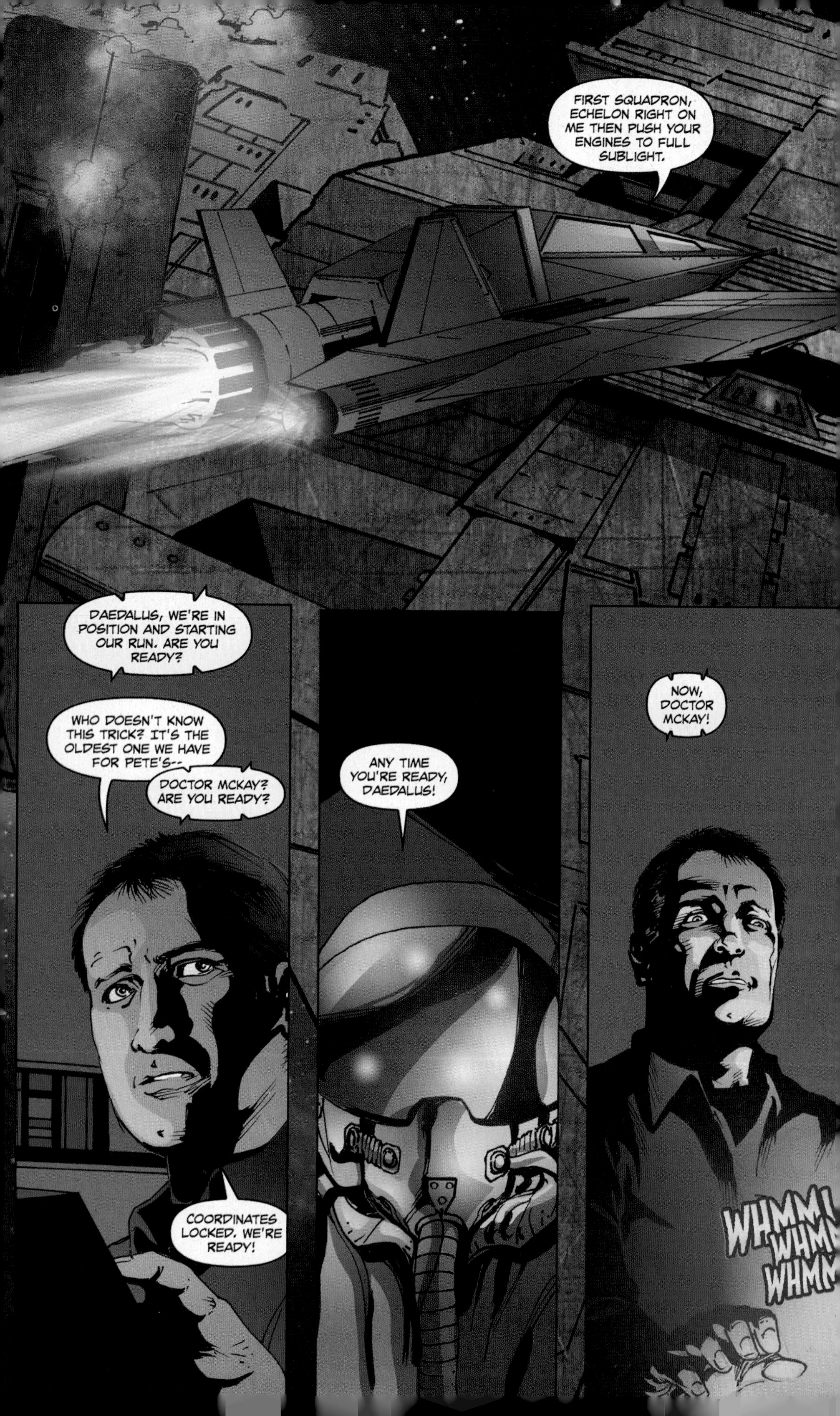
FIRST SQUADRON, ECHELON RIGHT ON ME THEN PUSH YOUR ENGINES TO FULL SUBLIGHT.
DAEDALUS, WE'RE IN POSITION AND STARTING OUR RUN. ARE YOU READY?
WHO DOESN'T KNOW THIS TRICK? IT'S THE OLDEST ONE WE HAVE FOR PETE'S--
DOCTOR MCKAY? ARE YOU READY?
COORDINATES LOCKED. WE'RE READY!
ANY TIME YOU'RE READY, DAEDALUS!
NOW, DOCTOR MCKAY!

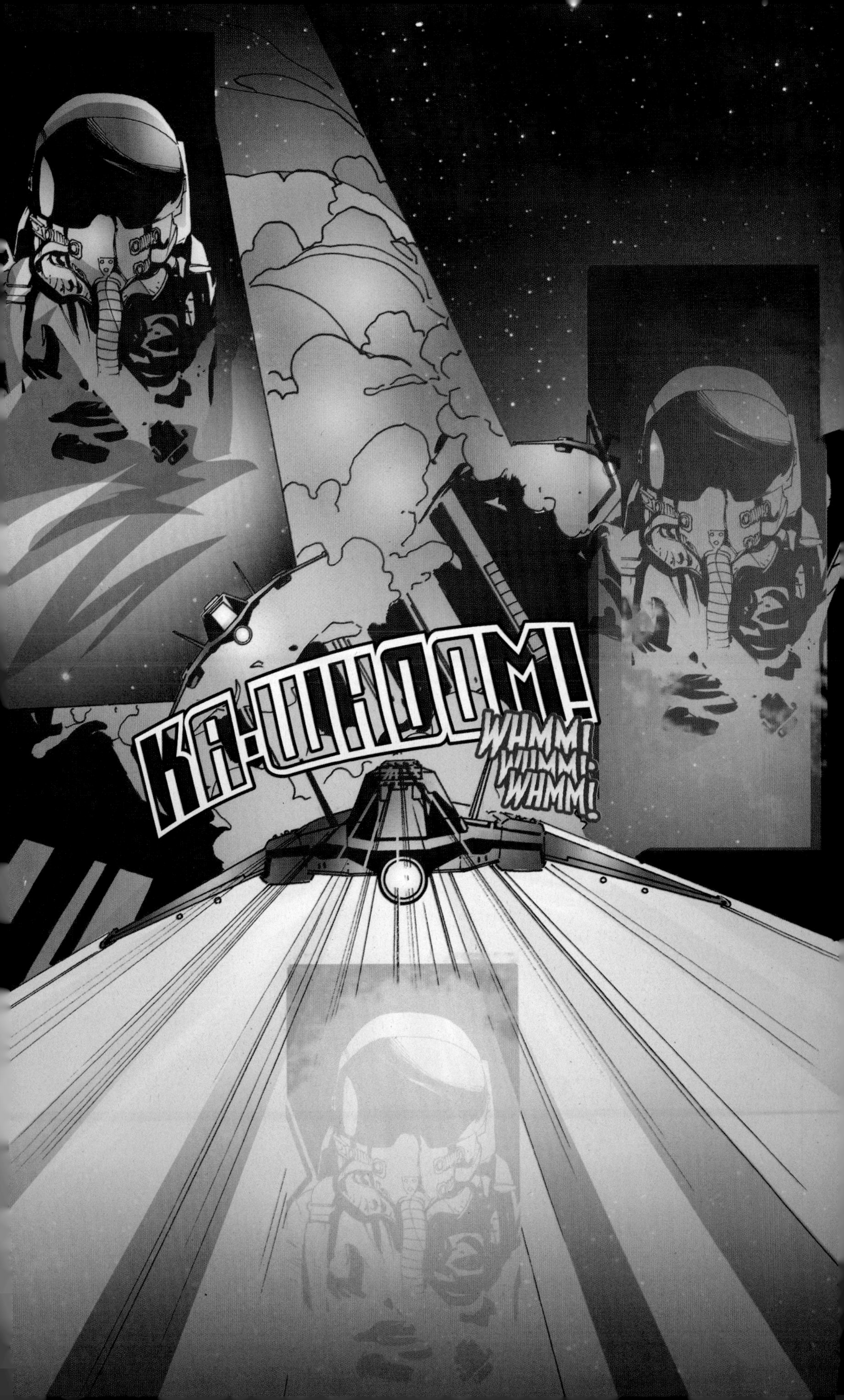
KA-WHOOM!
WHMM!
WHMM!
WHMM!

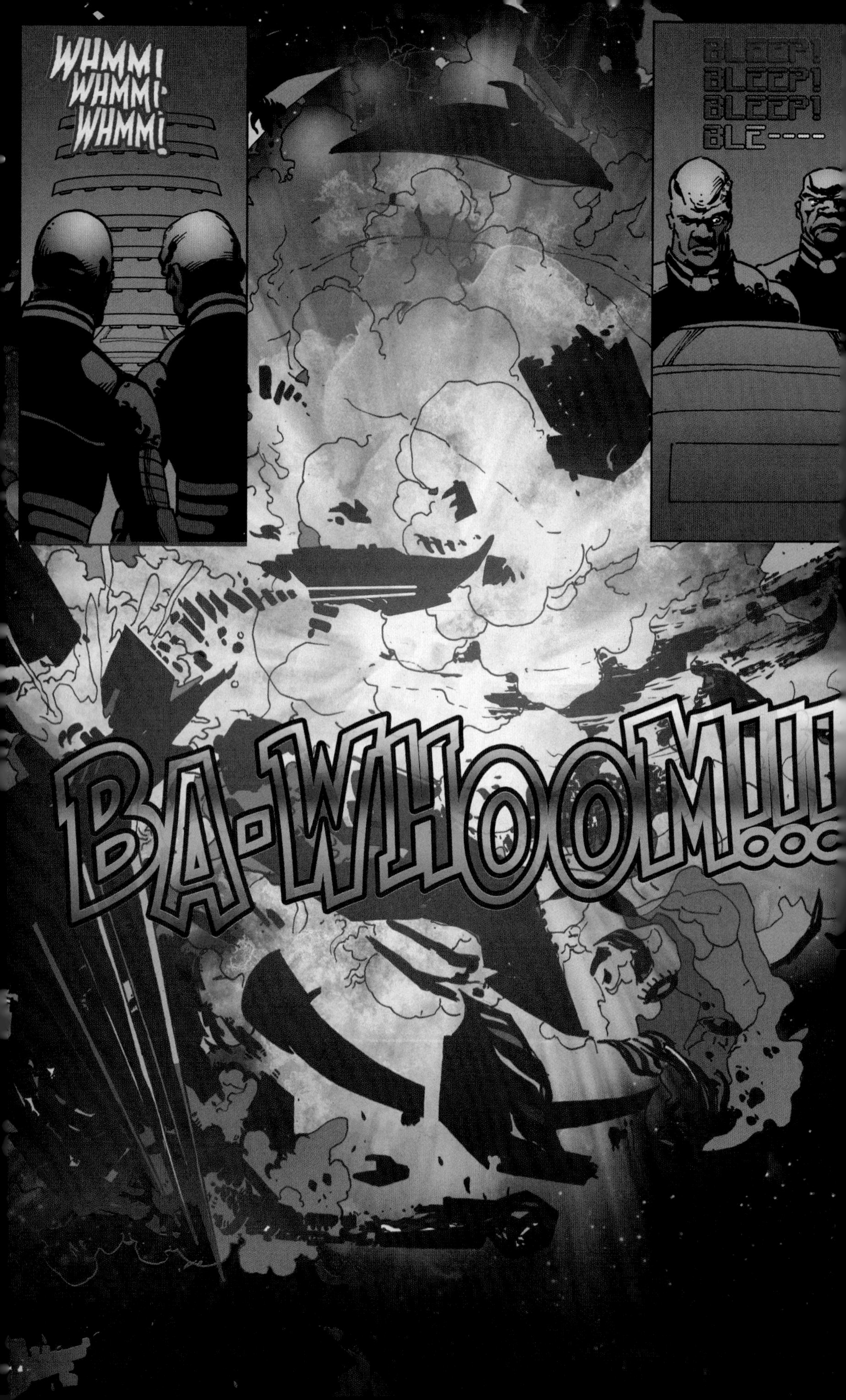
WHMM! WHMM! WHMM!
BLEEP! BLEEP! BLEEP! BLE----
BA-WHOOM!!!...

IT WORKED, SHEPPARD. GOOD CALL.

THANK YOU, SIR, AS LONG AS I DON'T HAVE TO PAY FOR THOSE 302S.

CAN WE CONTACT ATLANTIS?

UNFORTUNATELY, NO. LONG RANGE *COMMS SYSTEM* HAS BEEN *DESTROYED* AND OUR *HYPERDRIVE* IS GOING TO TAKE SEVERAL DAYS TO REPAIR, AT LEAST.

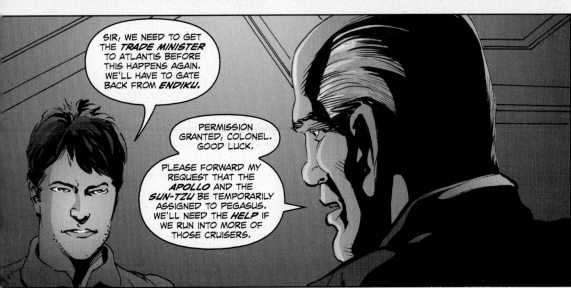

SIR, WE NEED TO GET THE *TRADE MINISTER* TO ATLANTIS BEFORE THIS HAPPENS AGAIN. WE'LL HAVE TO GATE BACK FROM *ENDIKU*.

PERMISSION GRANTED, COLONEL. GOOD LUCK.

PLEASE FORWARD MY REQUEST THAT THE *APOLLO* AND THE *SUN-TZU* BE TEMPORARILY ASSIGNED TO PEGASUS. WE'LL NEED THE *HELP* IF WE RUN INTO MORE OF THOSE CRUISERS.

WELCOME TO ATLANTIS. I'M RICHARD WOOLSEY. WE APPRECIATE YOUR WILLINGNESS TO COME FORWARD.

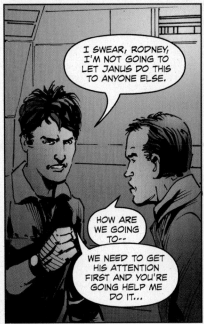

I SWEAR, RODNEY, I'M NOT GOING TO LET JANUS DO THIS TO ANYONE ELSE.

HOW ARE WE GOING TO--

WE NEED TO GET HIS ATTENTION FIRST AND YOU'RE GOING HELP ME DO IT...

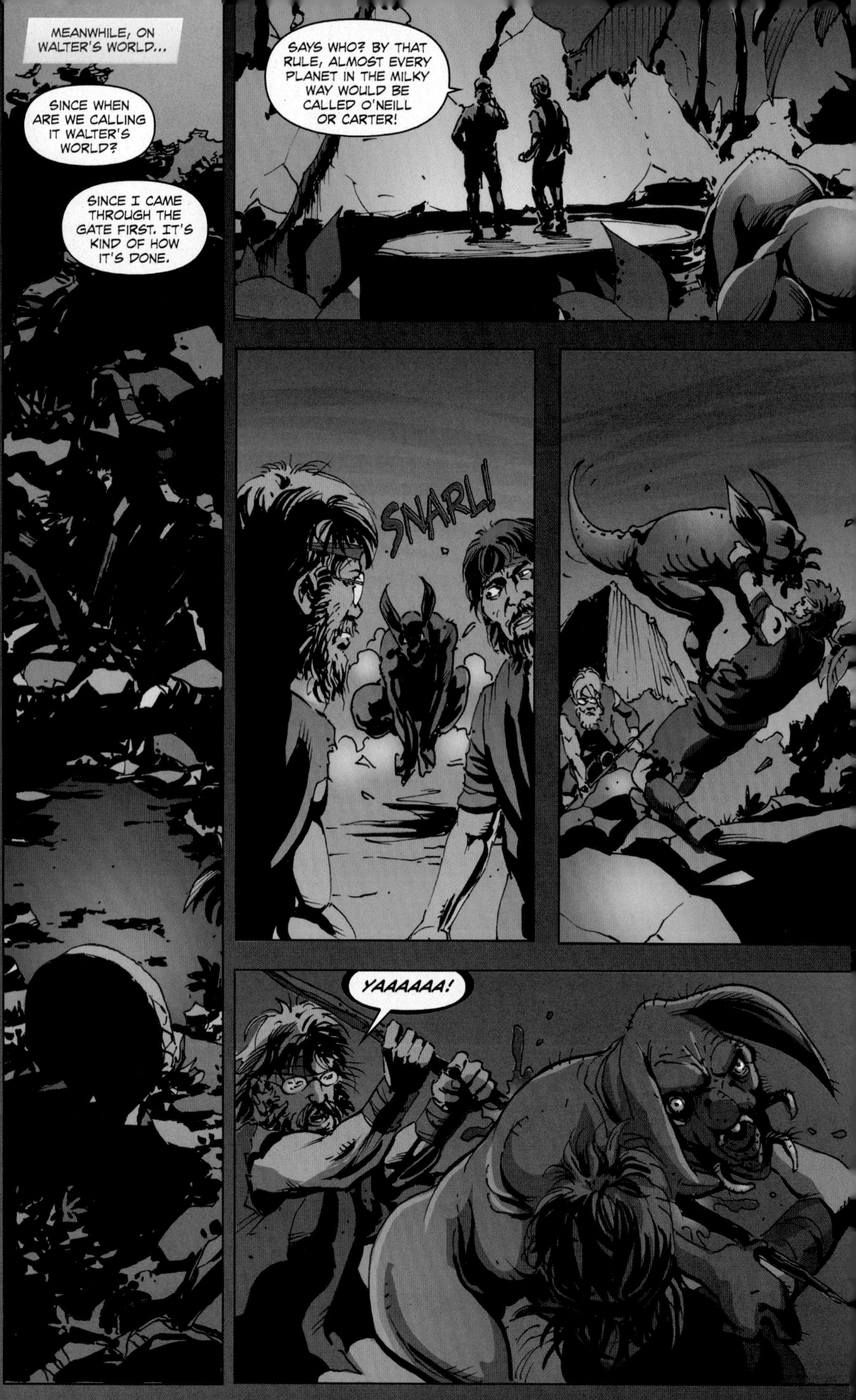
MEANWHILE, ON WALTER'S WORLD...
SINCE WHEN ARE WE CALLING IT WALTER'S WORLD?
SINCE I CAME THROUGH THE GATE FIRST. IT'S KIND OF HOW IT'S DONE.
SAYS WHO? BY THAT RULE, ALMOST EVERY PLANET IN THE MILKY WAY WOULD BE CALLED O'NEILL OR CARTER!
SNARL!
YAAAAAA!

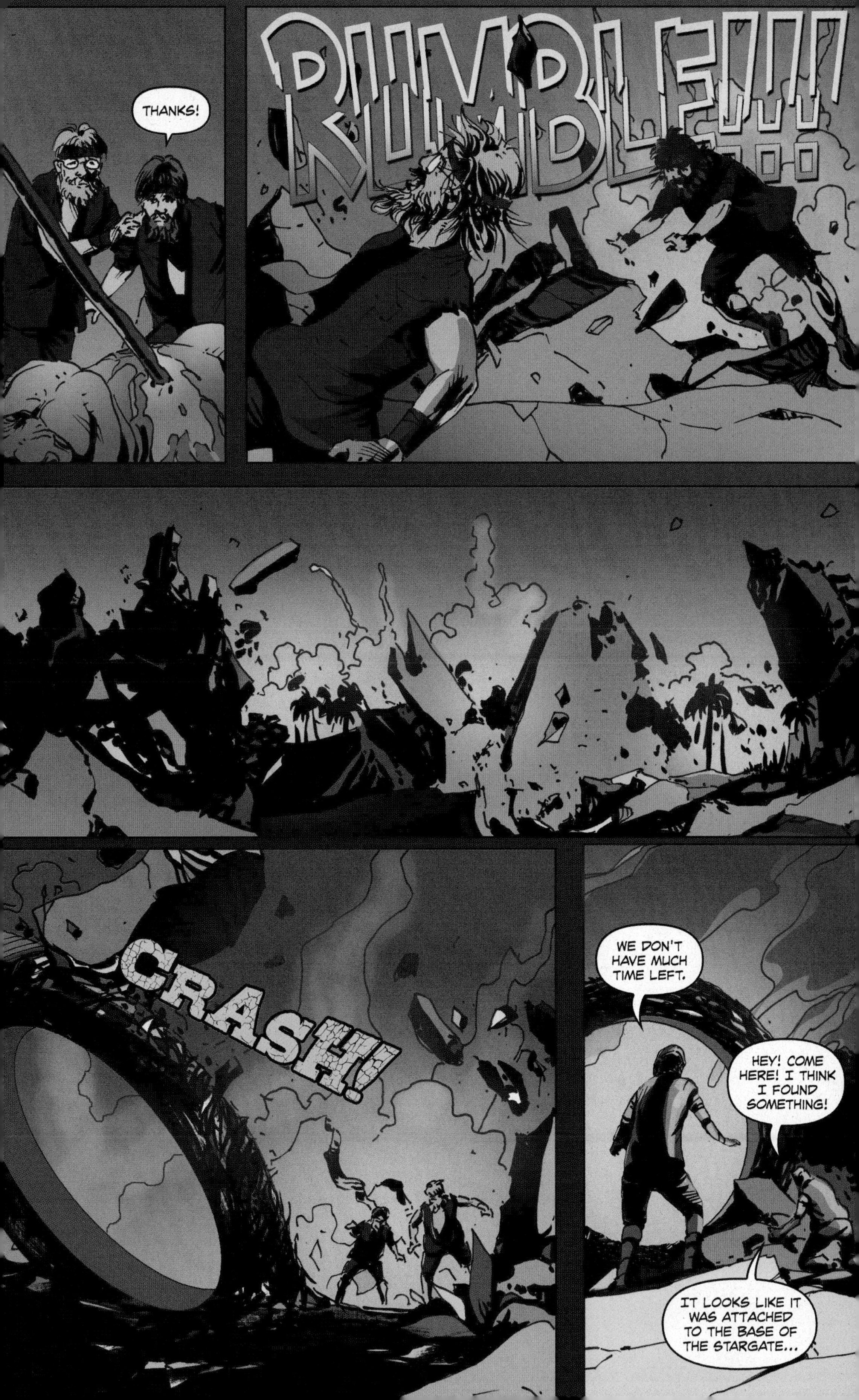
THANKS!
RUMBLE!!!
CRASH!!
WE DON'T HAVE MUCH TIME LEFT.
HEY! COME HERE! I THINK I FOUND SOMETHING!
IT LOOKS LIKE IT WAS ATTACHED TO THE BASE OF THE STARGATE...

WHAT THE HELL IS THAT?

BUT THE PROCEDURES WE DISCUSSED AT OUR LAST MEETING--

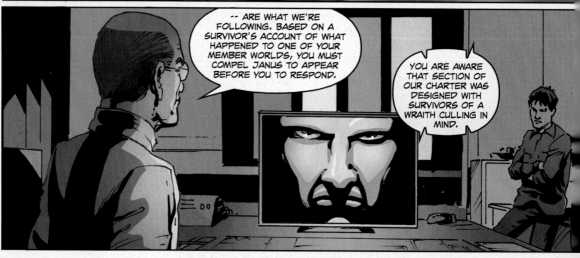

-- ARE WHAT WE'RE FOLLOWING. BASED ON A SURVIVOR'S ACCOUNT OF WHAT HAPPENED TO ONE OF YOUR MEMBER WORLDS, YOU MUST COMPEL JANUS TO APPEAR BEFORE YOU TO RESPOND.

YOU ARE AWARE THAT SECTION OF OUR CHARTER WAS DESIGNED WITH SURVIVORS OF A WRAITH CULLING IN MIND.

I DO, SIR, BUT THE LANGUAGE ISN'T THAT SPECIFIC.

THEY'RE YOUR RULES, AMBASSADOR. I DIDN'T WRITE THEM, BUT I DO INSIST YOU FOLLOW THEM.

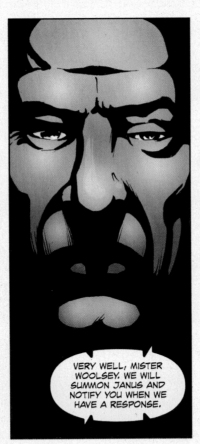

VERY WELL, MISTER WOOLSEY. WE WILL SUMMON JANUS AND NOTIFY YOU WHEN WE HAVE A RESPONSE.

REMIND ME TO CALL YOU THE NEXT TIME I GET A SPEEDING TICKET.

YOU THINK HE'LL SHOW?

I CERTAINLY HOPE SO OR ELSE WE, AND THIS ENTIRE PEGASUS GALAXY, MAY HAVE MORE TO CONTEND WITH THAN JUST THE REMNANTS OF THE WRAITH.

AM I INTERRUPTING?

COLONEL SHEPPARD, MAY I INTRODUCE YOU TO OUR NEW STAFF PSYCHOLOGIST.

WELCOME ABOARD, DOC. YOU'RE GONNA HAVE YOUR HANDS FULL WITH THIS BUNCH, ME INCLUDED.

LET ME GUESS, PROBLEMS WITH AUTHORITY?

THAT'S A RELIEF.

WHAT IS?

SOMEONE ACTUALLY READS MY MISSION REPORTS.

I'VE BROUGHT SHEN UP TO SPEED ON RECENT DEVELOPMENTS AND ASKED HER TO WEIGH IN ON OUR NEXT STEPS.

SPECIFICALLY, YOUR PROPOSAL TO CATCH JANUS OFF GUARD.

YEAH, I THINK IT'S --

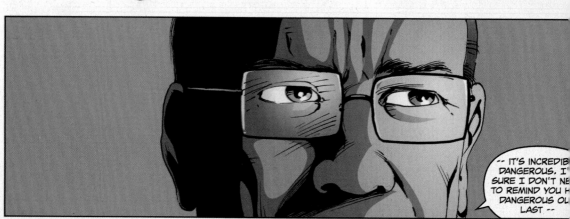

-- IT'S INCREDIB DANGEROUS, I' SURE I DON'T NE TO REMIND YOU H DANGEROUS OU LAST --

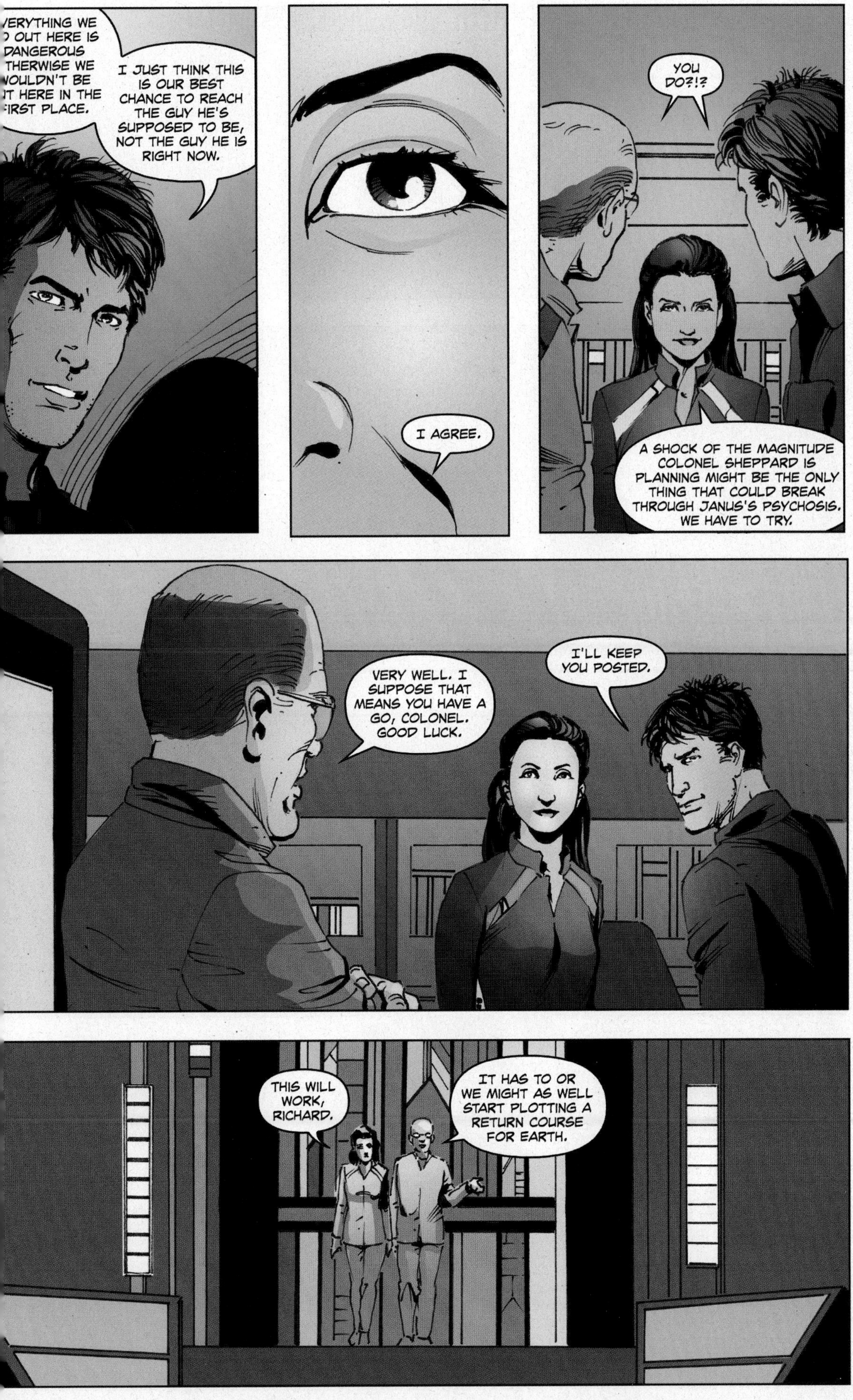

VERYTHING WE
O OUT HERE IS
DANGEROUS
THERWISE WE
VOULDN'T BE
UT HERE IN THE
FIRST PLACE.
I JUST THINK THIS IS OUR BEST CHANCE TO REACH THE GUY HE'S SUPPOSED TO BE, NOT THE GUY HE IS RIGHT NOW.
I AGREE.
YOU DO?!?
A SHOCK OF THE MAGNITUDE COLONEL SHEPPARD IS PLANNING MIGHT BE THE ONLY THING THAT COULD BREAK THROUGH JANUS'S PSYCHOSIS. WE HAVE TO TRY.
VERY WELL. I SUPPOSE THAT MEANS YOU HAVE A GO, COLONEL. GOOD LUCK.
I'LL KEEP YOU POSTED.
THIS WILL WORK, RICHARD.
IT HAS TO OR WE MIGHT AS WELL START PLOTTING A RETURN COURSE FOR EARTH.

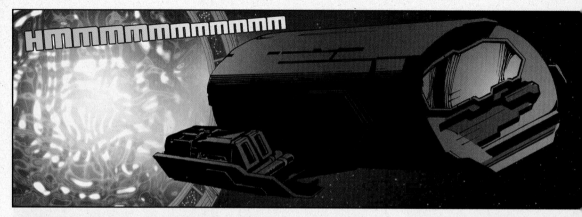

HMMMMMMMMMMMM

SEARCH PATTERN INITIATED. HOW LONG DO YOU THINK THIS WILL TAKE?

WE'RE NOT ORDERING TACOS AT A DRIVE-THRU, YOU KNOW.

WE DID GET SOME VELOCITY DATA FROM THE GATE ROOM SECURITY LOGS BUT WE DON'T KNOW ANYTHING ABOUT INITIAL TRAJECTORIES OR LOCAL GRAVITATIONAL EFFECTS --

SO WHAT YOU'RE SAYING IS IT WILL TAKE AS LONG AS IT TAKES.

WELL, YEAH...

BLEEP... BLEEP... BLEEP...

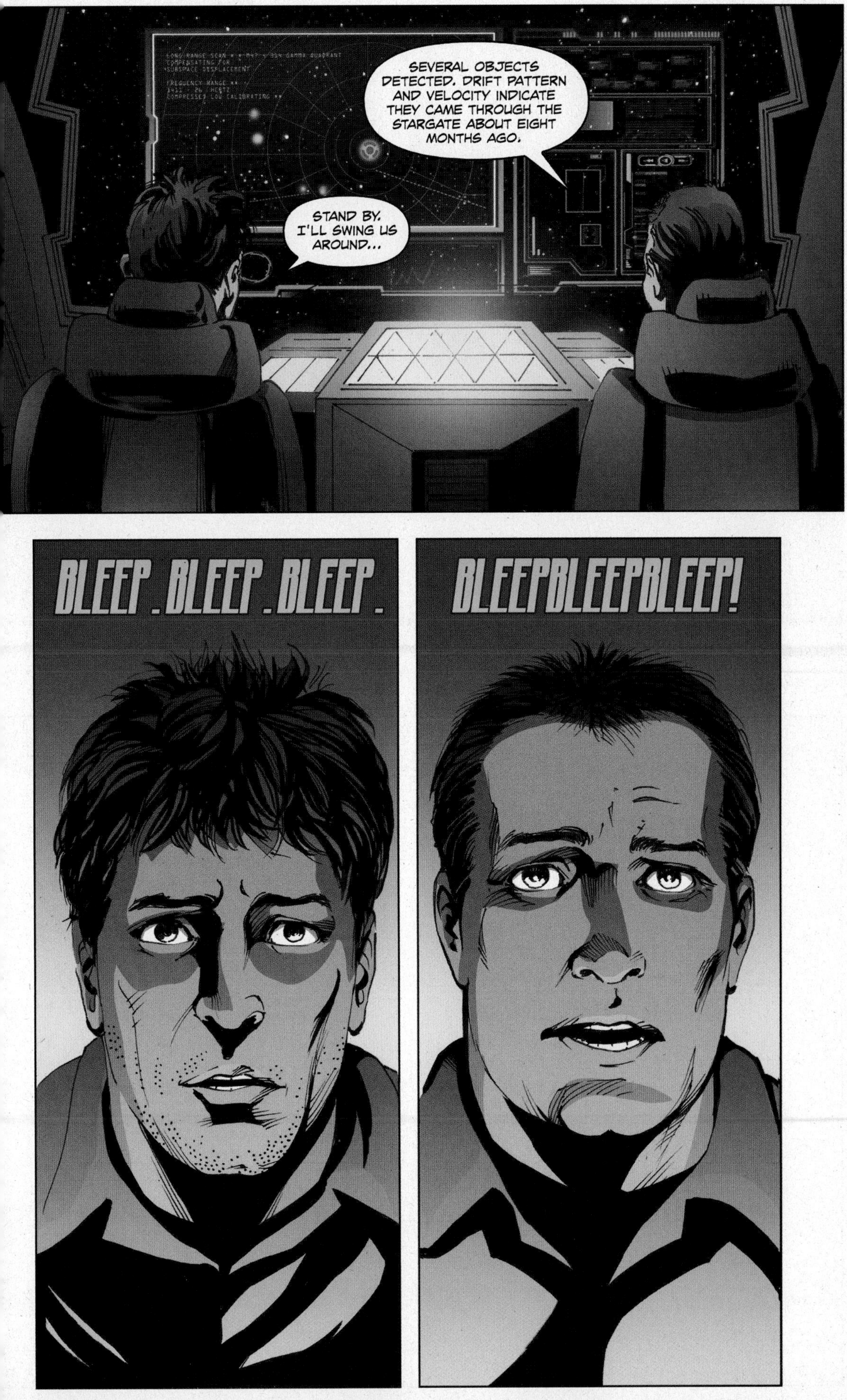
SEVERAL OBJECTS DETECTED. DRIFT PATTERN AND VELOCITY INDICATE THEY CAME THROUGH THE STARGATE ABOUT EIGHT MONTHS AGO.
STAND BY. I'LL SWING US AROUND...
BLEEP. BLEEP. BLEEP.
BLEEPBLEEPBLEEP!

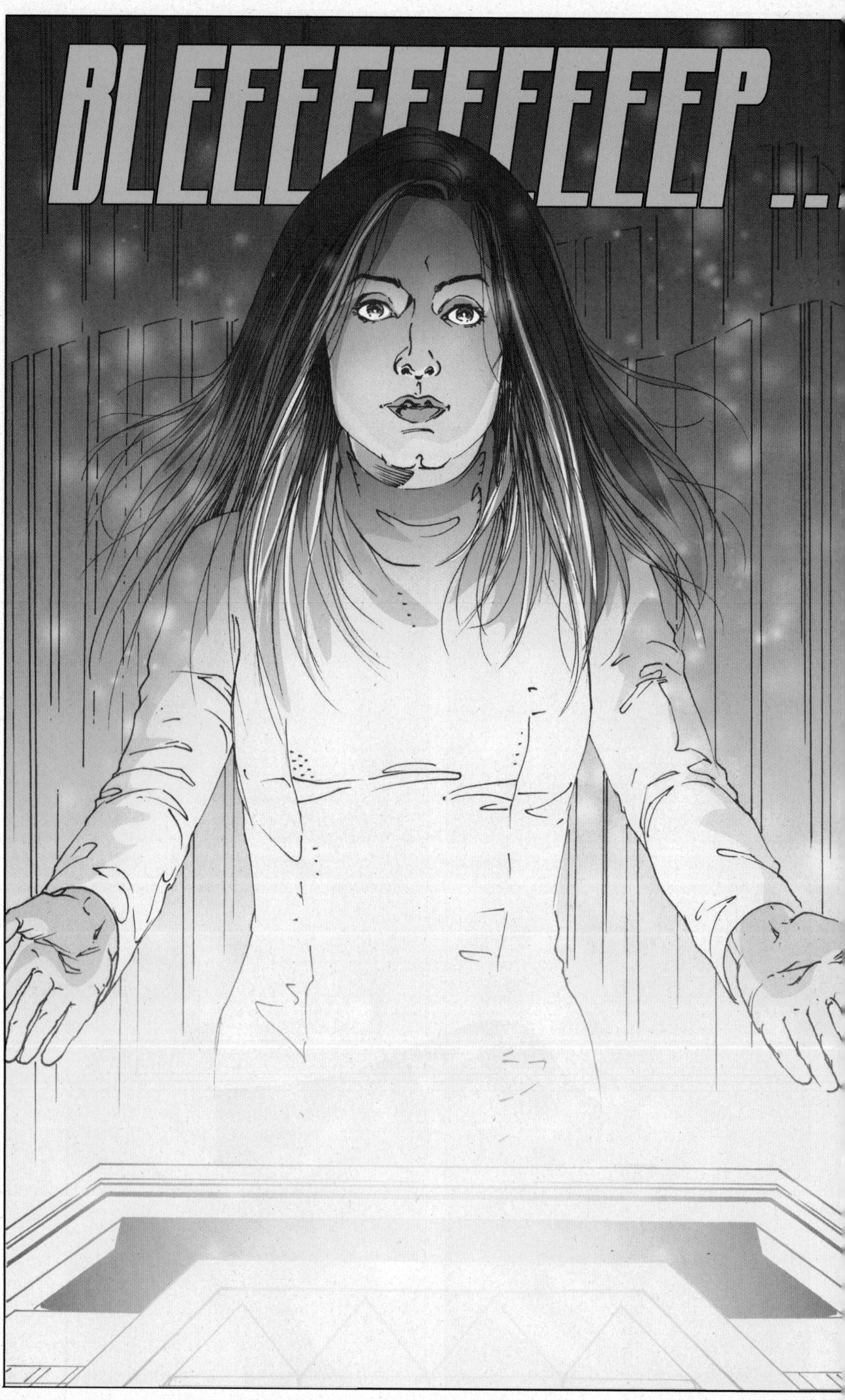
BLEEEEEEEEEEP...

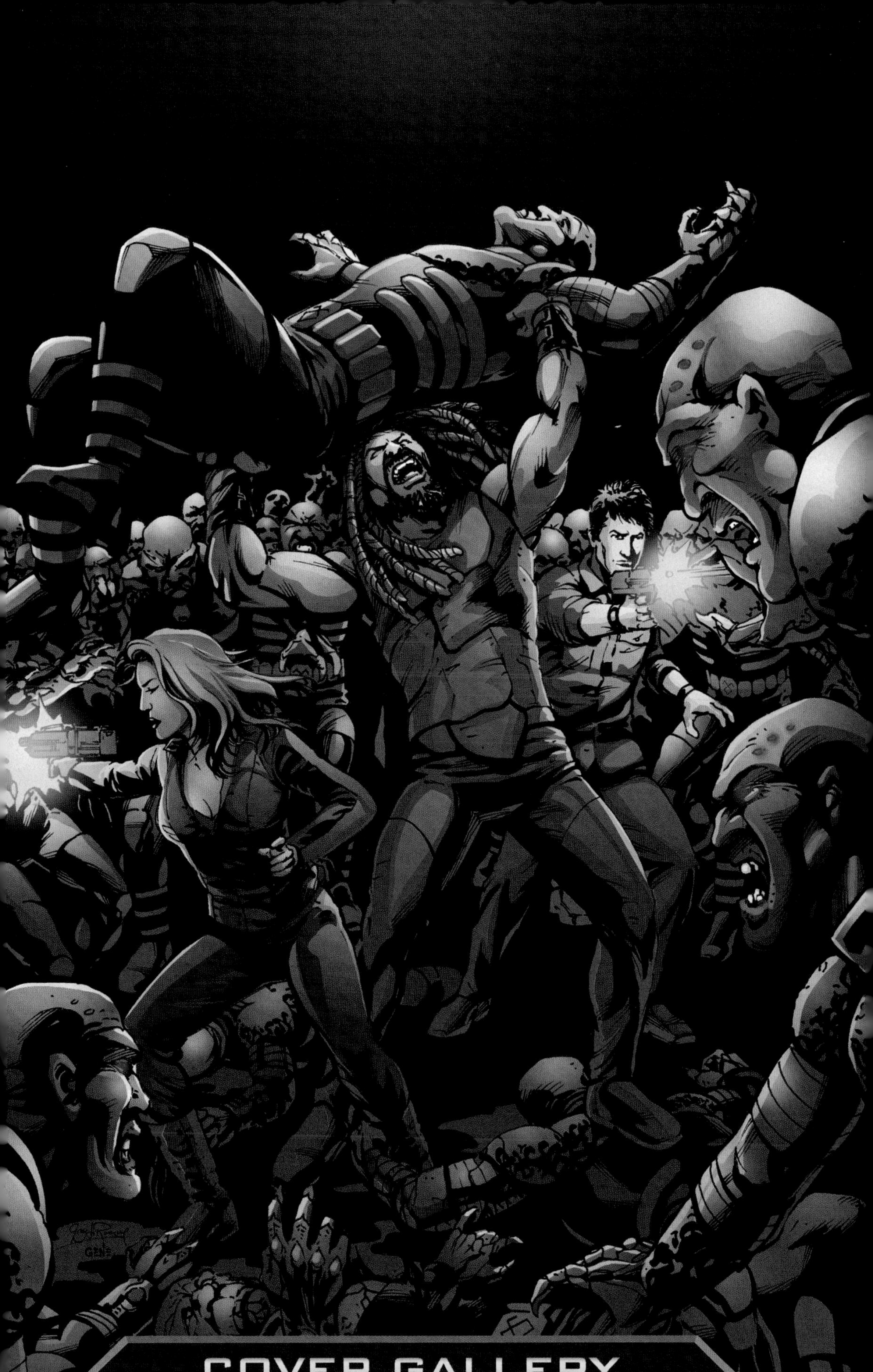

COVER GALLERY

SINGULARITY #1 MAIN COVER

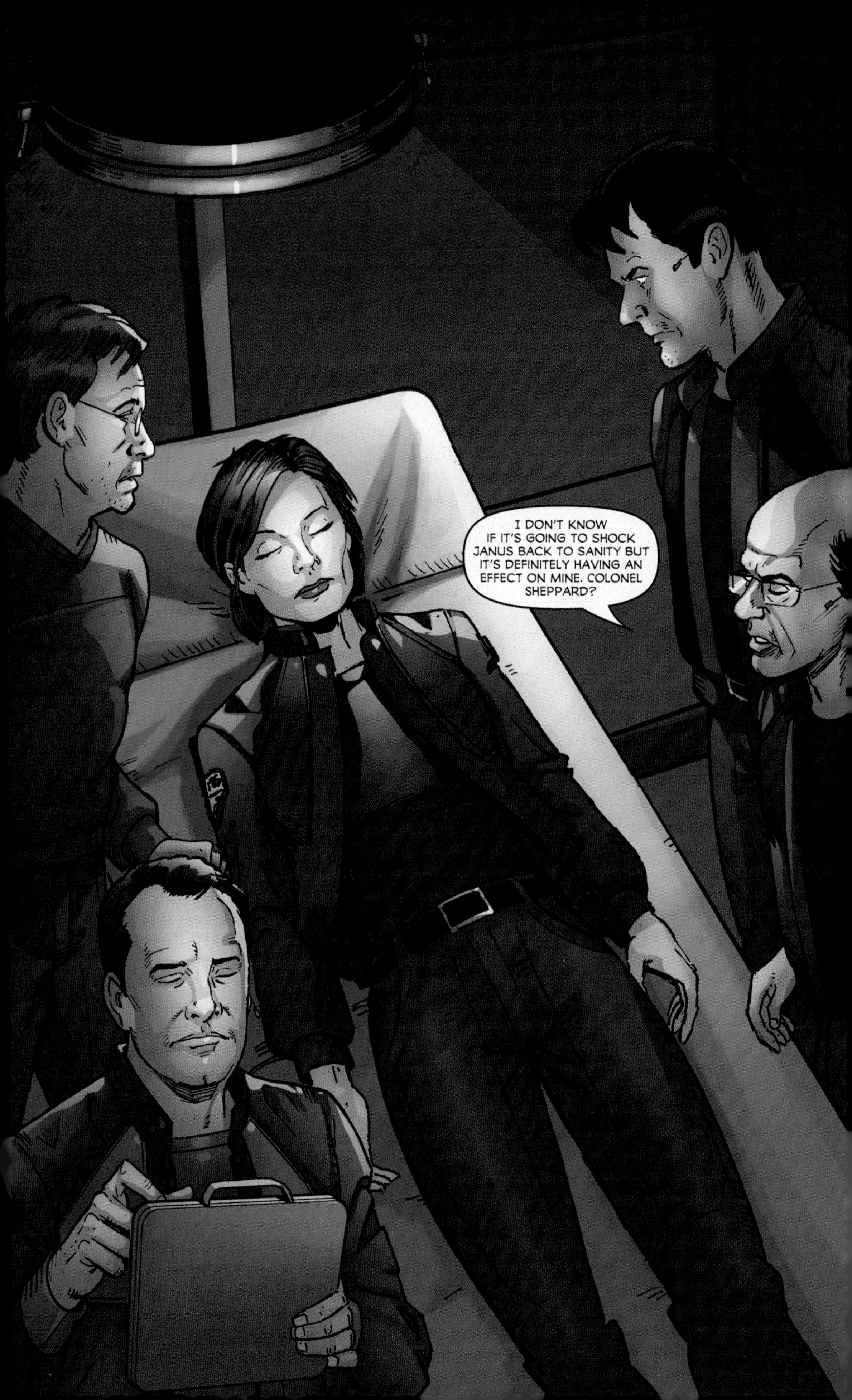
I DON'T KNOW IF IT'S GOING TO SHOCK JANUS BACK TO SANITY BUT IT'S DEFINITELY HAVING AN EFFECT ON MINE. COLONEL SHEPPARD?

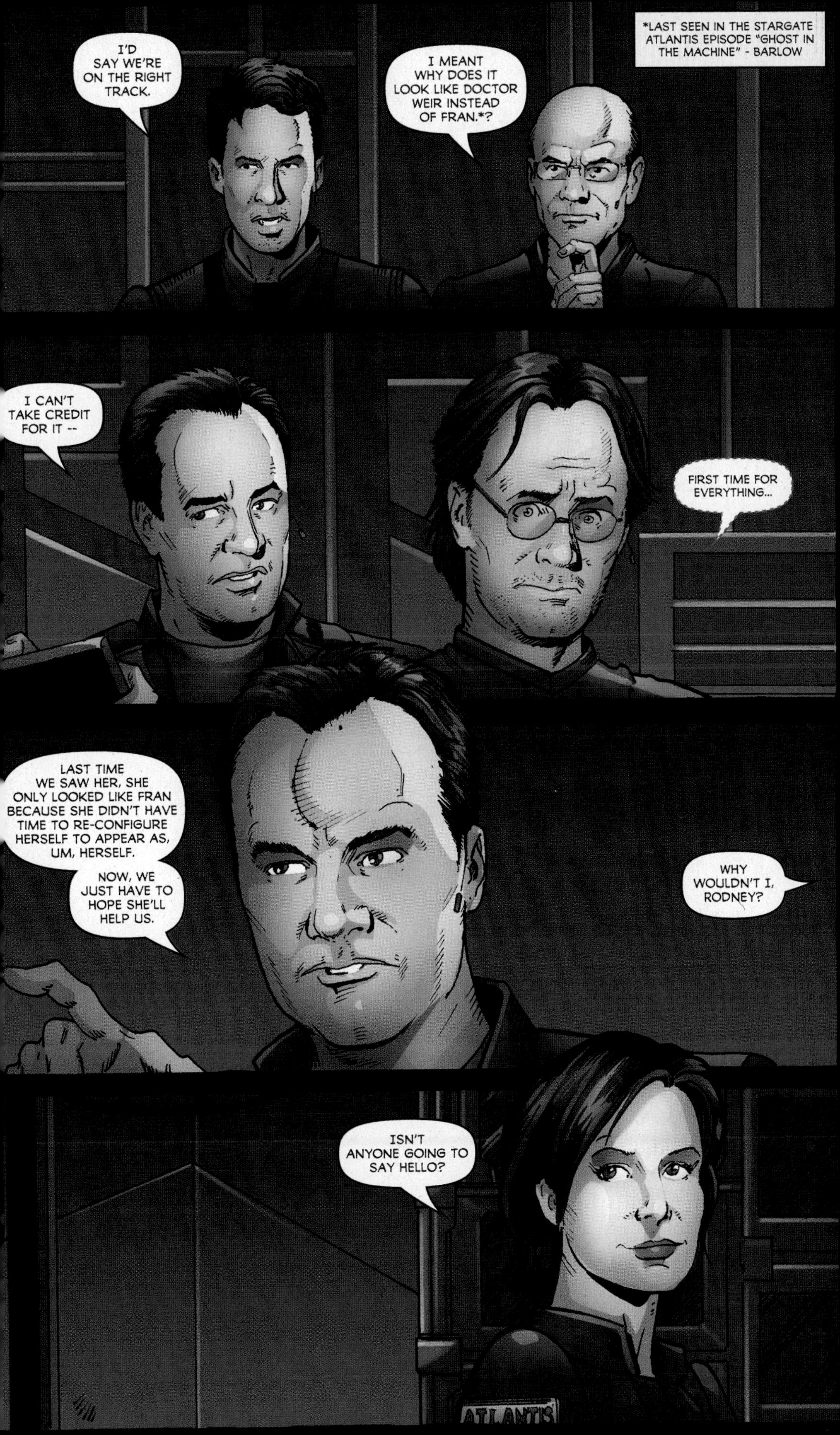
*LAST SEEN IN THE STARGATE ATLANTIS EPISODE "GHOST IN THE MACHINE" - BARLOW
I'D SAY WE'RE ON THE RIGHT TRACK.
I MEANT WHY DOES IT LOOK LIKE DOCTOR WEIR INSTEAD OF FRAN.*?
I CAN'T TAKE CREDIT FOR IT --
FIRST TIME FOR EVERYTHING...
LAST TIME WE SAW HER, SHE ONLY LOOKED LIKE FRAN BECAUSE SHE DIDN'T HAVE TIME TO RE-CONFIGURE HERSELF TO APPEAR AS, UM, HERSELF.
NOW, WE JUST HAVE TO HOPE SHE'LL HELP US.
WHY WOULDN'T I, RODNEY?
ISN'T ANYONE GOING TO SAY HELLO?
ATLANTIS

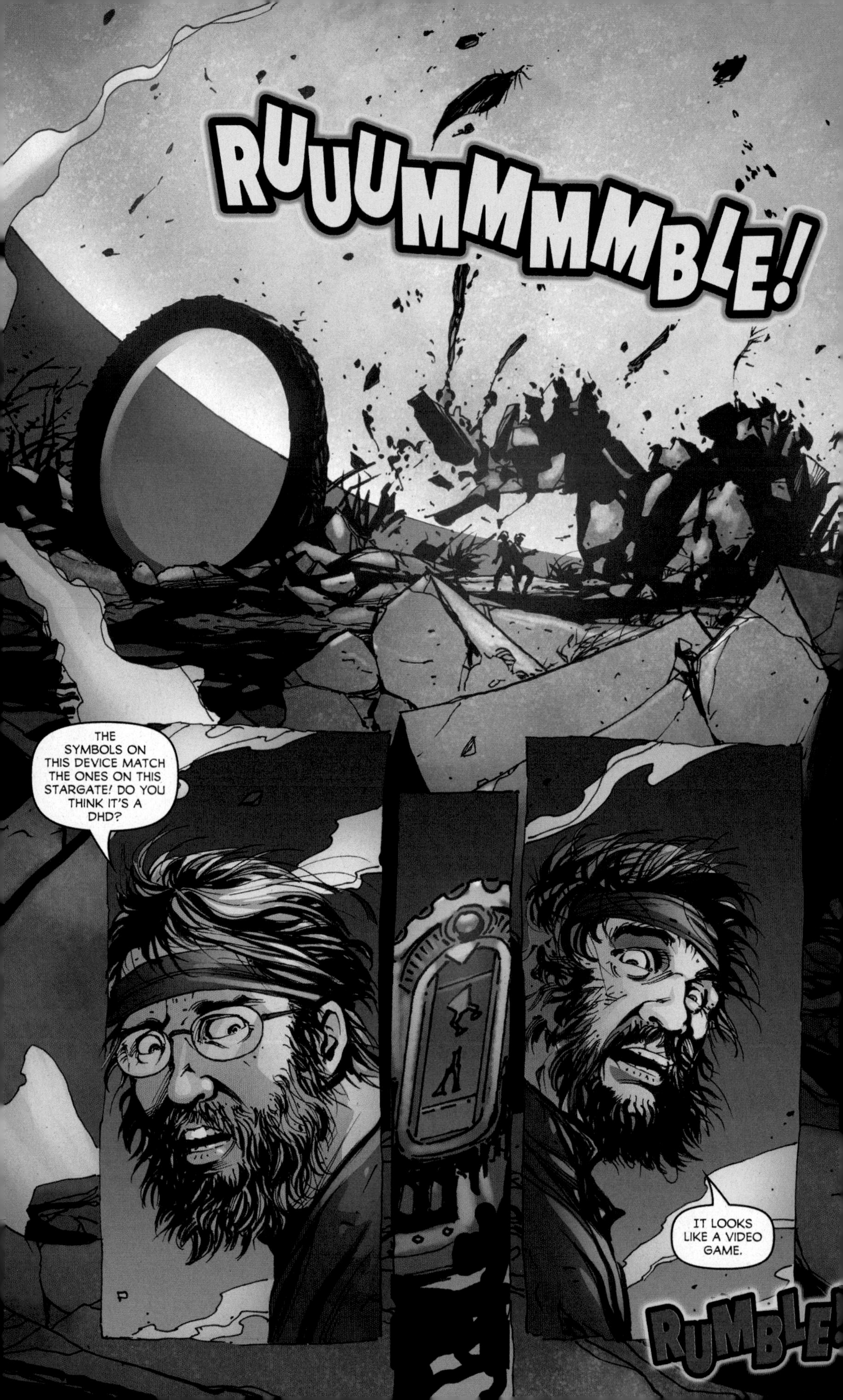
RUUUMMMMMBLE!
THE SYMBOLS ON THIS DEVICE MATCH THE ONES ON THIS STARGATE! DO YOU THINK IT'S A DHD?
IT LOOKS LIKE A VIDEO GAME.
RUMBLE

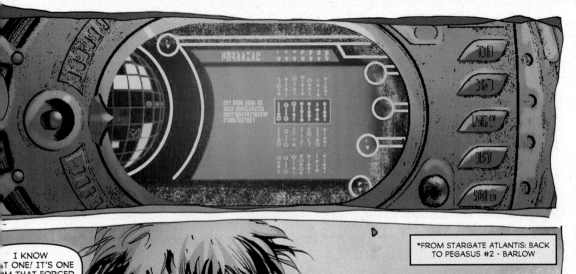

I KNOW
[TH]AT ONE! IT'S ONE
[FRO]M THAT FORCED
[ ]DOWNLOAD.*

*FROM STARGATE ATLANTIS: BACK TO PEGASUS #2 - BARLOW

YOU'RE RIGHT!
I SAW THAT ONE,
TOO!

HERE GOES
NOTHING...

MAKE IT
SPIN!

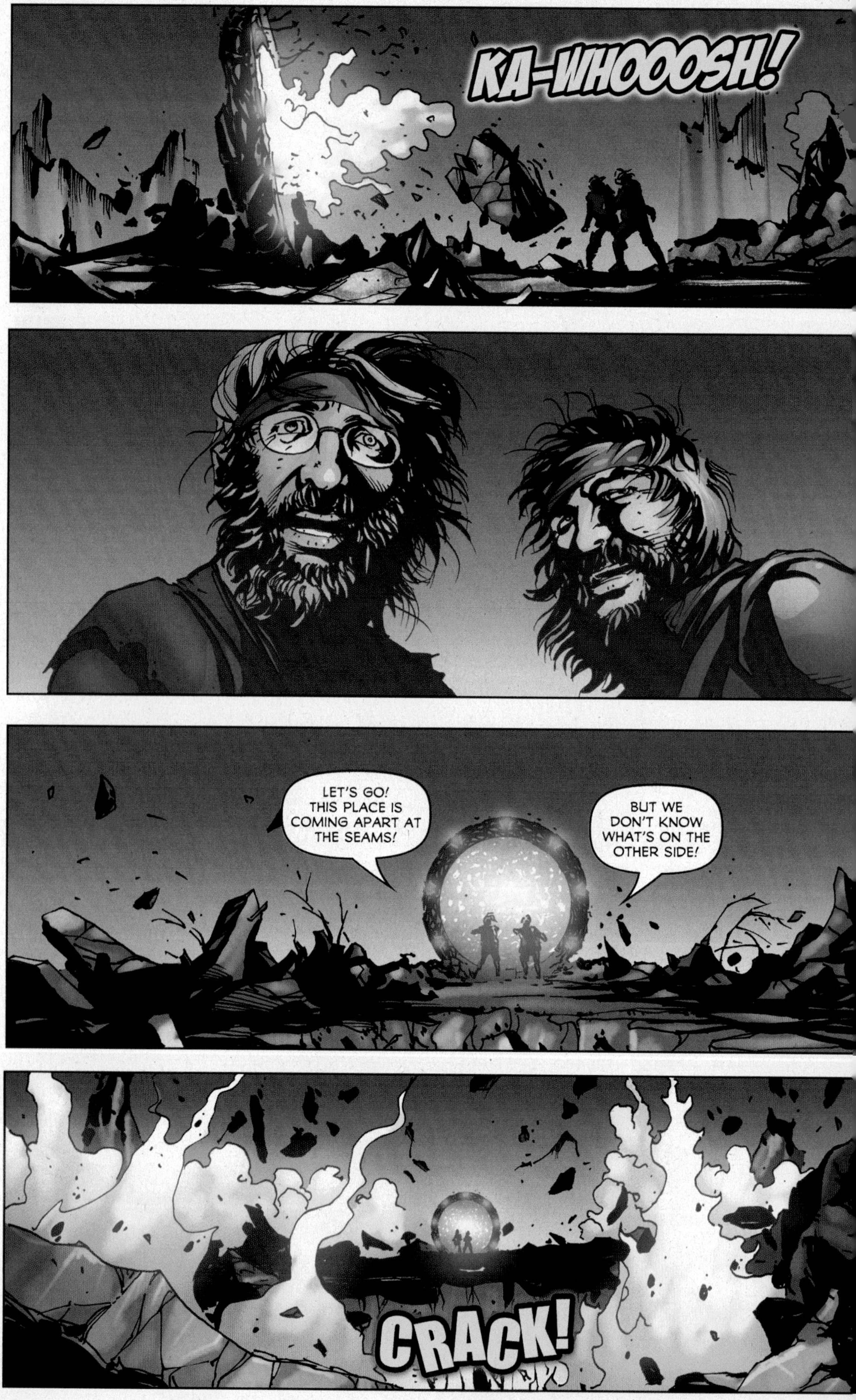
KA-WHOOOSH!
LET'S GO! THIS PLACE IS COMING APART AT THE SEAMS!
BUT WE DON'T KNOW WHAT'S ON THE OTHER SIDE!
CRACK!

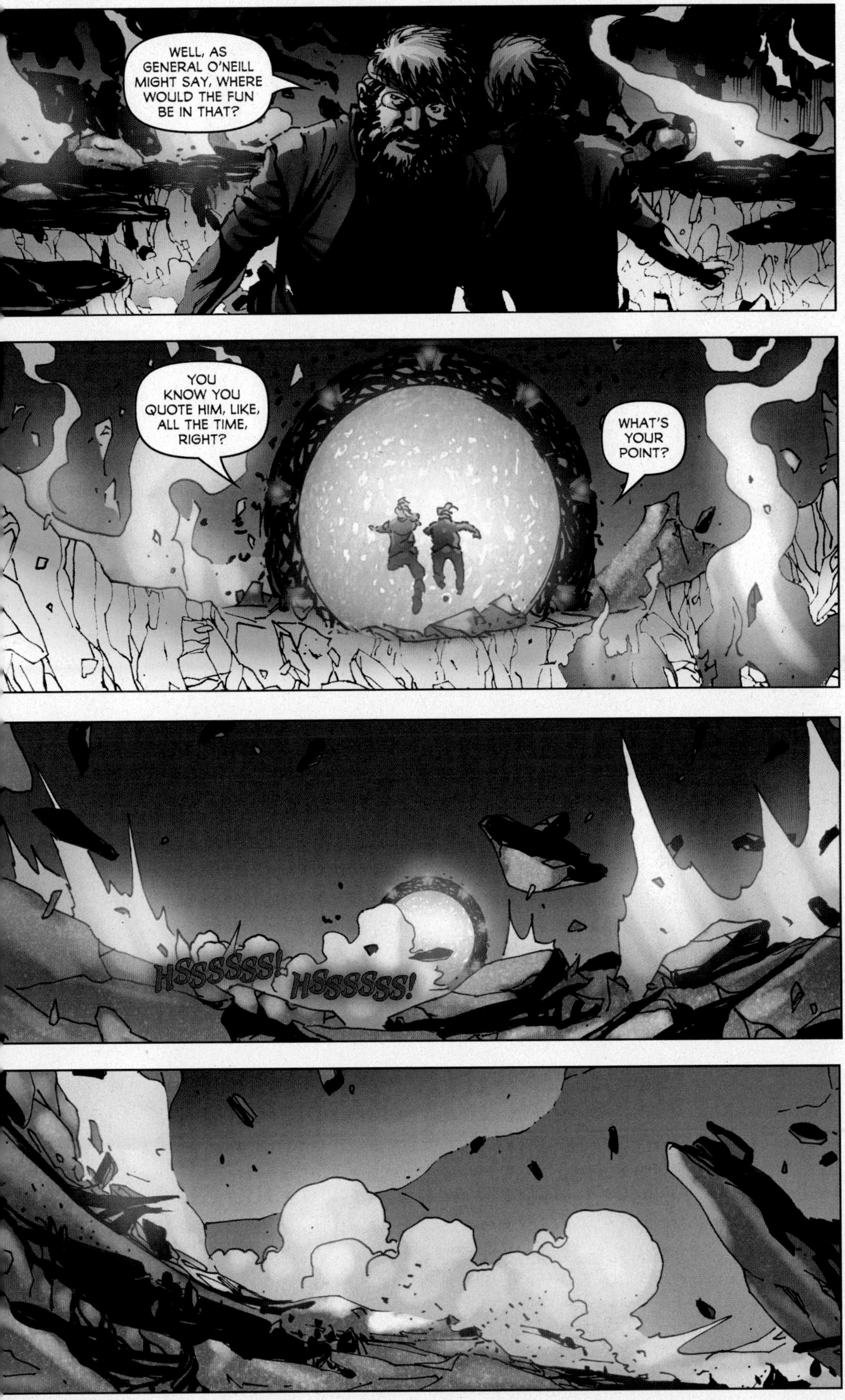
WELL, AS GENERAL O'NEILL MIGHT SAY, WHERE WOULD THE FUN BE IN THAT?
YOU KNOW YOU QUOTE HIM, LIKE, ALL THE TIME, RIGHT?
WHAT'S YOUR POINT?
HSSSSSS!
HSSSSSS!

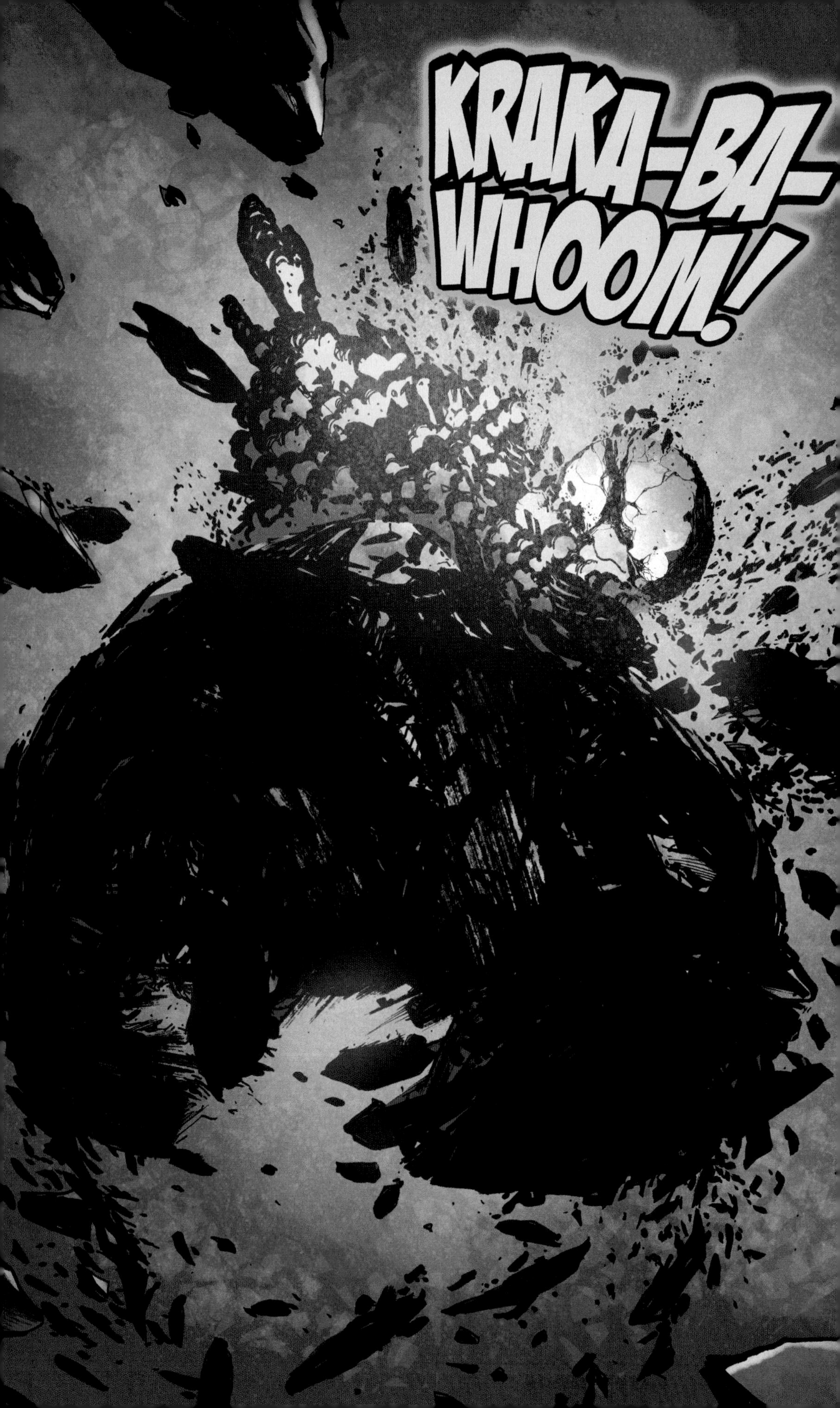
KRAKA-BA-WHOOM!

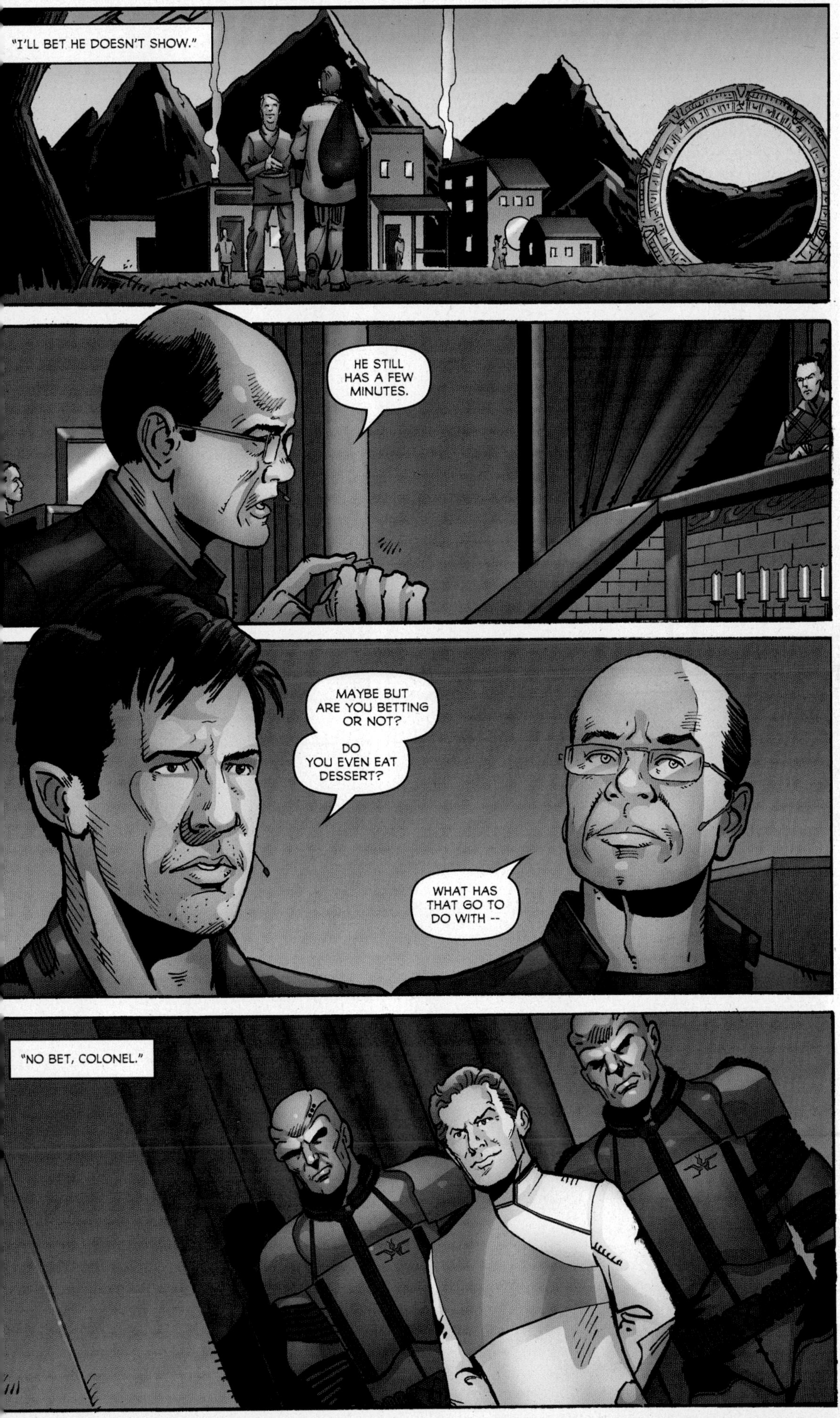
"I'LL BET HE DOESN'T SHOW."
HE STILL HAS A FEW MINUTES.
MAYBE BUT ARE YOU BETTING OR NOT?
DO YOU EVEN EAT DESSERT?
WHAT HAS THAT GO TO DO WITH --
"NO BET, COLONEL."

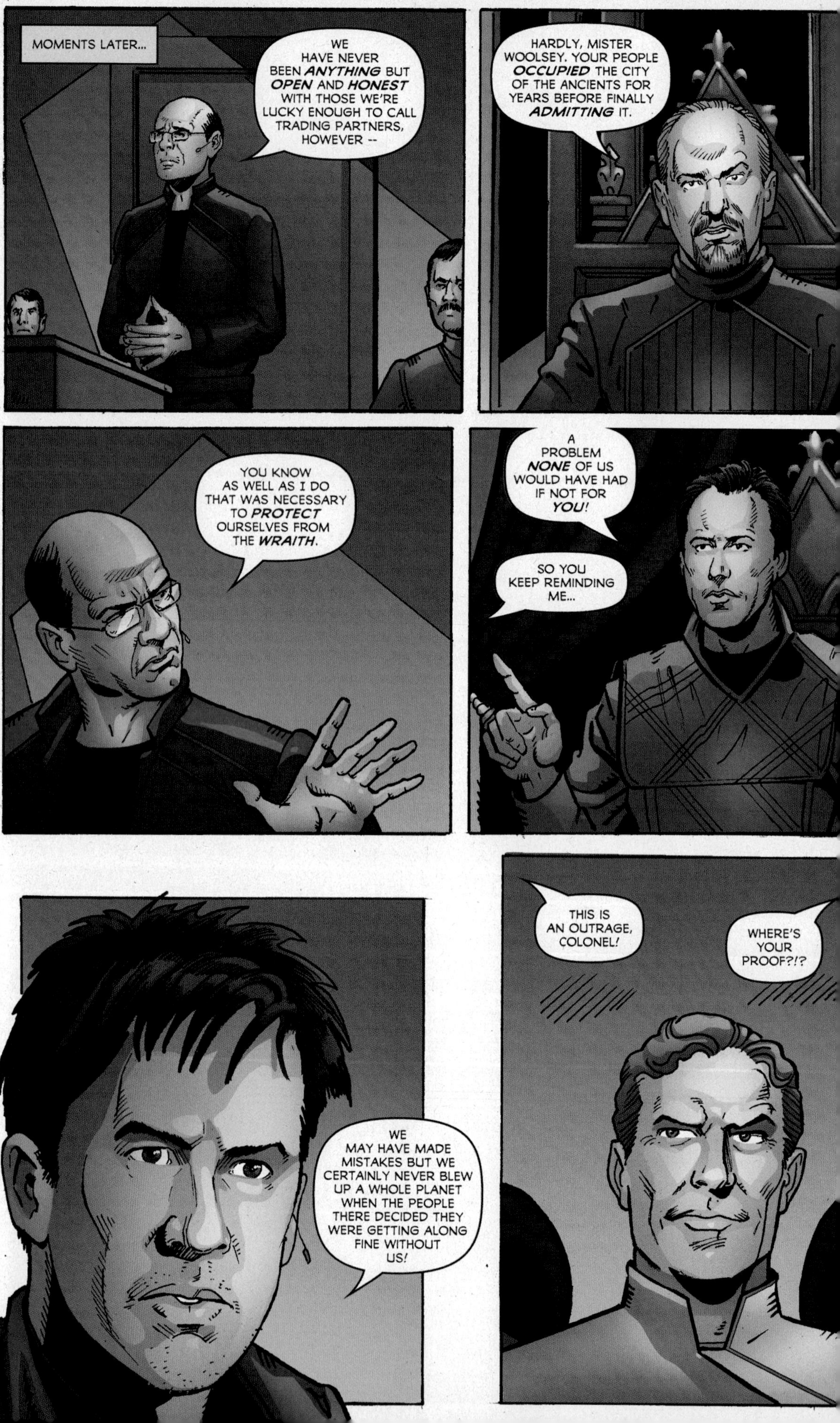

MOMENTS LATER...
WE HAVE NEVER BEEN ANYTHING BUT OPEN AND HONEST WITH THOSE WE'RE LUCKY ENOUGH TO CALL TRADING PARTNERS, HOWEVER --
HARDLY, MISTER WOOLSEY. YOUR PEOPLE OCCUPIED THE CITY OF THE ANCIENTS FOR YEARS BEFORE FINALLY ADMITTING IT.
YOU KNOW AS WELL AS I DO THAT WAS NECESSARY TO PROTECT OURSELVES FROM THE WRAITH.
A PROBLEM NONE OF US WOULD HAVE HAD IF NOT FOR YOU!
SO YOU KEEP REMINDING ME...
WE MAY HAVE MADE MISTAKES BUT WE CERTAINLY NEVER BLEW UP A WHOLE PLANET WHEN THE PEOPLE THERE DECIDED THEY WERE GETTING ALONG FINE WITHOUT US!
THIS IS AN OUTRAGE, COLONEL!
WHERE'S YOUR PROOF?!?

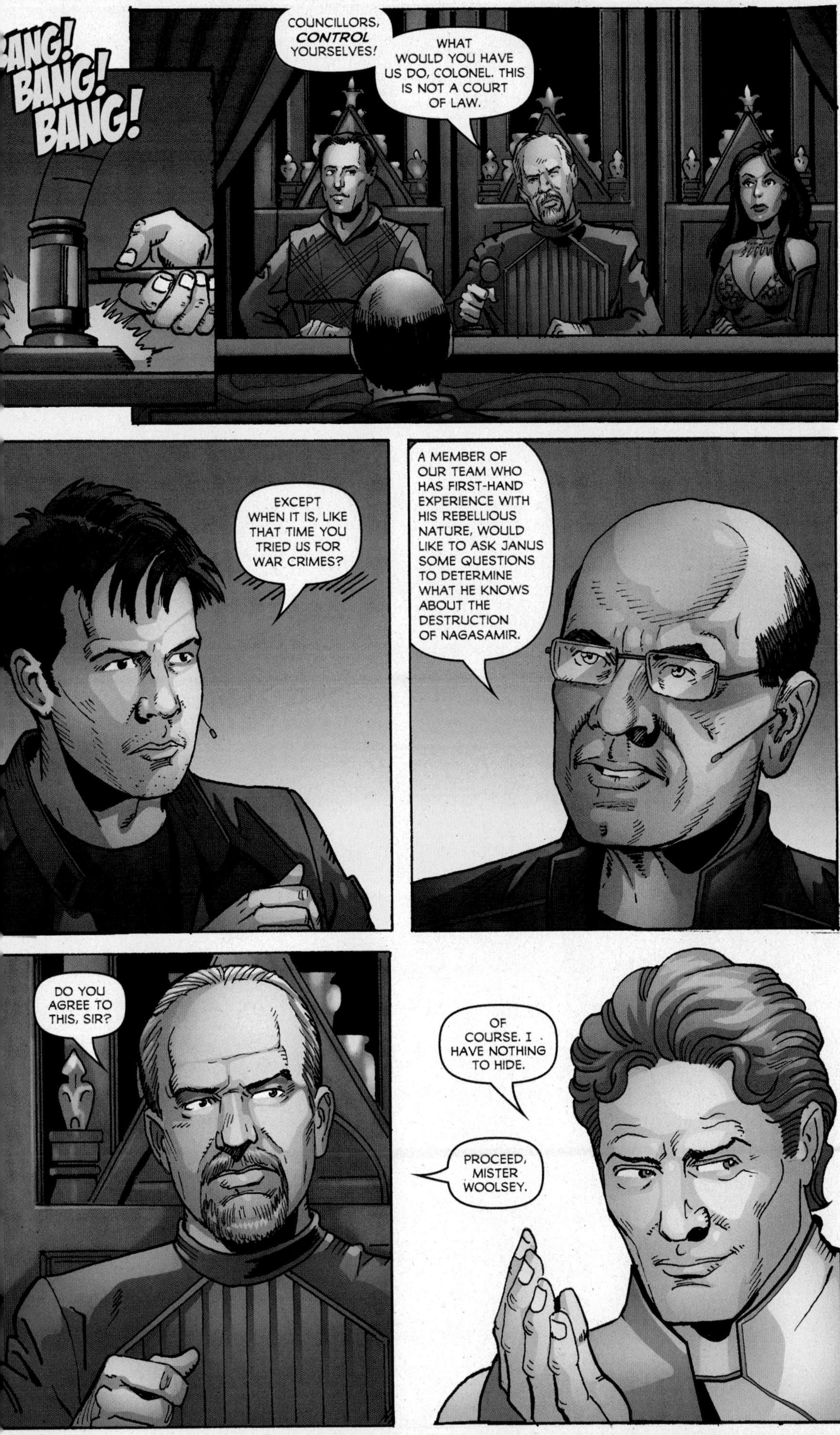
BANG! BANG! BANG!
COUNCILLORS, CONTROL YOURSELVES!
WHAT WOULD YOU HAVE US DO, COLONEL. THIS IS NOT A COURT OF LAW.
EXCEPT WHEN IT IS, LIKE THAT TIME YOU TRIED US FOR WAR CRIMES?
A MEMBER OF OUR TEAM WHO HAS FIRST-HAND EXPERIENCE WITH HIS REBELLIOUS NATURE, WOULD LIKE TO ASK JANUS SOME QUESTIONS TO DETERMINE WHAT HE KNOWS ABOUT THE DESTRUCTION OF NAGASAMIR.
DO YOU AGREE TO THIS, SIR?
OF COURSE. I HAVE NOTHING TO HIDE.
PROCEED, MISTER WOOLSEY.

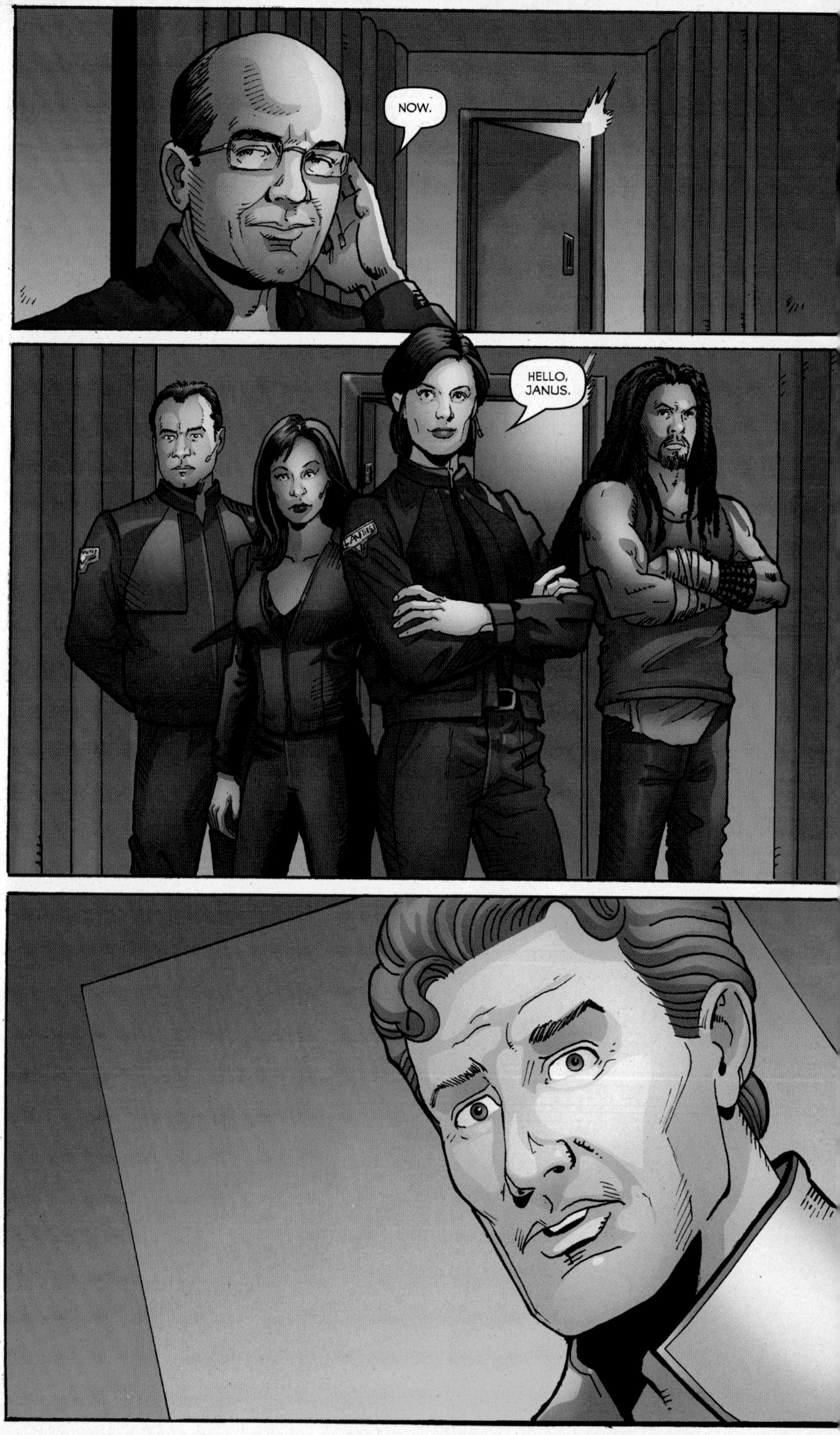
NOW.
HELLO, JANUS.

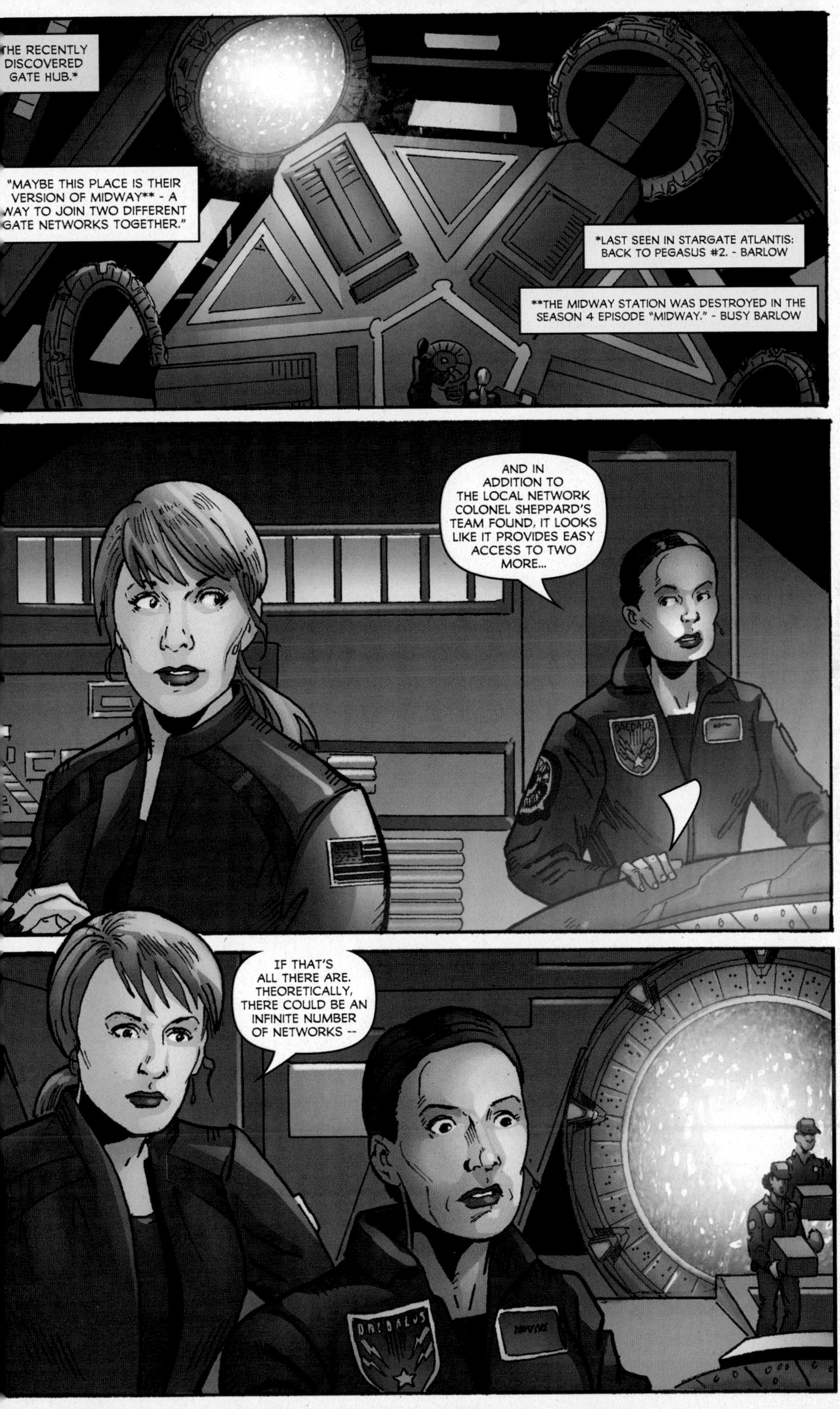

THE RECENTLY DISCOVERED GATE HUB.*
"MAYBE THIS PLACE IS THEIR VERSION OF MIDWAY** - A WAY TO JOIN TWO DIFFERENT GATE NETWORKS TOGETHER."
*LAST SEEN IN STARGATE ATLANTIS: BACK TO PEGASUS #2. - BARLOW
**THE MIDWAY STATION WAS DESTROYED IN THE SEASON 4 EPISODE "MIDWAY." - BUSY BARLOW
AND IN ADDITION TO THE LOCAL NETWORK COLONEL SHEPPARD'S TEAM FOUND, IT LOOKS LIKE IT PROVIDES EASY ACCESS TO TWO MORE...
IF THAT'S ALL THERE ARE. THEORETICALLY, THERE COULD BE AN INFINITE NUMBER OF NETWORKS --
DAEDALUS

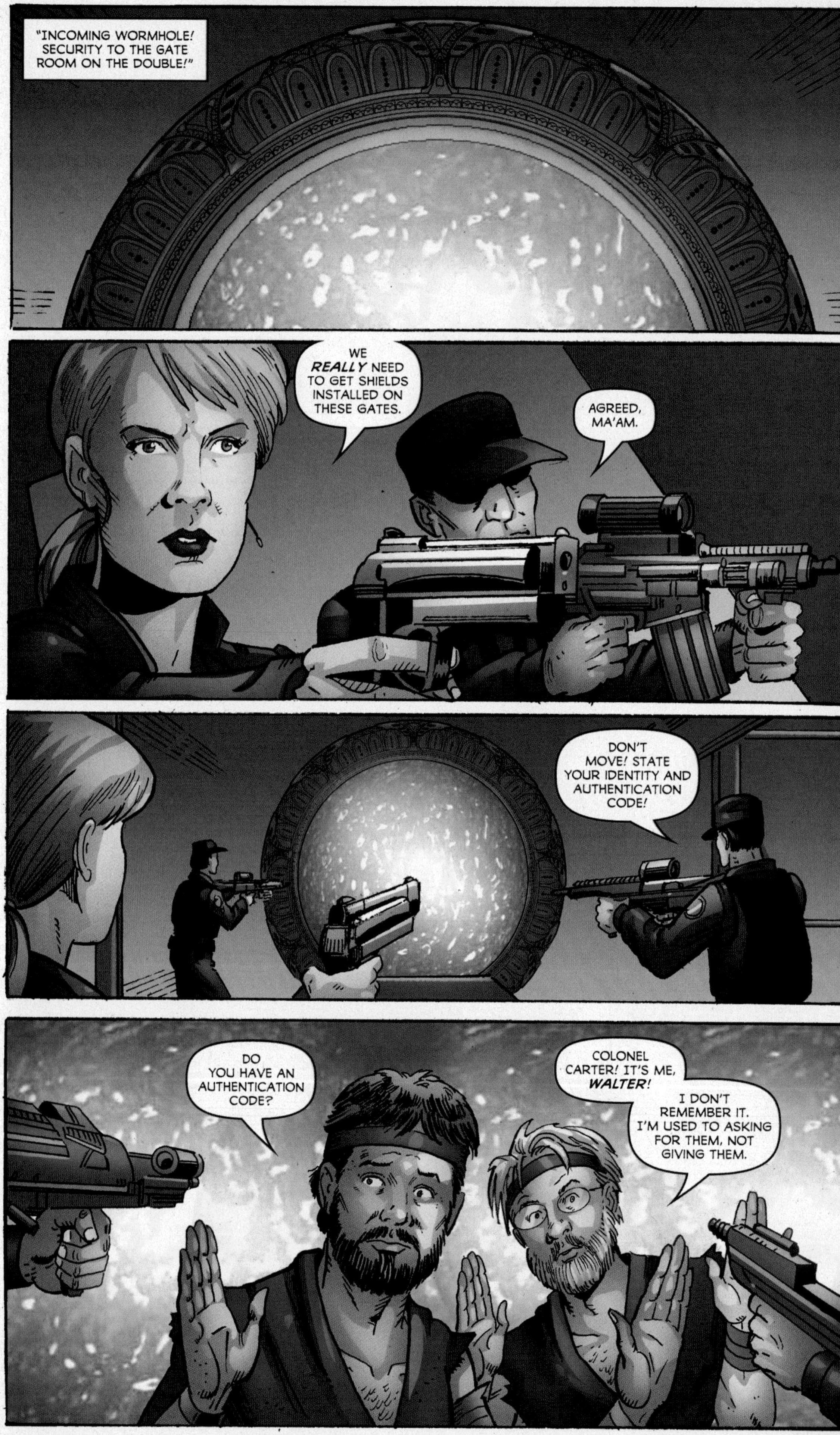
"INCOMING WORMHOLE! SECURITY TO THE GATE ROOM ON THE DOUBLE!"
WE *REALLY* NEED TO GET SHIELDS INSTALLED ON THESE GATES.
AGREED, MA'AM.
DON'T MOVE! STATE YOUR IDENTITY AND AUTHENTICATION CODE!
DO YOU HAVE AN AUTHENTICATION CODE?
COLONEL CARTER! IT'S ME, *WALTER*!
I DON'T REMEMBER IT. I'M USED TO ASKING FOR THEM, NOT GIVING THEM.

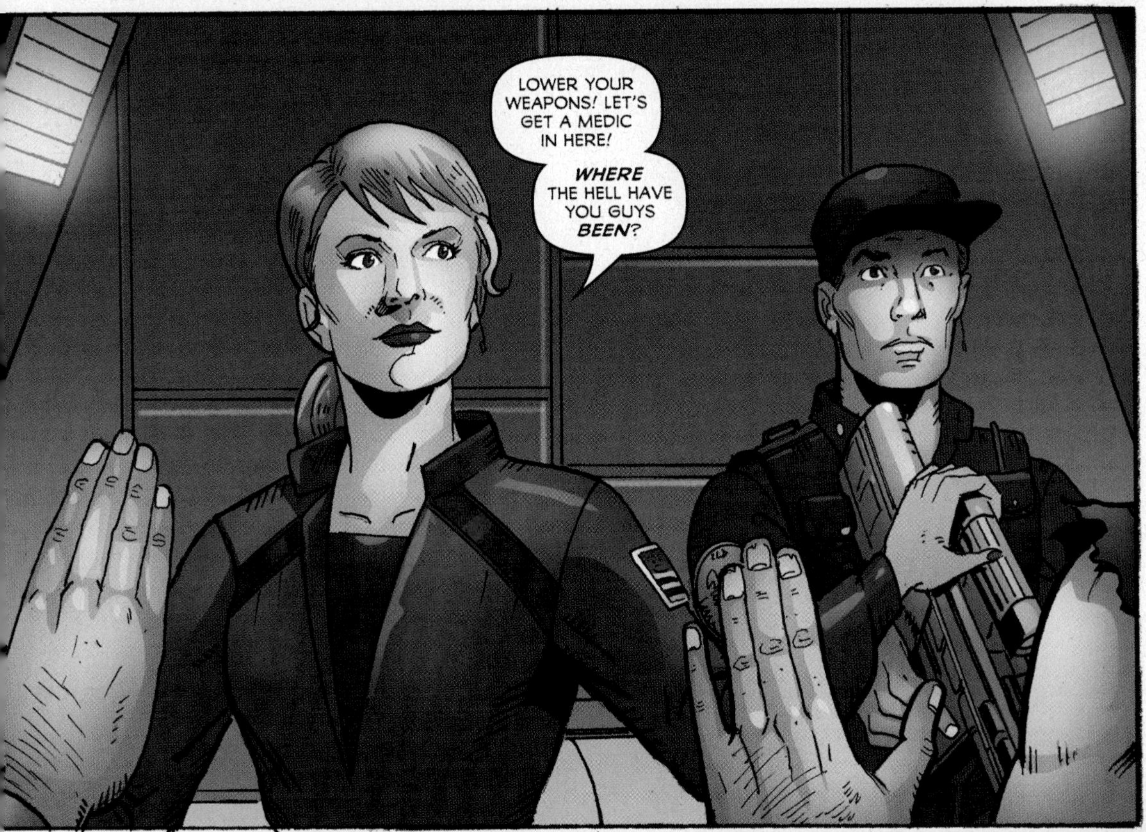
LOWER YOUR WEAPONS! LET'S GET A MEDIC IN HERE!
WHERE THE HELL HAVE YOU GUYS *BEEN*?

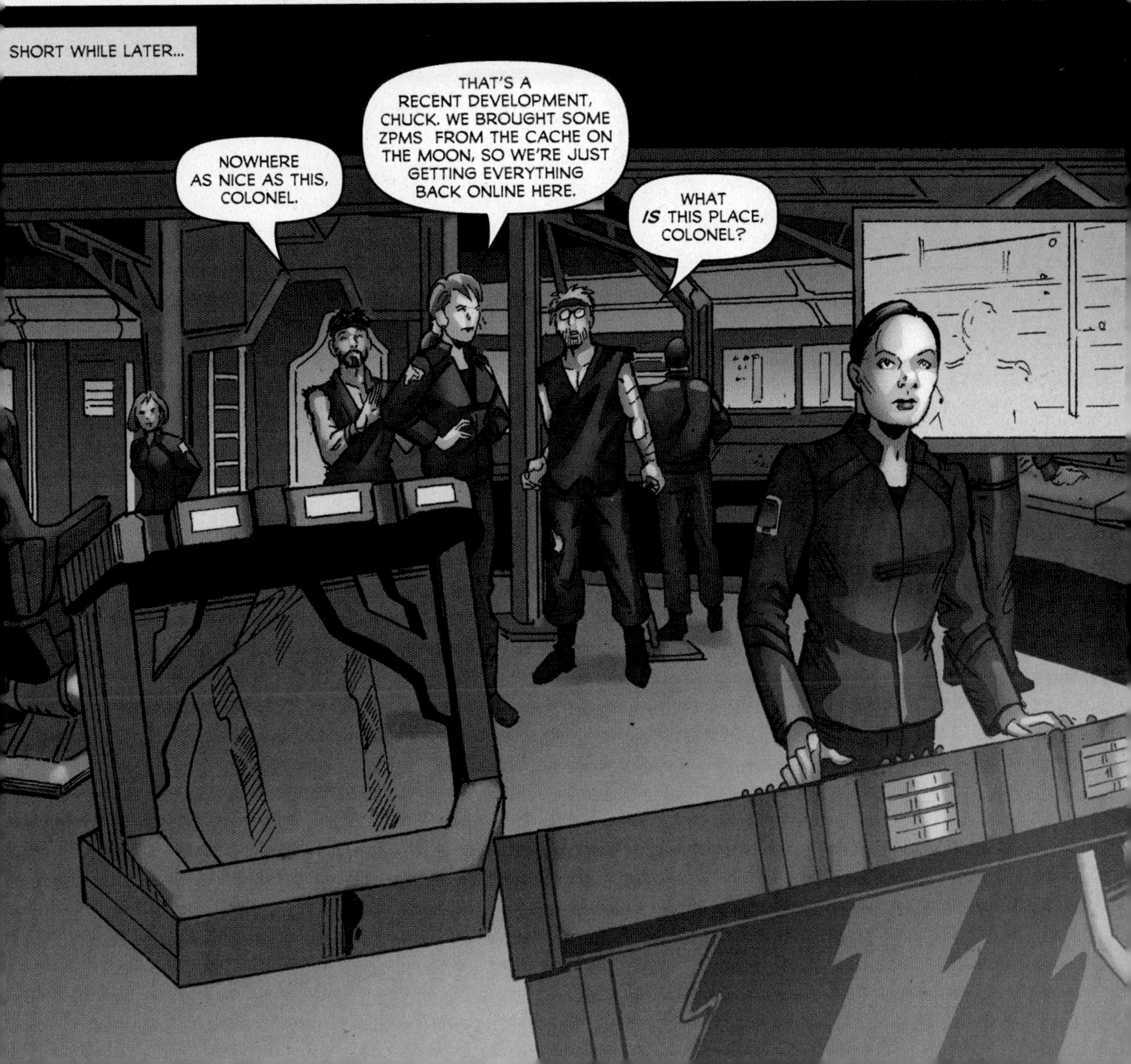
SHORT WHILE LATER...
NOWHERE AS NICE AS THIS, COLONEL.
THAT'S A RECENT DEVELOPMENT, CHUCK. WE BROUGHT SOME ZPMS FROM THE CACHE ON THE MOON, SO WE'RE JUST GETTING EVERYTHING BACK ONLINE HERE.
WHAT *IS* THIS PLACE, COLONEL?

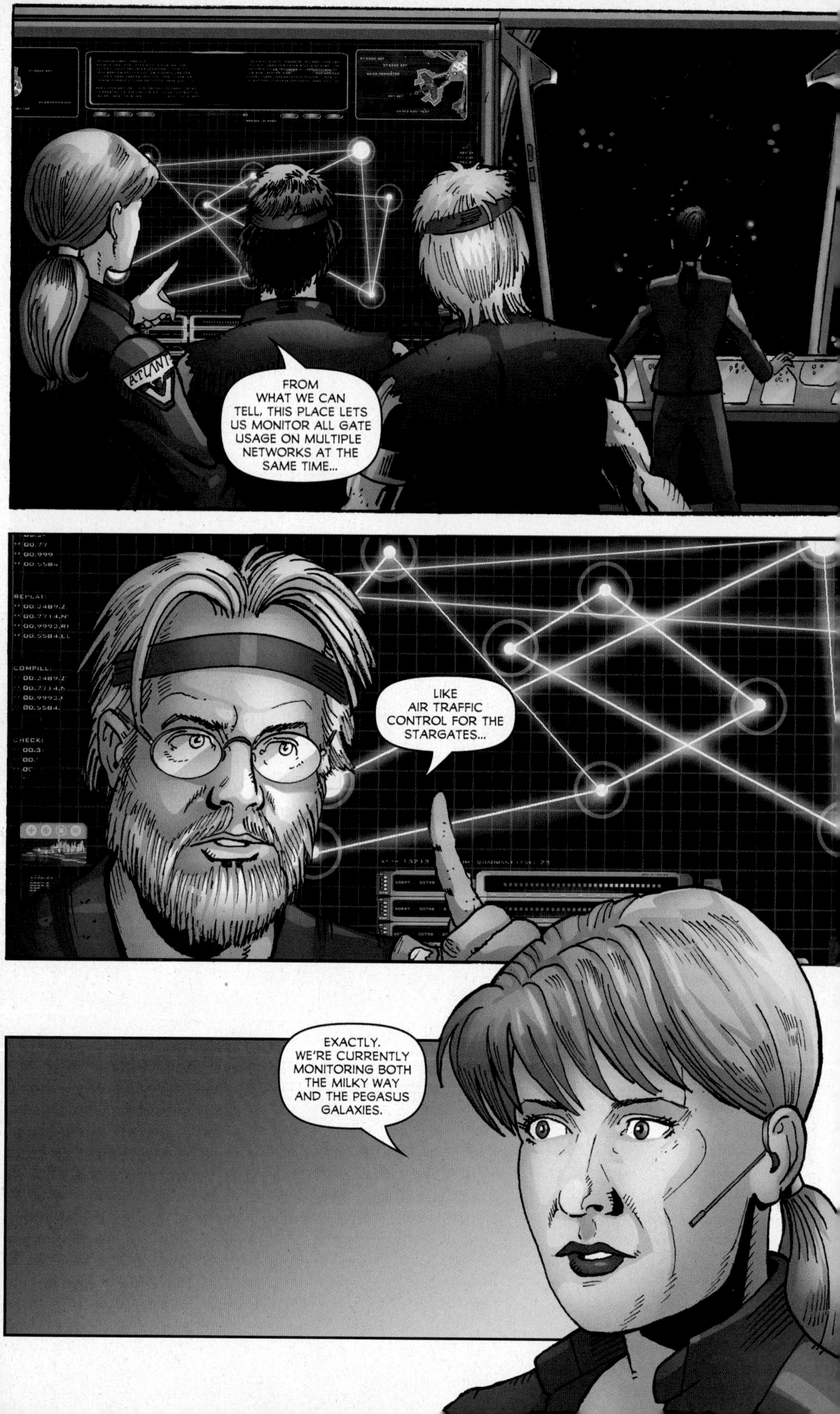
FROM WHAT WE CAN TELL, THIS PLACE LETS US MONITOR ALL GATE USAGE ON MULTIPLE NETWORKS AT THE SAME TIME...
LIKE AIR TRAFFIC CONTROL FOR THE STARGATES...
EXACTLY. WE'RE CURRENTLY MONITORING BOTH THE MILKY WAY AND THE PEGASUS GALAXIES.

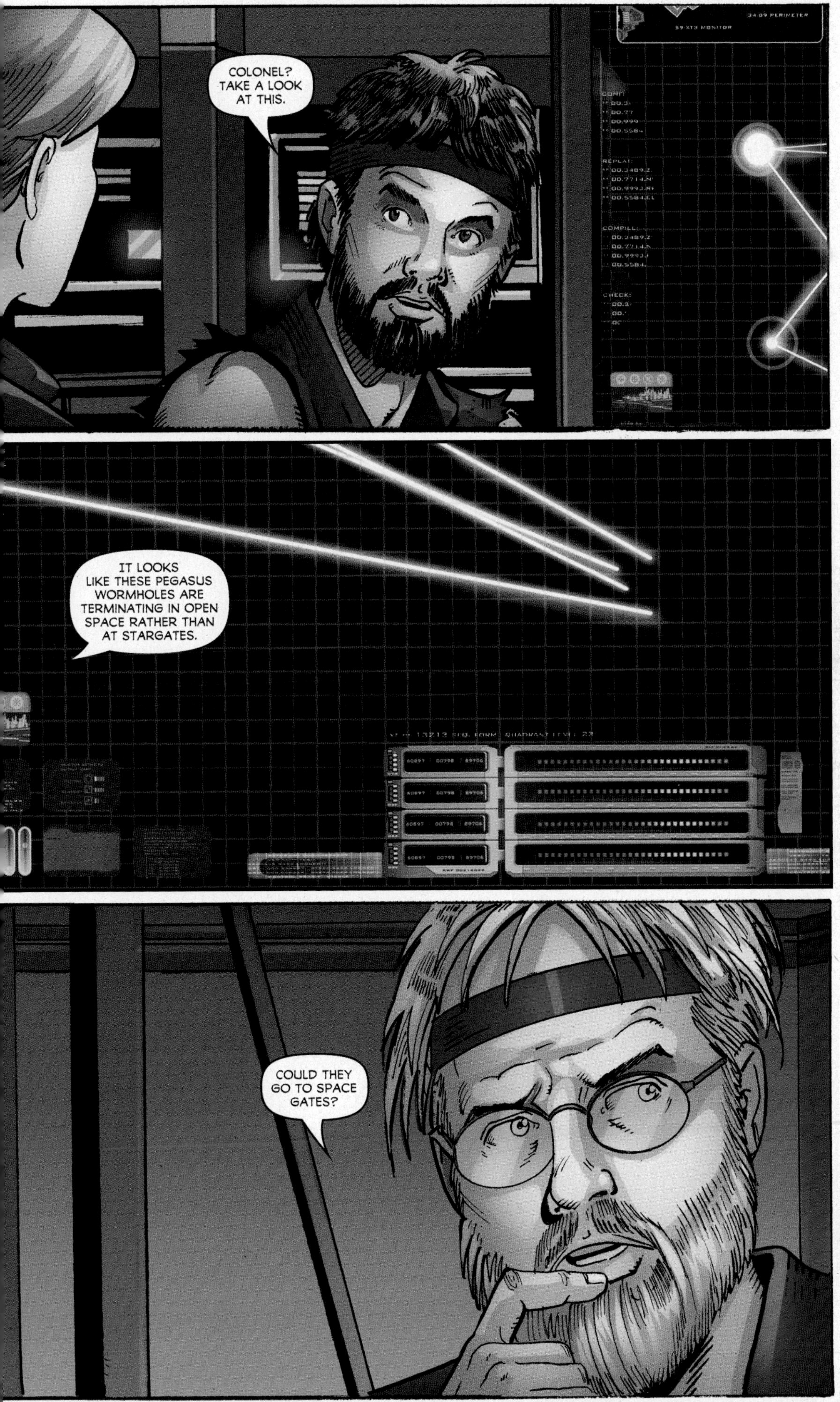
COLONEL? TAKE A LOOK AT THIS.
IT LOOKS LIKE THESE PEGASUS WORMHOLES ARE TERMINATING IN OPEN SPACE RATHER THAN AT STARGATES.
COULD THEY GO TO SPACE GATES?

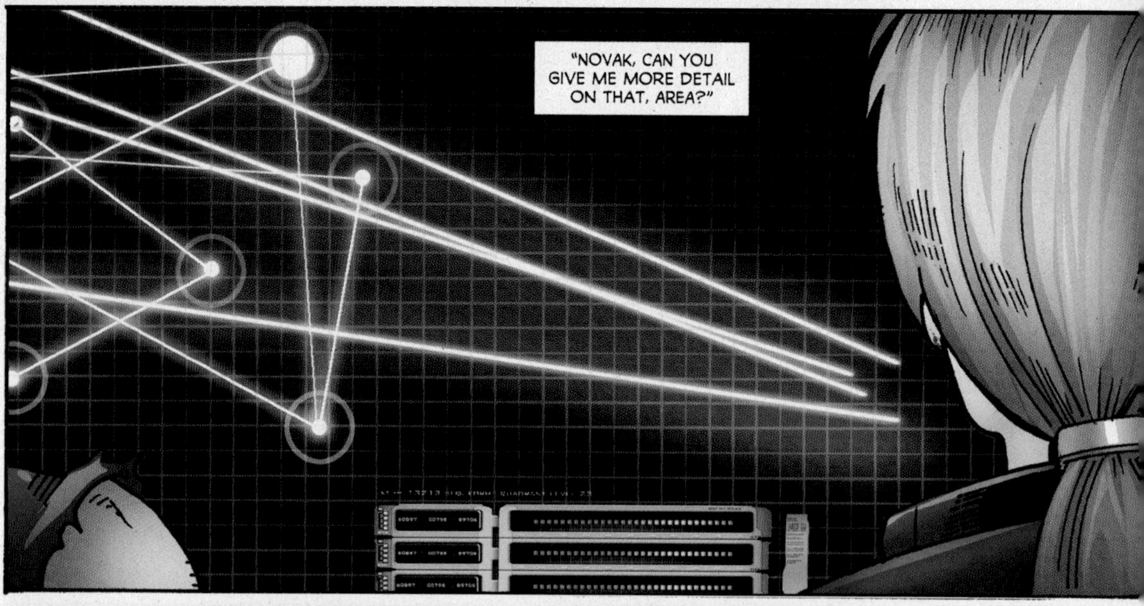
"NOVAK, CAN YOU GIVE ME MORE DETAIL ON THAT, AREA?"

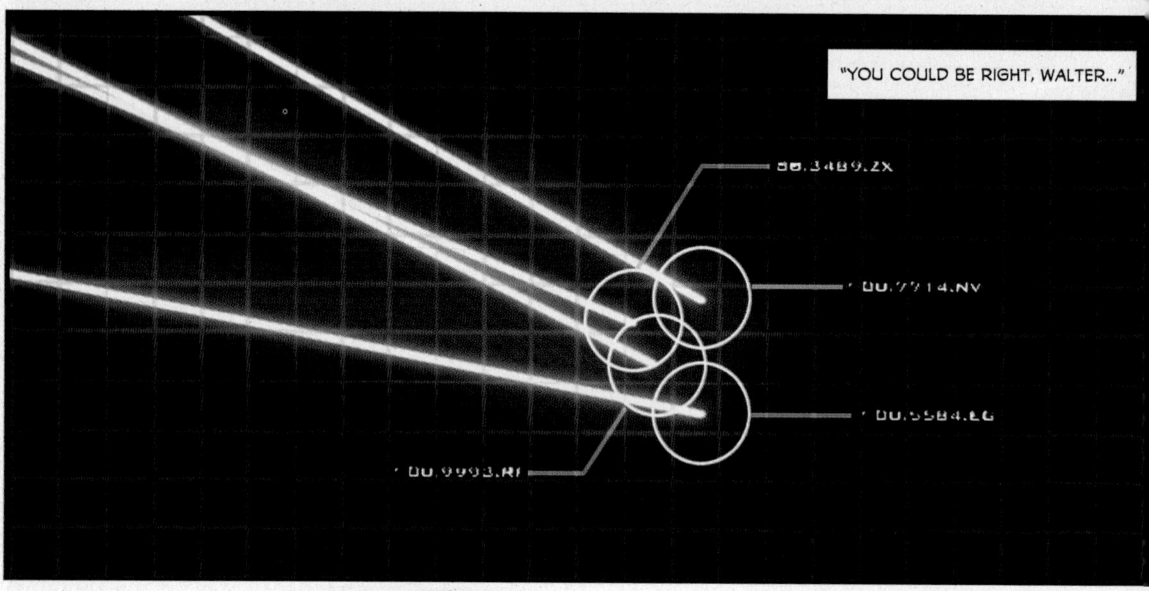
"YOU COULD BE RIGHT, WALTER..."

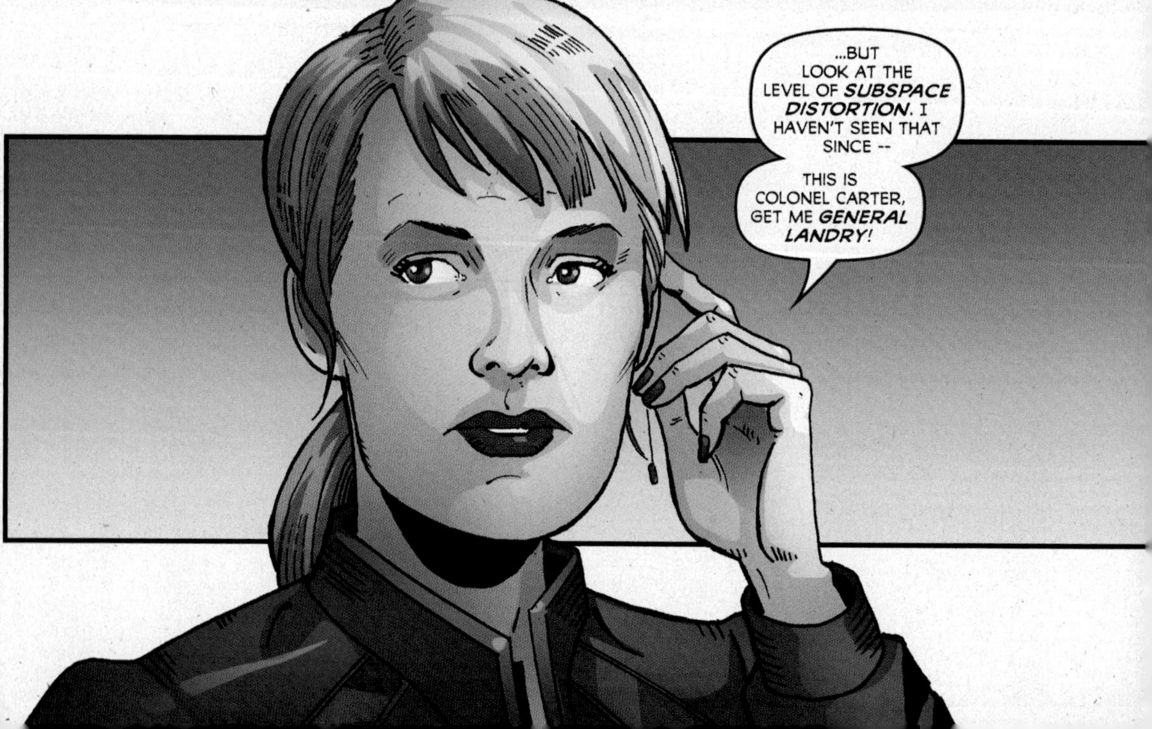
...BUT LOOK AT THE LEVEL OF SUBSPACE DISTORTION. I HAVEN'T SEEN THAT SINCE --
THIS IS COLONEL CARTER, GET ME GENERAL LANDRY!

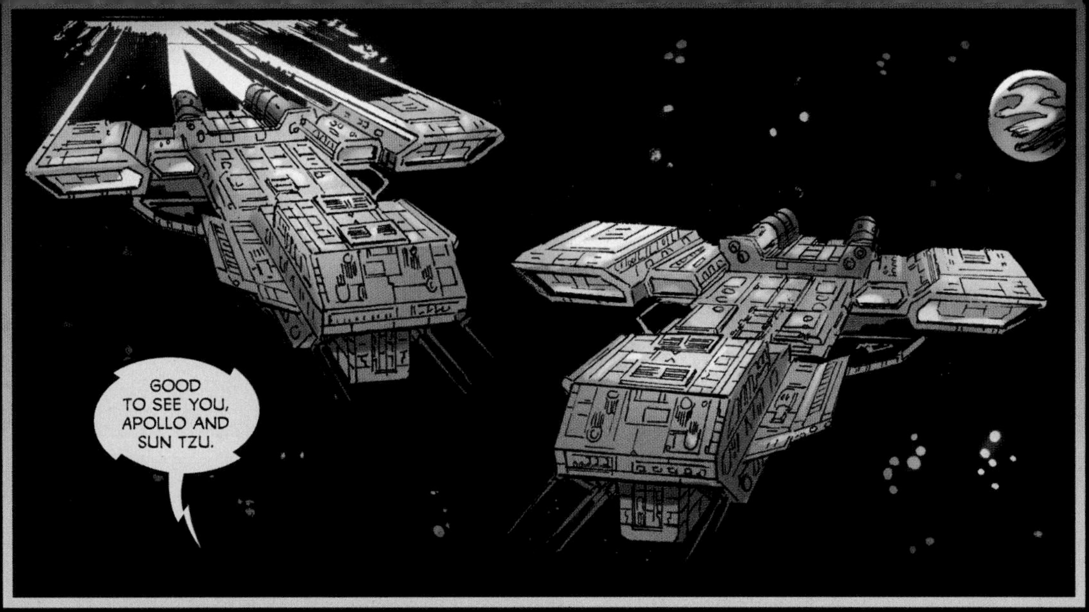
GOOD TO SEE YOU, APOLLO AND SUN TZU.

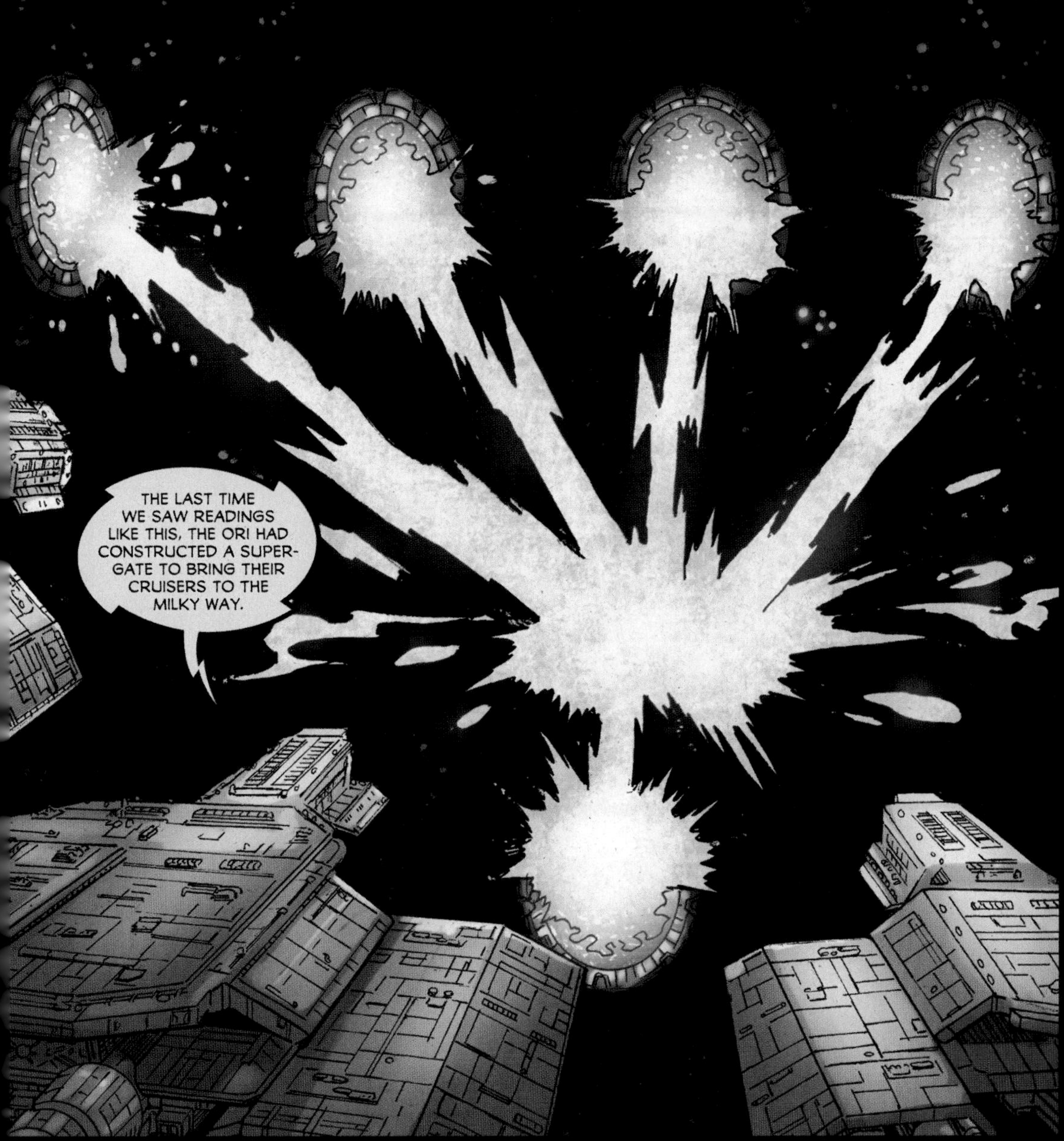
THE LAST TIME WE SAW READINGS LIKE THIS, THE ORI HAD CONSTRUCTED A SUPER-GATE TO BRING THEIR CRUISERS TO THE MILKY WAY.

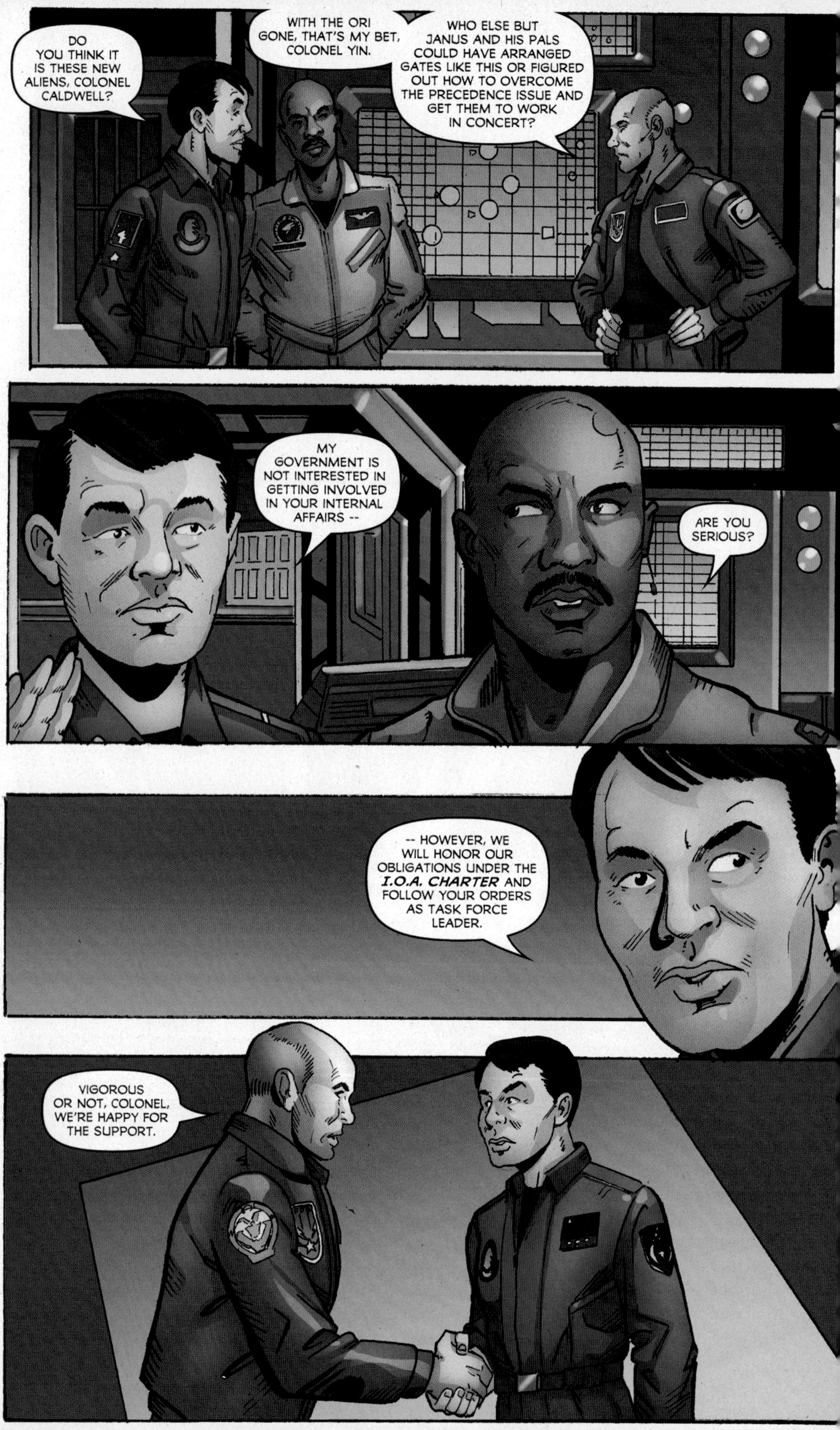
DO YOU THINK IT IS THESE NEW ALIENS, COLONEL CALDWELL?
WITH THE ORI GONE, THAT'S MY BET, COLONEL YIN.
WHO ELSE BUT JANUS AND HIS PALS COULD HAVE ARRANGED GATES LIKE THIS OR FIGURED OUT HOW TO OVERCOME THE PRECEDENCE ISSUE AND GET THEM TO WORK IN CONCERT?
MY GOVERNMENT IS NOT INTERESTED IN GETTING INVOLVED IN YOUR INTERNAL AFFAIRS --
ARE YOU SERIOUS?
-- HOWEVER, WE WILL HONOR OUR OBLIGATIONS UNDER THE *I.O.A. CHARTER* AND FOLLOW YOUR ORDERS AS TASK FORCE LEADER.
VIGOROUS OR NOT, COLONEL, WE'RE HAPPY FOR THE SUPPORT.

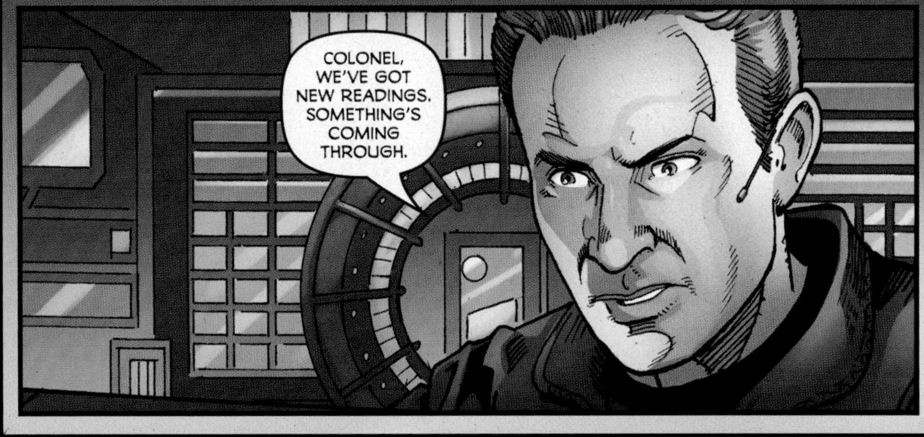
COLONEL, WE'VE GOT NEW READINGS. SOMETHING'S COMING THROUGH.

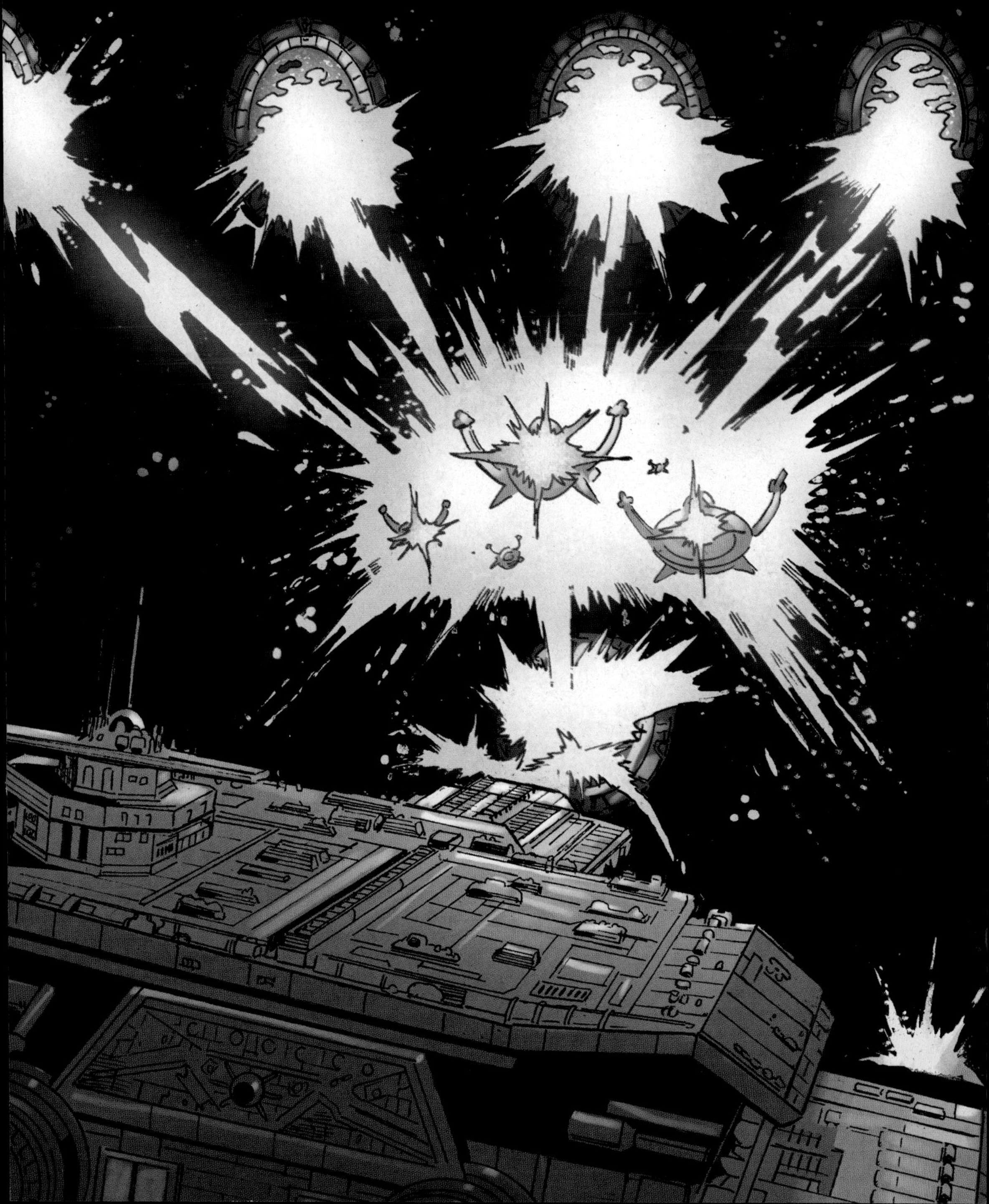

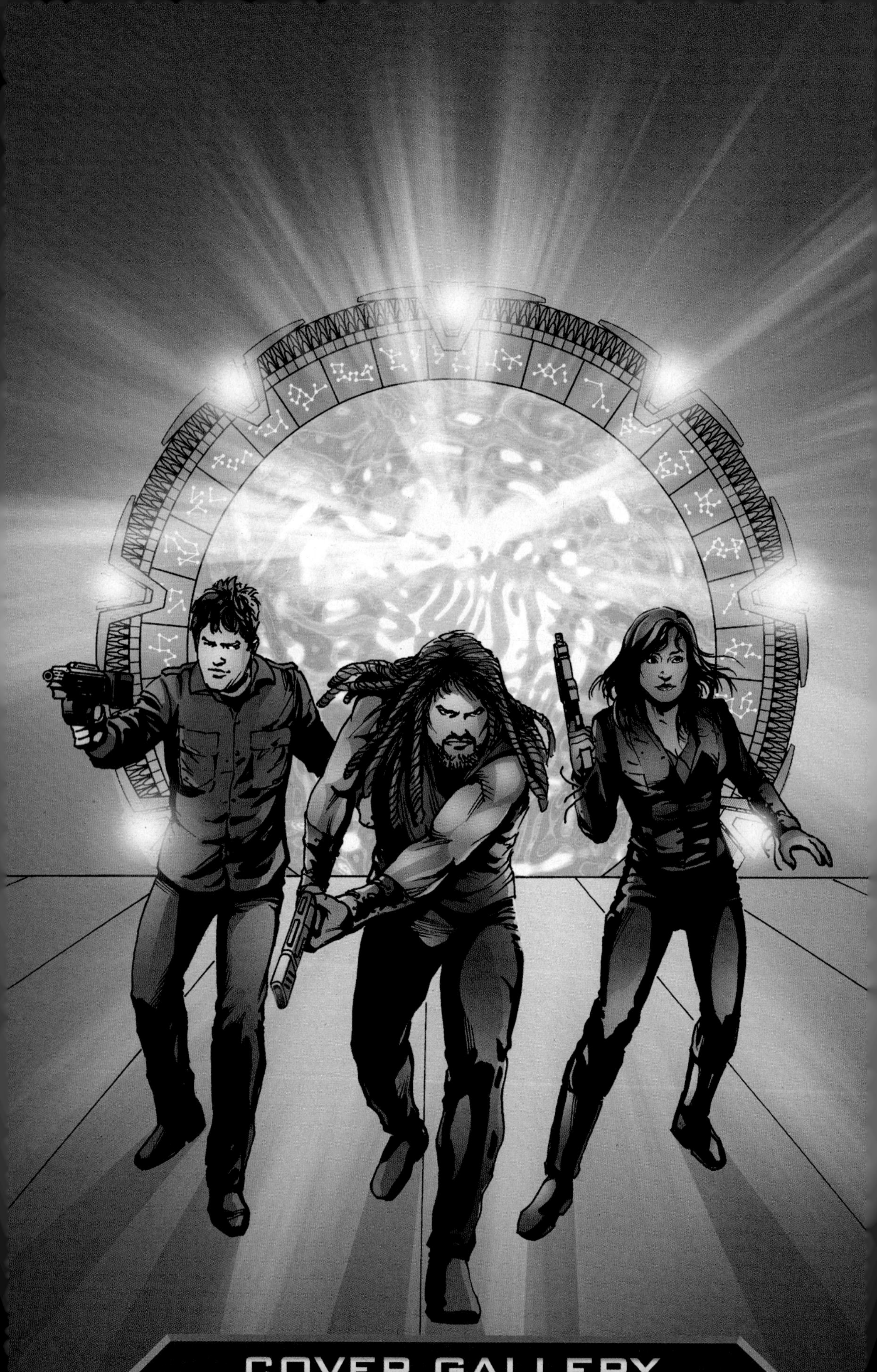

COVER GALLERY
SINGULARITY #2 MAIN COVER

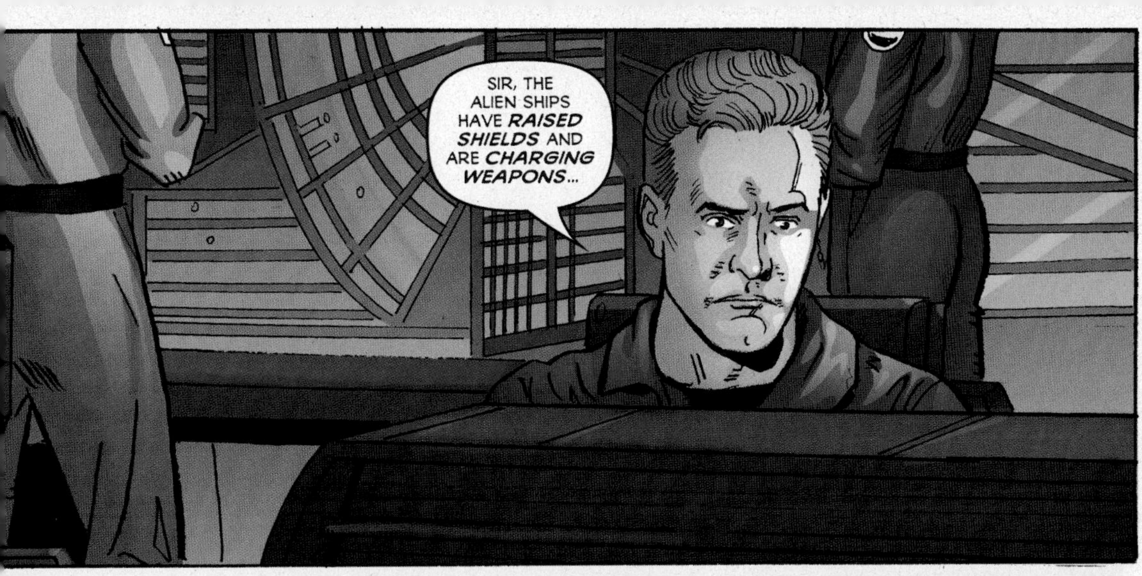
SIR, THE ALIEN SHIPS HAVE RAISED SHIELDS AND ARE CHARGING WEAPONS...

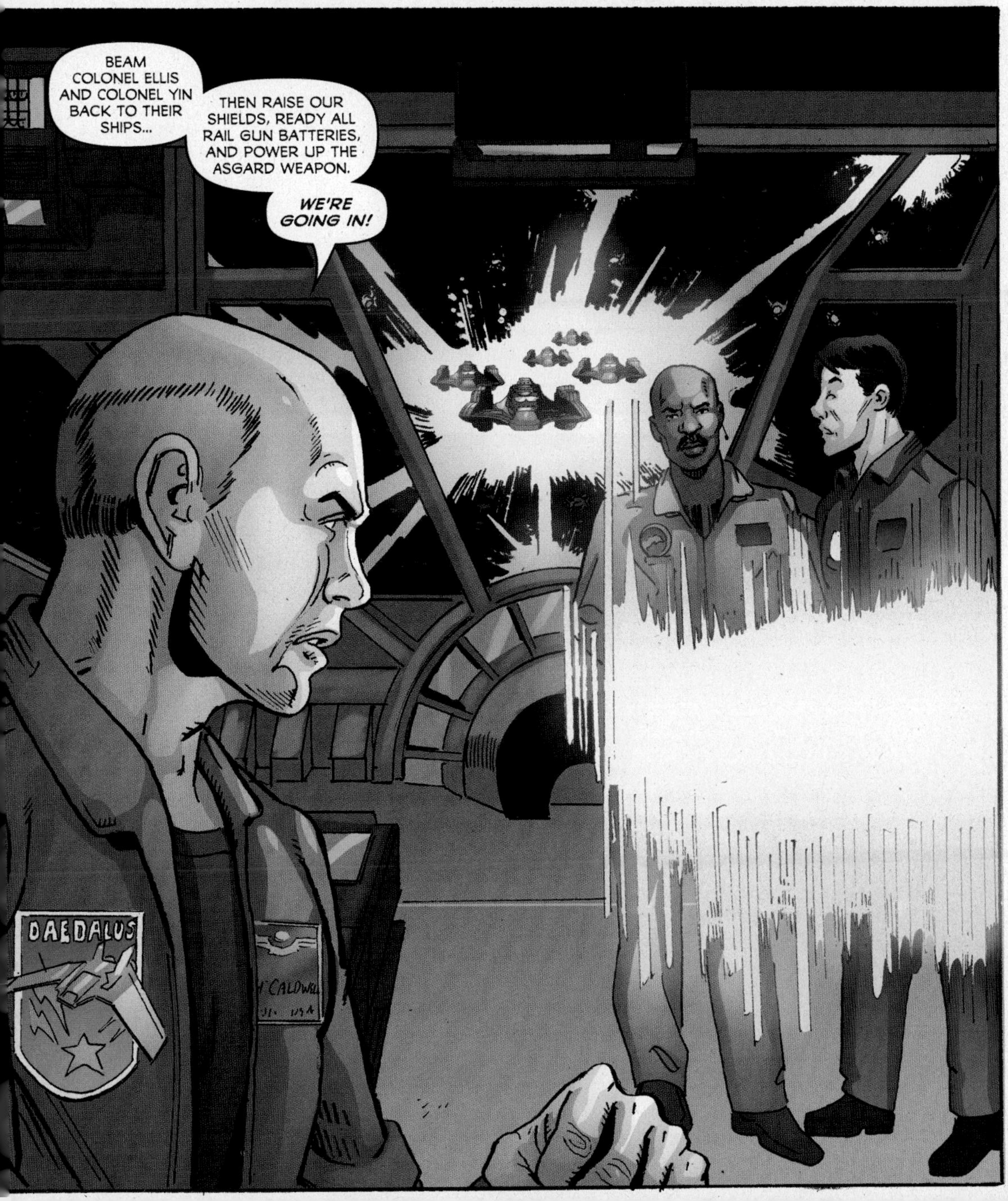
BEAM COLONEL ELLIS AND COLONEL YIN BACK TO THEIR SHIPS...
THEN RAISE OUR SHIELDS, READY ALL RAIL GUN BATTERIES, AND POWER UP THE ASGARD WEAPON.
WE'RE GOING IN!
DAEDALUS
CALDWELL

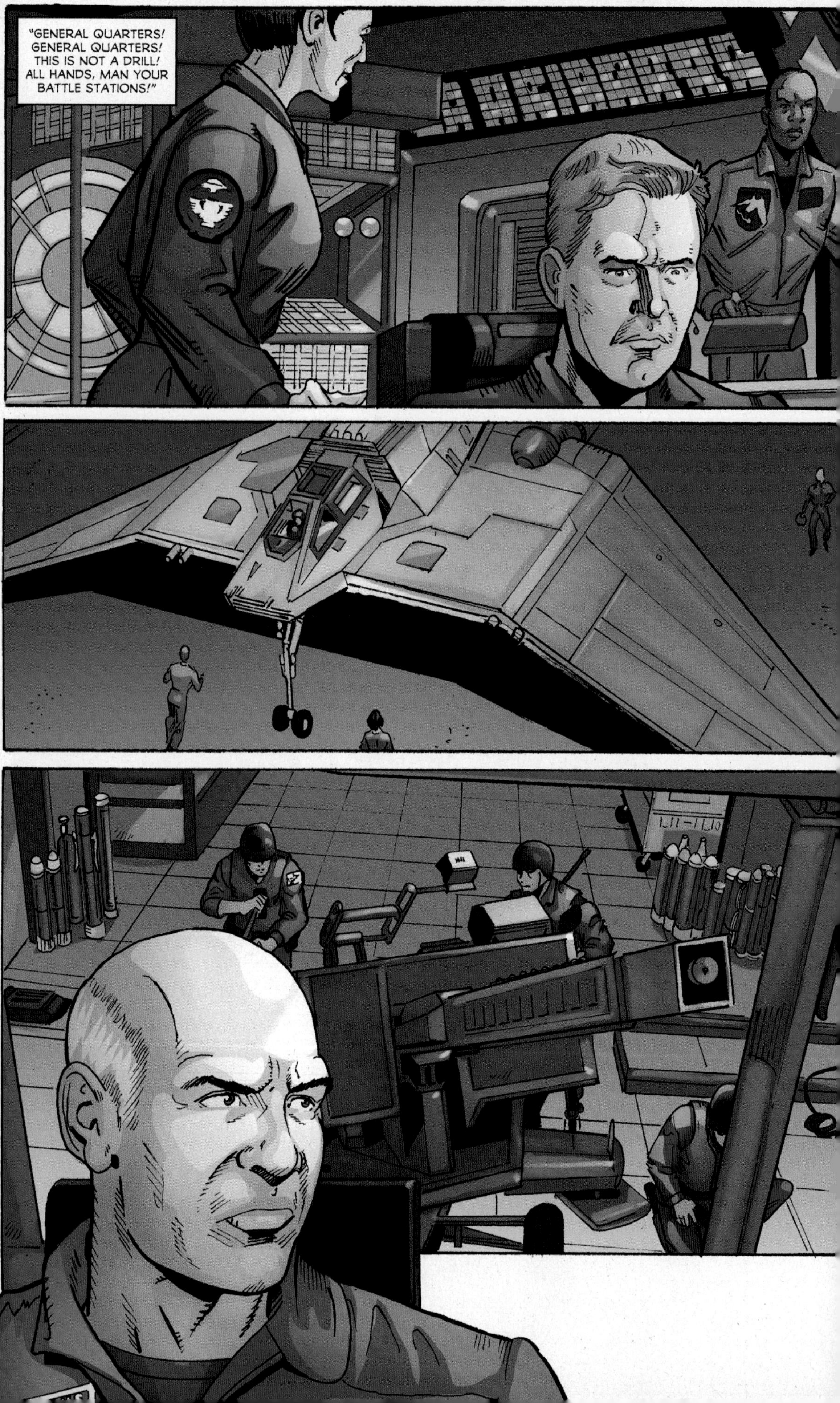
"GENERAL QUARTERS! GENERAL QUARTERS! THIS IS NOT A DRILL! ALL HANDS, MAN YOUR BATTLE STATIONS!"

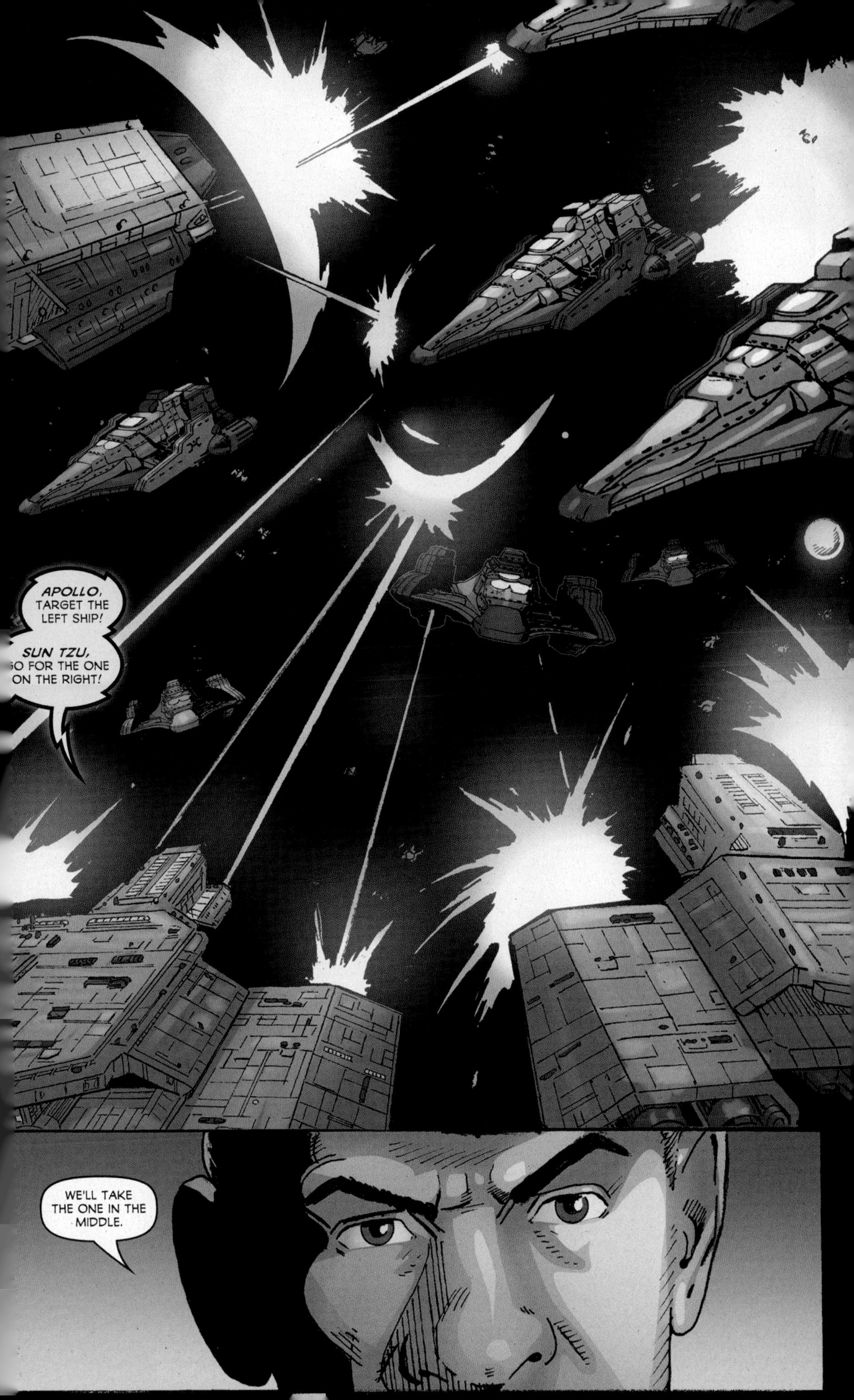
APOLLO, TARGET THE LEFT SHIP!
SUN TZU, GO FOR THE ONE ON THE RIGHT!
WE'LL TAKE THE ONE IN THE MIDDLE.

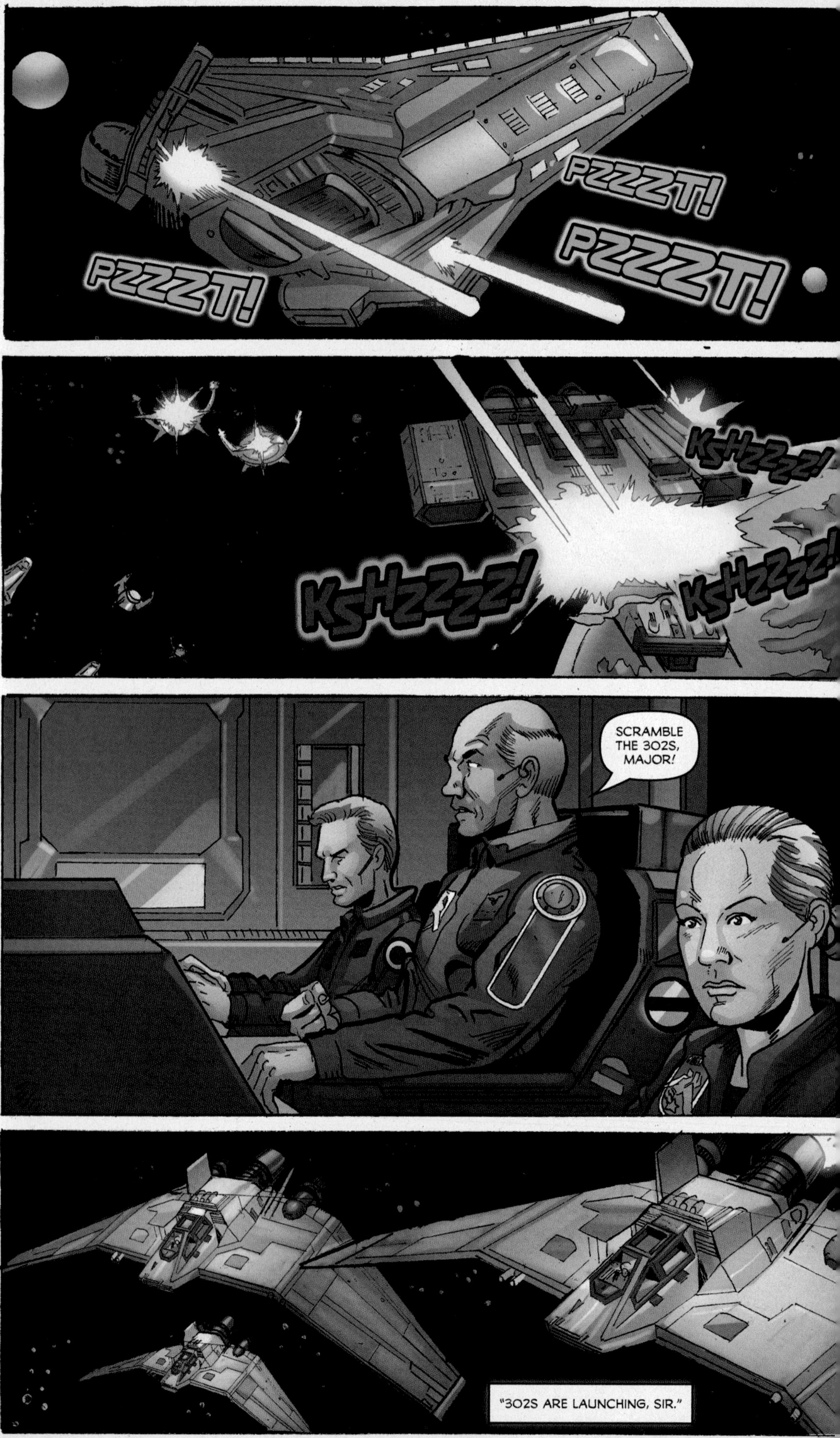
PZZZT!
PZZZT!
PZZZT!
KSHZZZZZ!
KSHZZZZZ!
KSHZZZZZ!
SCRAMBLE THE 302S, MAJOR!
"302S ARE LAUNCHING, SIR."

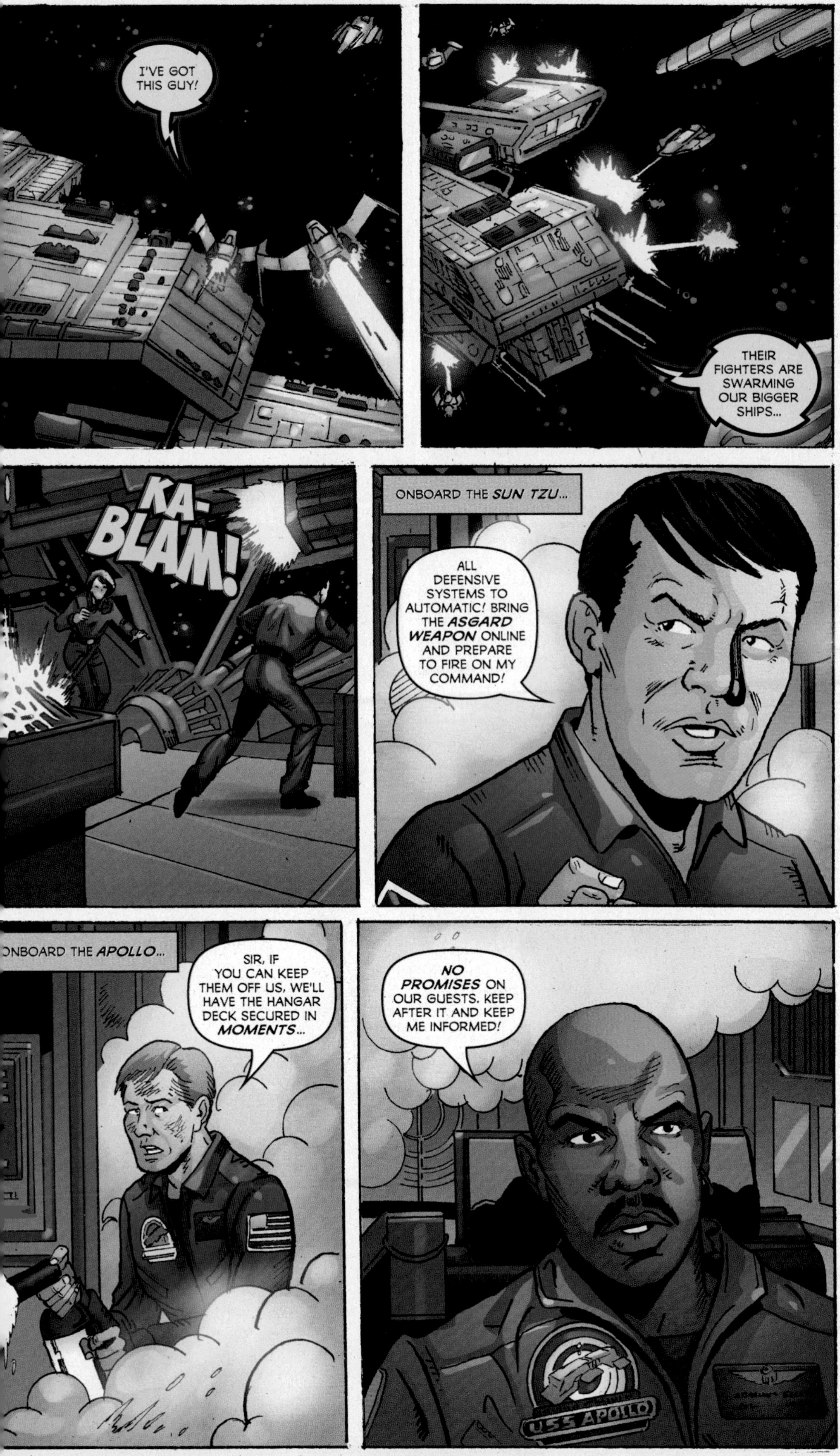
I'VE GOT THIS GUY!
THEIR FIGHTERS ARE SWARMING OUR BIGGER SHIPS...
KA-BLAM!
ONBOARD THE *SUN TZU*...
ALL DEFENSIVE SYSTEMS TO AUTOMATIC! BRING THE ***ASGARD WEAPON*** ONLINE AND PREPARE TO FIRE ON MY COMMAND!
ONBOARD THE *APOLLO*...
SIR, IF YOU CAN KEEP THEM OFF US, WE'LL HAVE THE HANGAR DECK SECURED IN ***MOMENTS***...
NO PROMISES ON OUR GUESTS. KEEP AFTER IT AND KEEP ME INFORMED!
USS APOLLO

SIR, THE DISTORTION FIELD IS DISSIPATING...

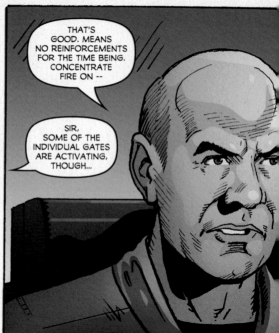

THAT'S GOOD. MEANS NO REINFORCEMENTS FOR THE TIME BEING. CONCENTRATE FIRE ON --

SIR, SOME OF THE INDIVIDUAL GATES ARE ACTIVATING, THOUGH...

"BUT WHAT'S COMING THROUGH? IT COULDN'T BE...

"PEOPLE?!?"

ORDER THE SUN TZU AND THE APOLLO TO COVER US!

THEN DROP SHIELDS AND BEAM AS MANY OF THOSE PEOPLE ON BOARD AS POSSIBLE!

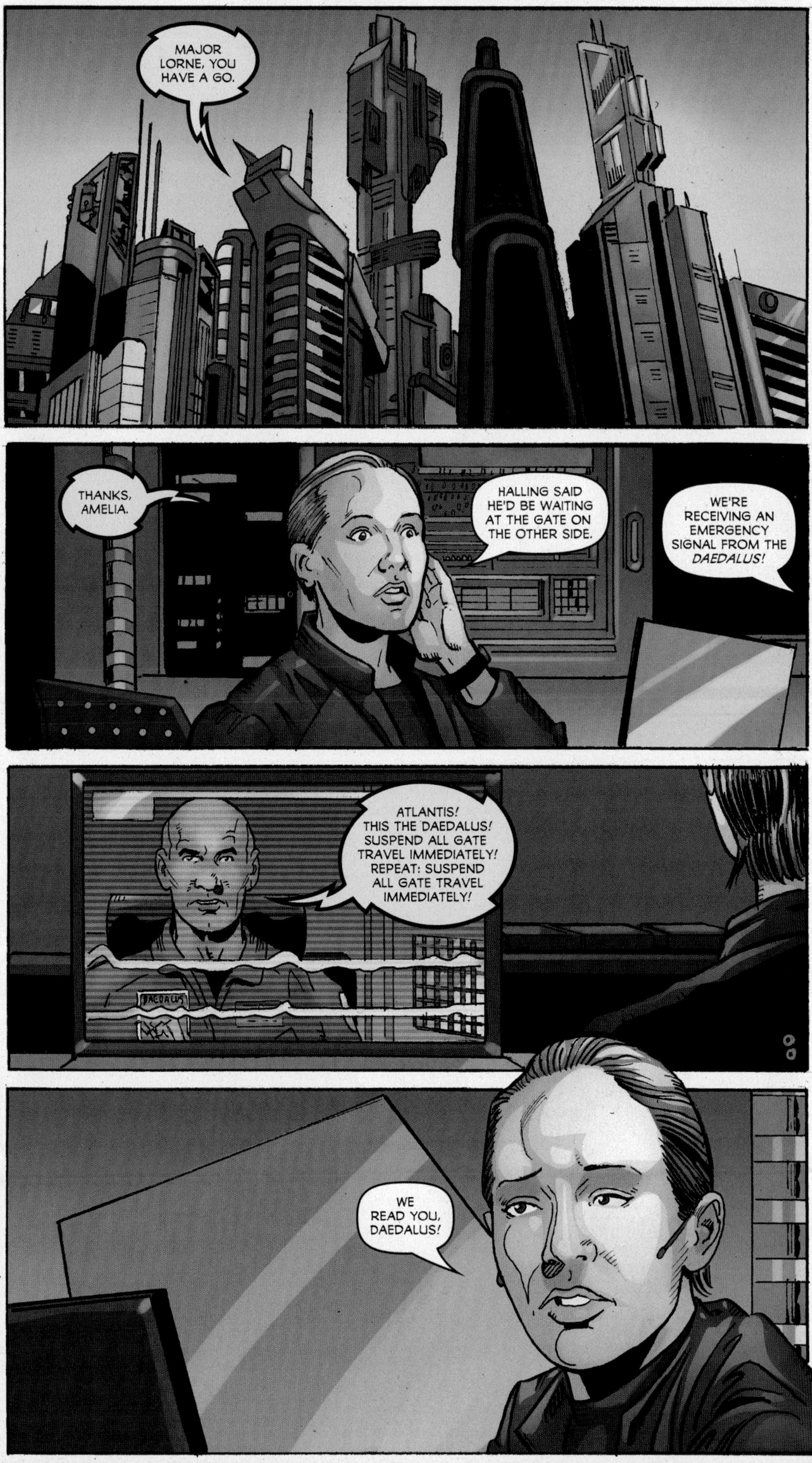
MAJOR LORNE, YOU HAVE A GO.
THANKS, AMELIA.
HALLING SAID HE'D BE WAITING AT THE GATE ON THE OTHER SIDE.
WE'RE RECEIVING AN EMERGENCY SIGNAL FROM THE *DAEDALUS!*
ATLANTIS! THIS THE DAEDALUS! SUSPEND ALL GATE TRAVEL IMMEDIATELY! REPEAT: SUSPEND ALL GATE TRAVEL IMMEDIATELY!
WE READ YOU, DAEDALUS!

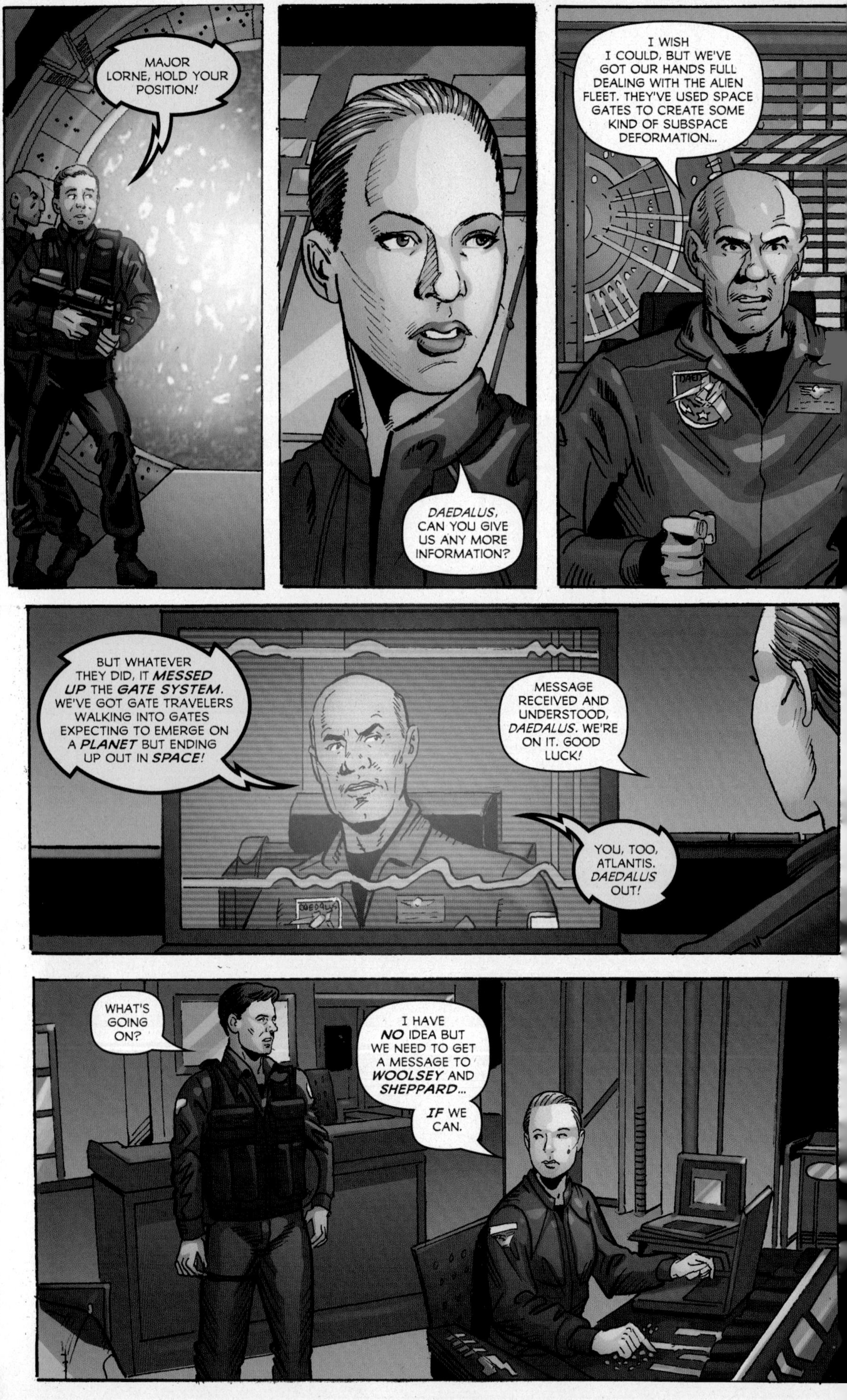
MAJOR LORNE, HOLD YOUR POSITION!
DAEDALUS, CAN YOU GIVE US ANY MORE INFORMATION?
I WISH I COULD, BUT WE'VE GOT OUR HANDS FULL DEALING WITH THE ALIEN FLEET. THEY'VE USED SPACE GATES TO CREATE SOME KIND OF SUBSPACE DEFORMATION...
BUT WHATEVER THEY DID, IT MESSED UP THE GATE SYSTEM. WE'VE GOT GATE TRAVELERS WALKING INTO GATES EXPECTING TO EMERGE ON A PLANET BUT ENDING UP OUT IN SPACE!
MESSAGE RECEIVED AND UNDERSTOOD, DAEDALUS. WE'RE ON IT. GOOD LUCK!
YOU, TOO, ATLANTIS. DAEDALUS OUT!
WHAT'S GOING ON?
I HAVE NO IDEA BUT WE NEED TO GET A MESSAGE TO WOOLSEY AND SHEPPARD...
IF WE CAN.

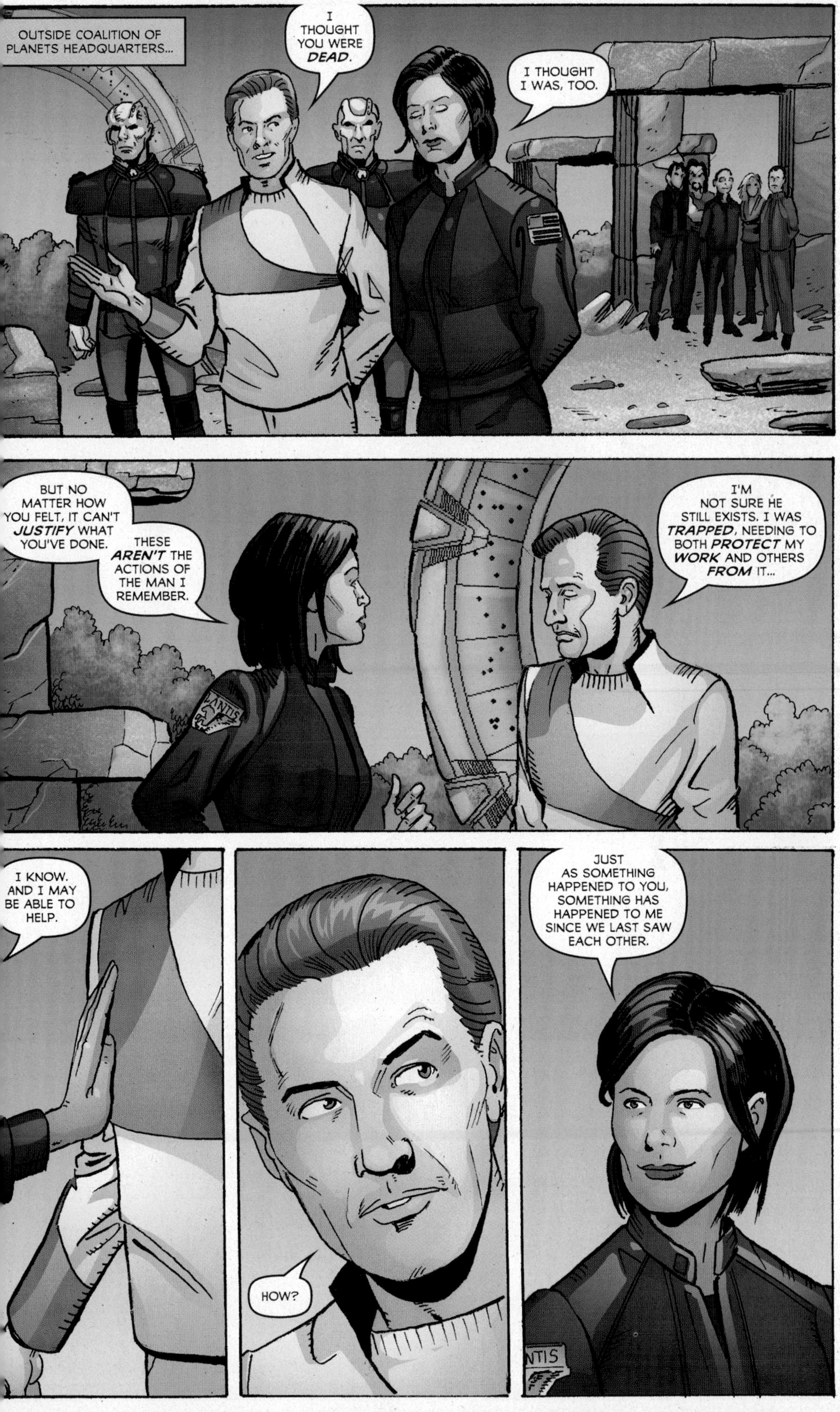
OUTSIDE COALITION OF PLANETS HEADQUARTERS...
I THOUGHT YOU WERE DEAD.
I THOUGHT I WAS, TOO.
BUT NO MATTER HOW YOU FELT, IT CAN'T JUSTIFY WHAT YOU'VE DONE.
THESE AREN'T THE ACTIONS OF THE MAN I REMEMBER.
I'M NOT SURE HE STILL EXISTS. I WAS TRAPPED, NEEDING TO BOTH PROTECT MY WORK AND OTHERS FROM IT...
I KNOW. AND I MAY BE ABLE TO HELP.
HOW?
JUST AS SOMETHING HAPPENED TO YOU, SOMETHING HAS HAPPENED TO ME SINCE WE LAST SAW EACH OTHER.

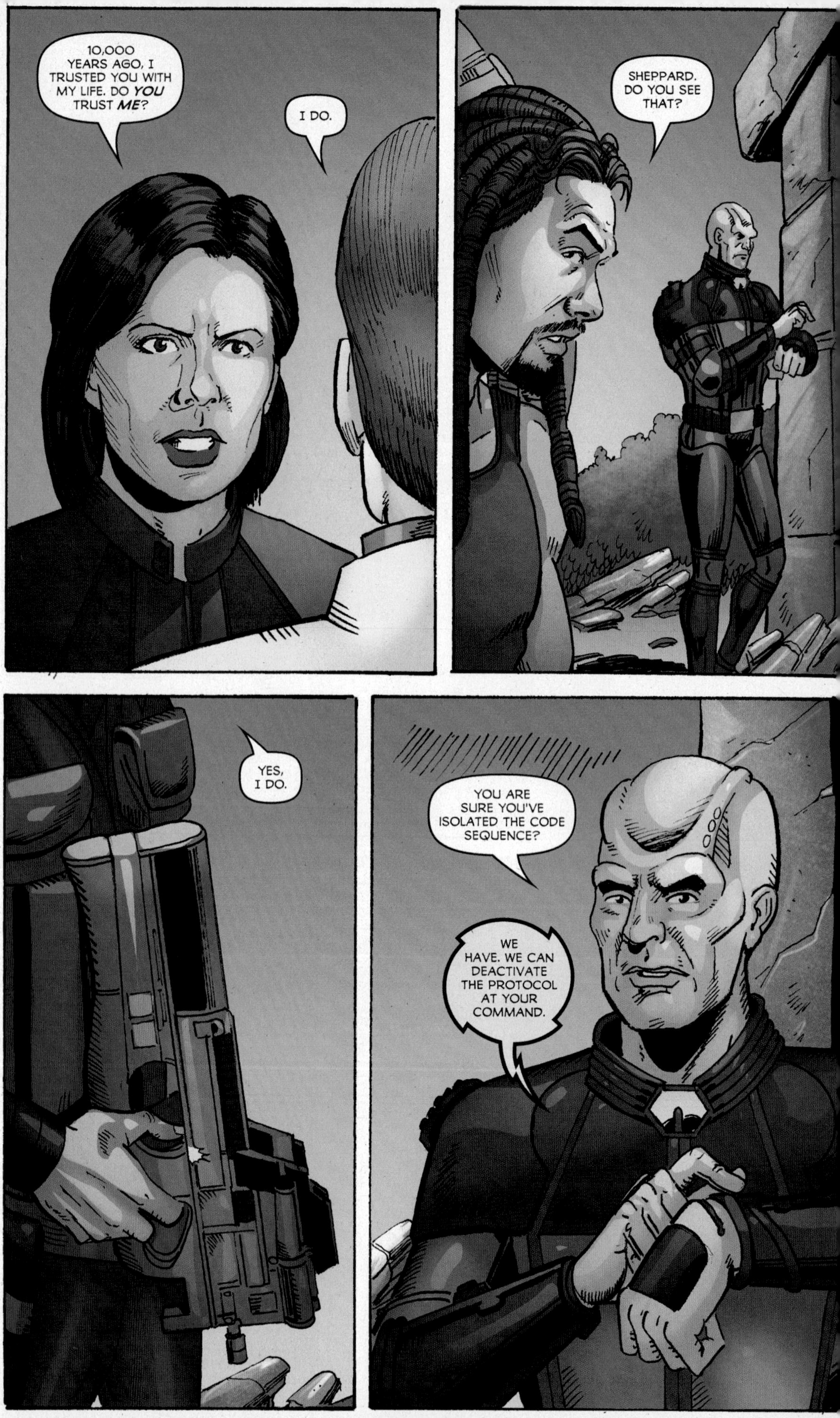
10,000 YEARS AGO, I TRUSTED YOU WITH MY LIFE. DO *YOU* TRUST *ME*?
I DO.
SHEPPARD. DO YOU SEE THAT?
YES, I DO.
YOU ARE SURE YOU'VE ISOLATED THE CODE SEQUENCE?
WE HAVE. WE CAN DEACTIVATE THE PROTOCOL AT YOUR COMMAND.

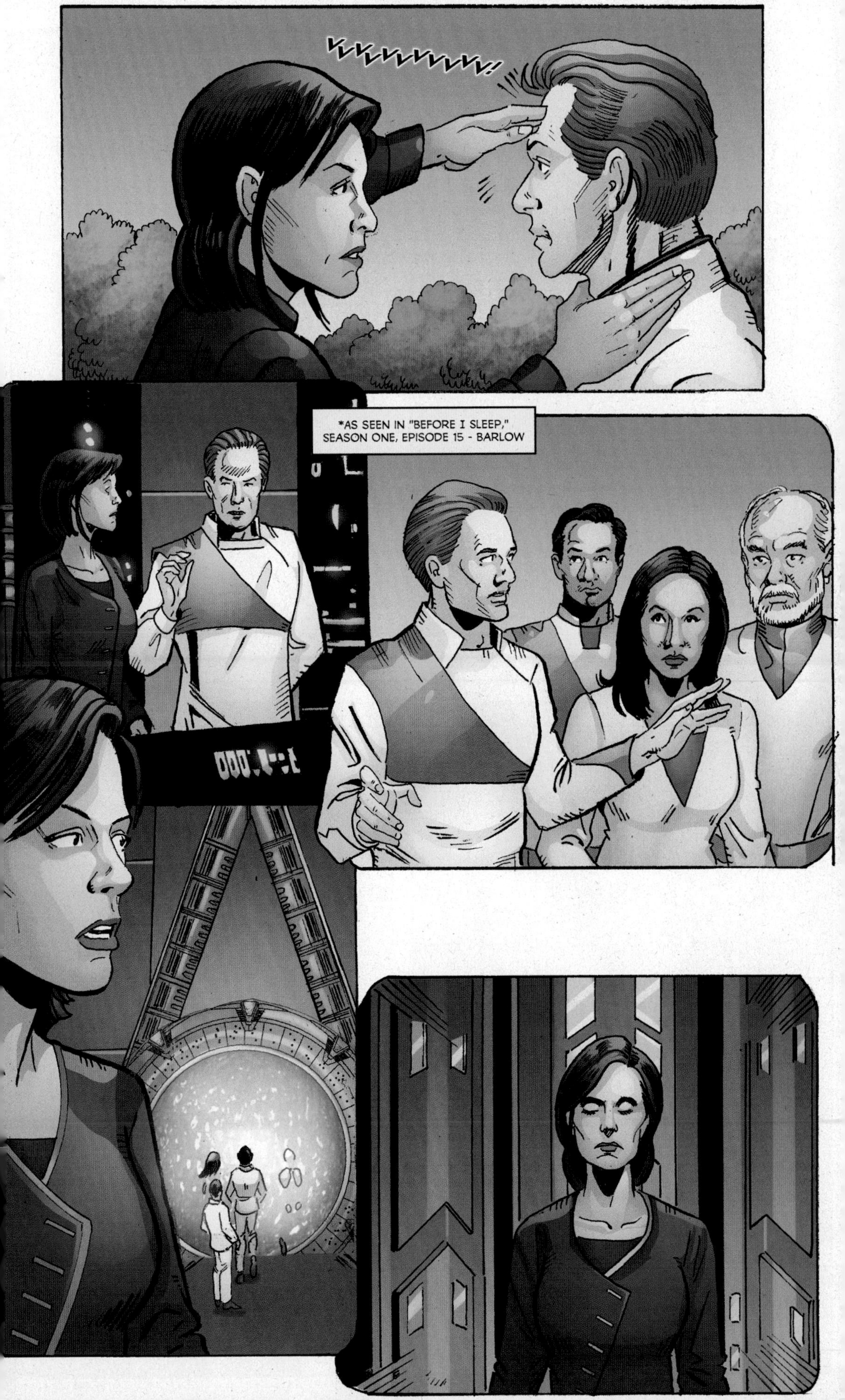
VVVVVVVVVVV!
*AS SEEN IN "BEFORE I SLEEP," SEASON ONE, EPISODE 15 - BARLOW

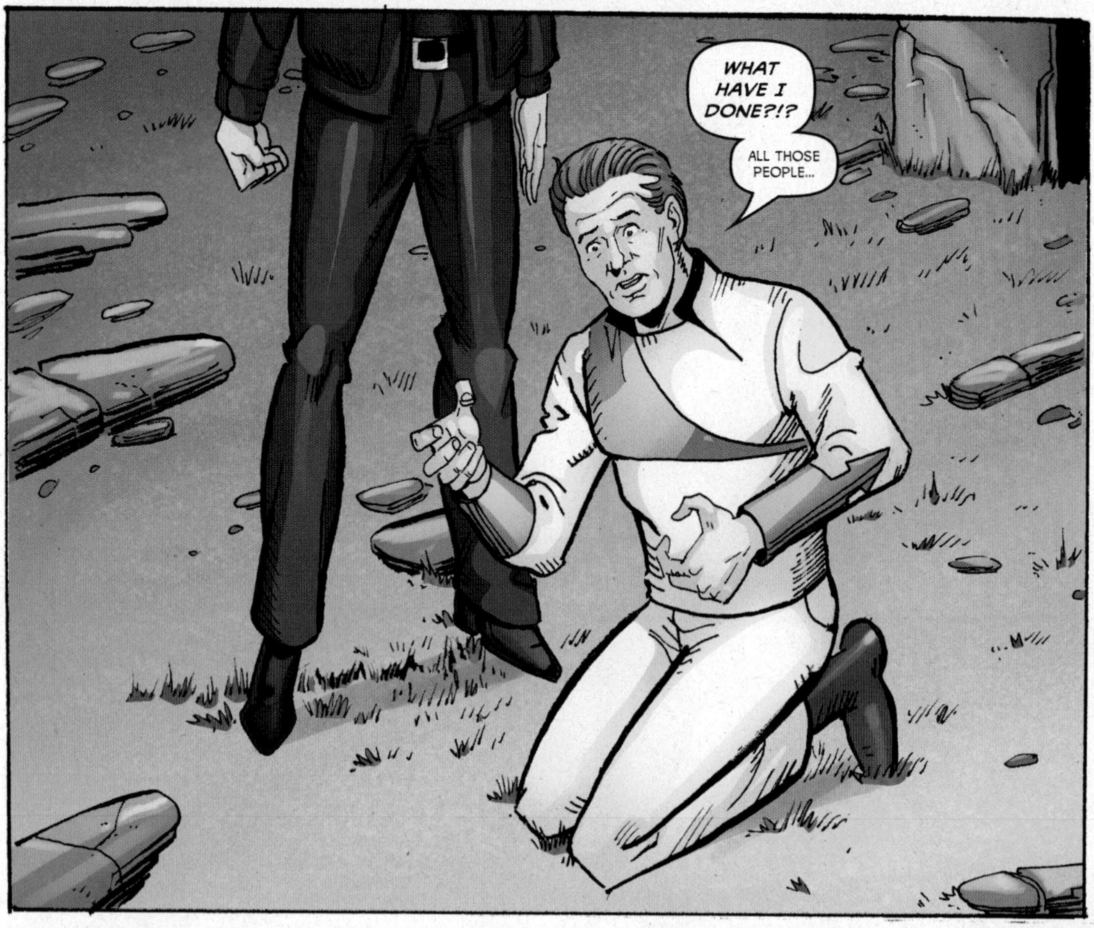
WHAT HAVE I DONE?!?
ALL THOSE PEOPLE...

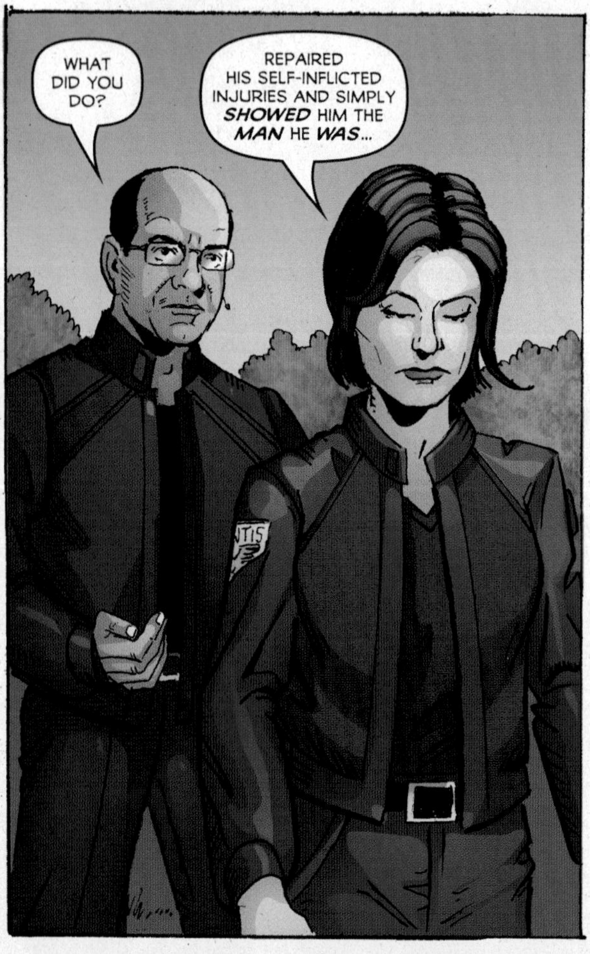
WHAT DID YOU DO?
REPAIRED HIS SELF-INFLICTED INJURIES AND SIMPLY SHOWED HIM THE MAN HE WAS...

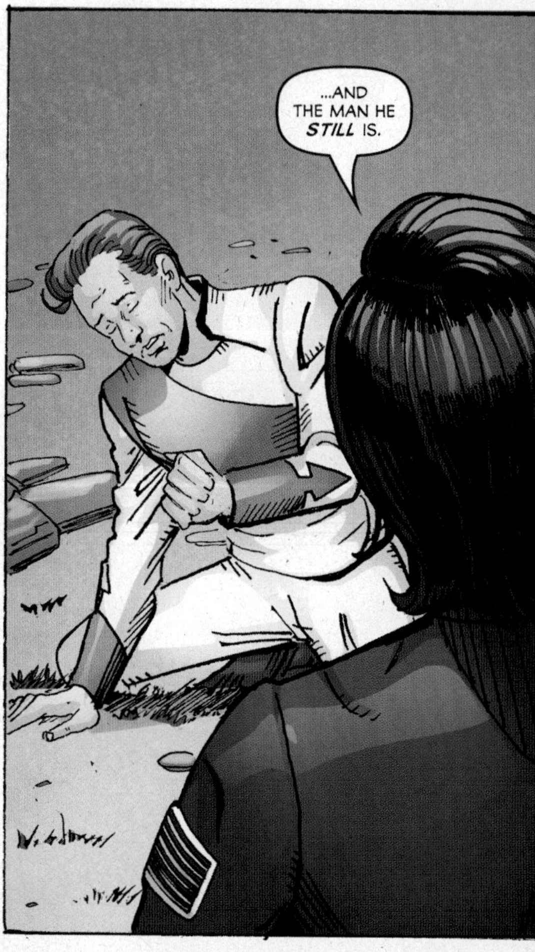
...AND THE MAN HE STILL IS.

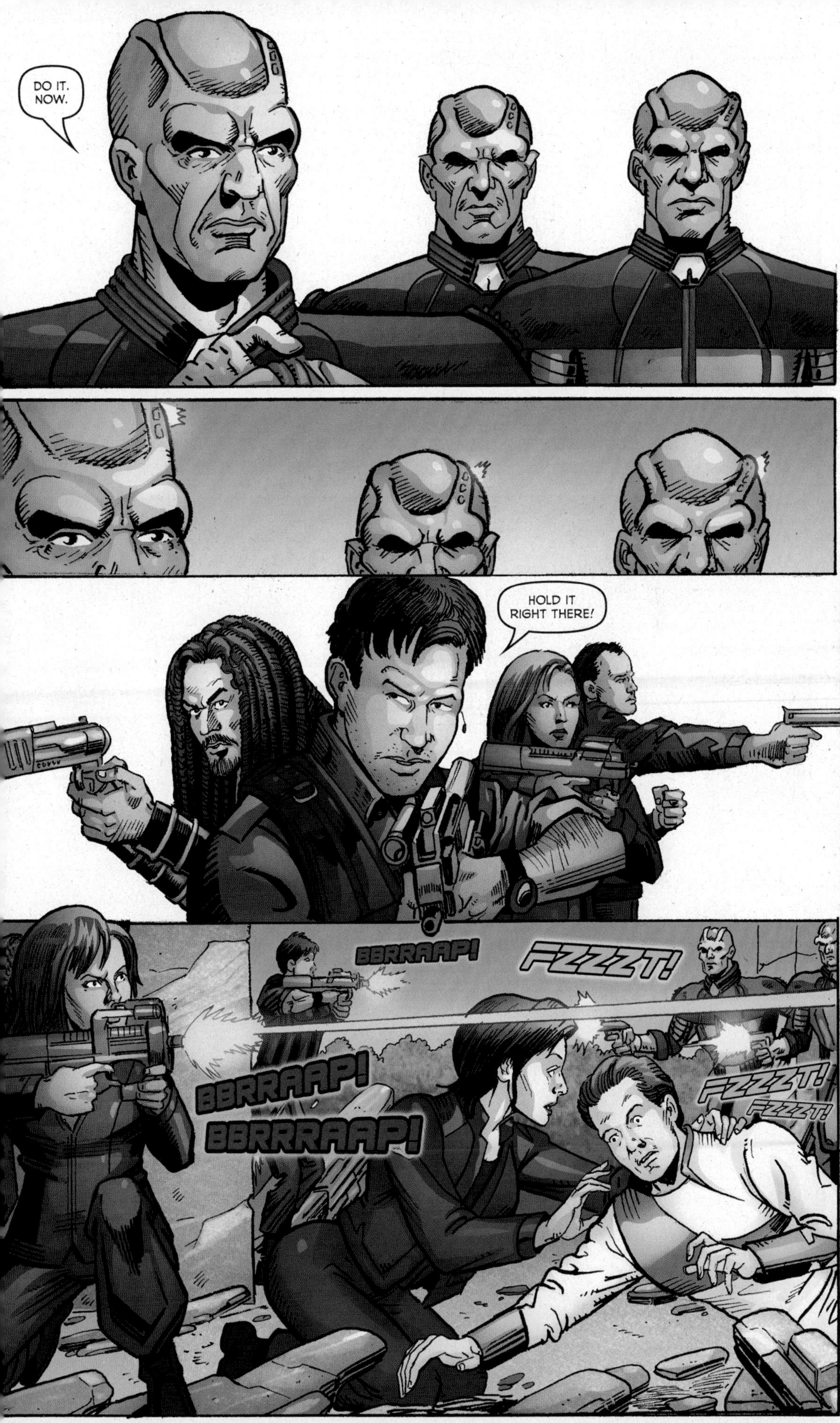
DO IT. NOW.
HOLD IT RIGHT THERE!
BBRRAAP!
FZZZT!
BBRRAAP!
BBRRRAAP!
FZZZT!
FZZZT!

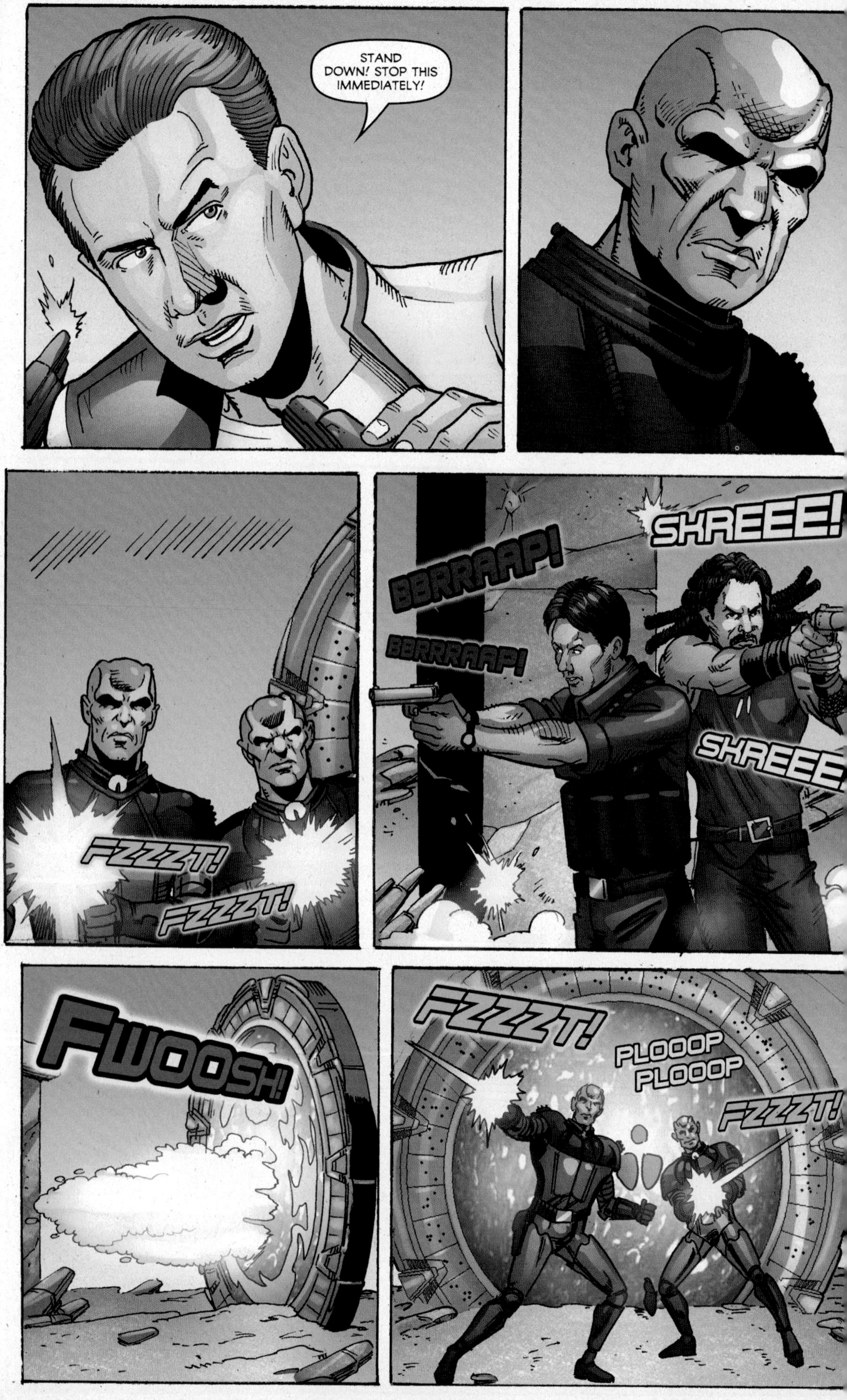
STAND DOWN! STOP THIS IMMEDIATELY!
FZZZT!
FZZZT!
SHREEE!
BBRRAAP!
BBRRRAAP!
SHREEE
FWOOSH!
FZZZT!
PLOOOP PLOOOP
FZZZT!

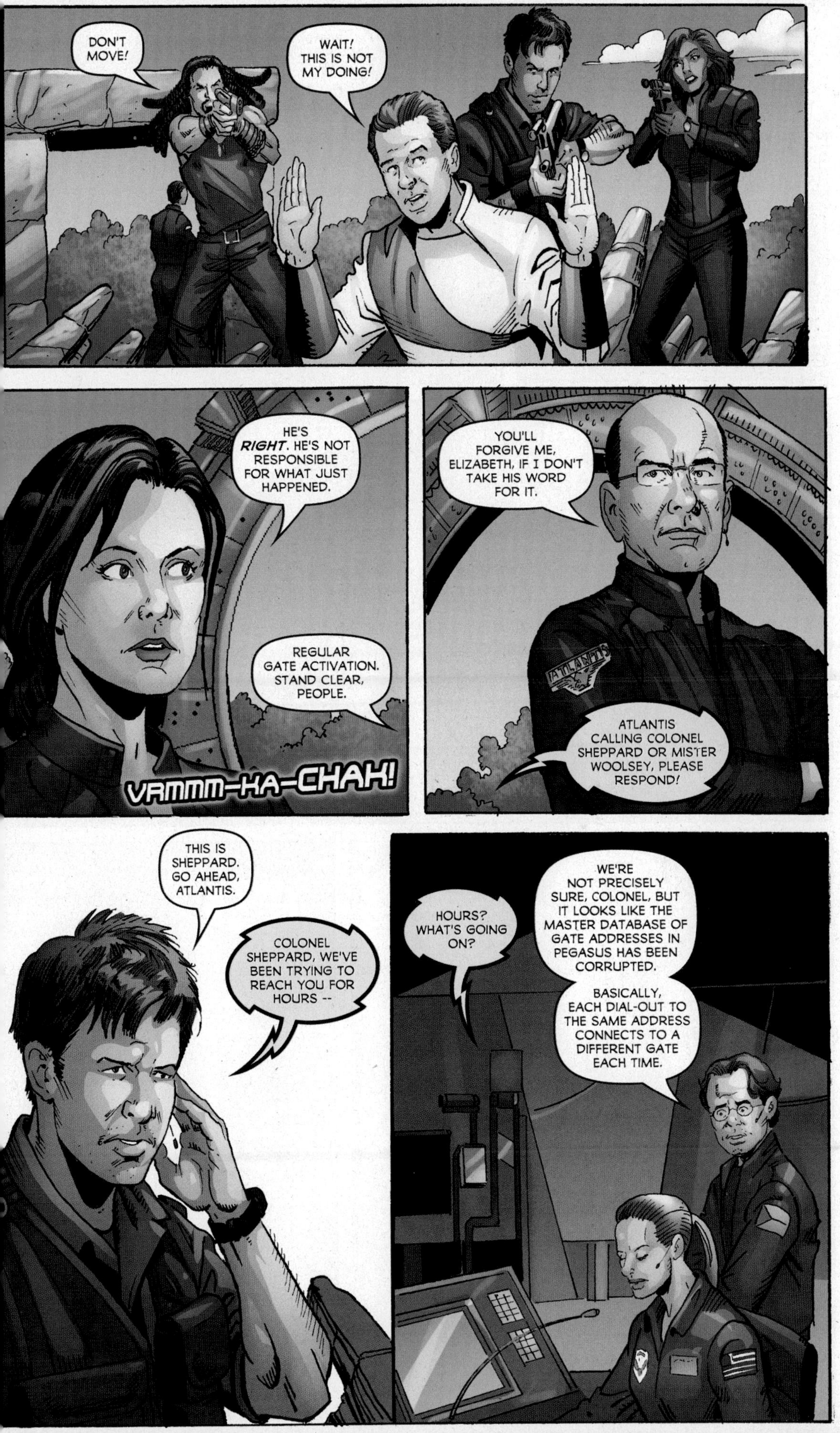
DON'T MOVE!
WAIT! THIS IS NOT MY DOING!
HE'S RIGHT. HE'S NOT RESPONSIBLE FOR WHAT JUST HAPPENED.
REGULAR GATE ACTIVATION. STAND CLEAR, PEOPLE.
VRMMM-KA-CHAK!
YOU'LL FORGIVE ME, ELIZABETH, IF I DON'T TAKE HIS WORD FOR IT.
ATLANTIS CALLING COLONEL SHEPPARD OR MISTER WOOLSEY, PLEASE RESPOND!
THIS IS SHEPPARD. GO AHEAD, ATLANTIS.
COLONEL SHEPPARD, WE'VE BEEN TRYING TO REACH YOU FOR HOURS --
HOURS? WHAT'S GOING ON?
WE'RE NOT PRECISELY SURE, COLONEL, BUT IT LOOKS LIKE THE MASTER DATABASE OF GATE ADDRESSES IN PEGASUS HAS BEEN CORRUPTED.
BASICALLY, EACH DIAL-OUT TO THE SAME ADDRESS CONNECTS TO A DIFFERENT GATE EACH TIME.

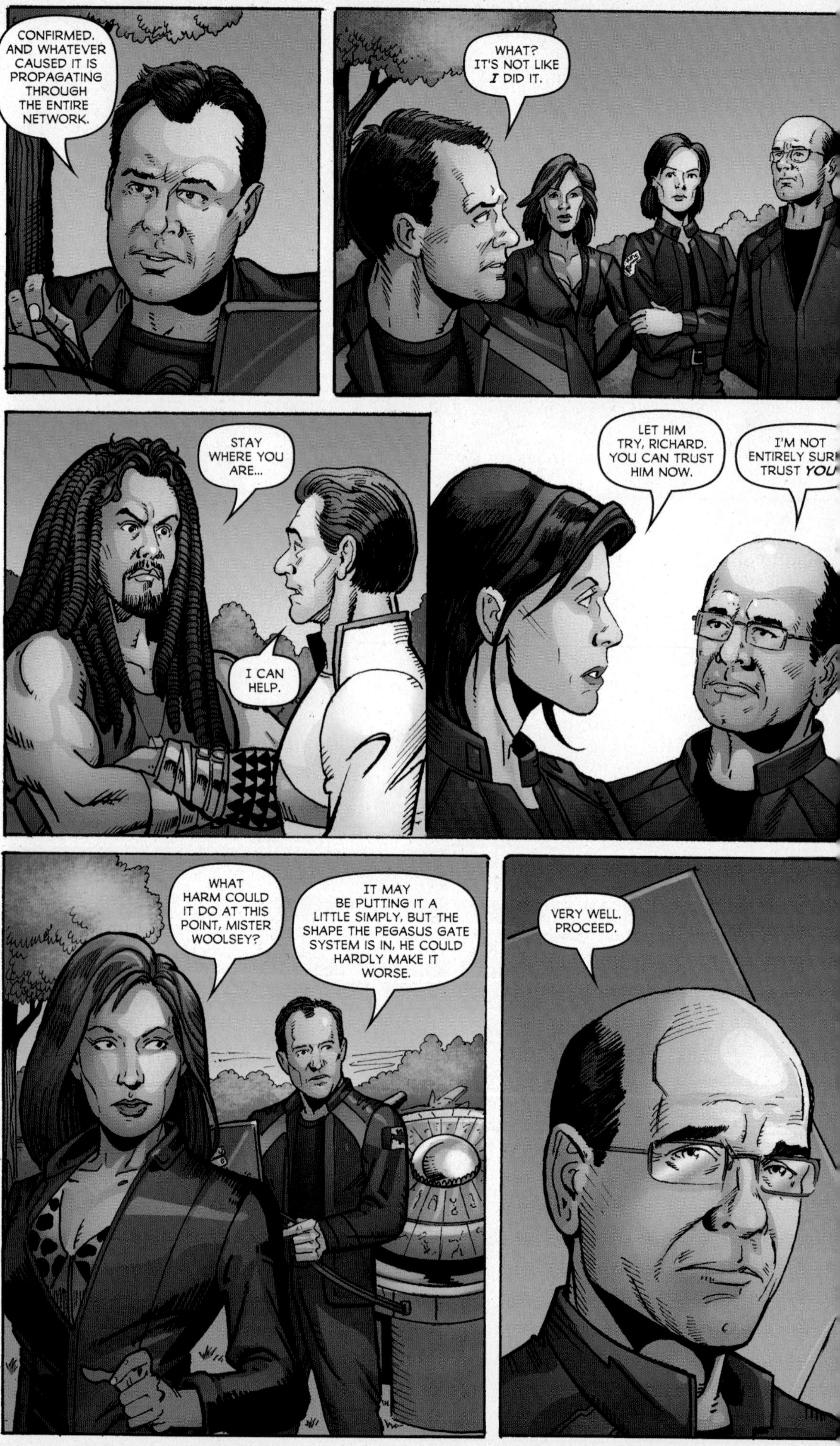
CONFIRMED. AND WHATEVER CAUSED IT IS PROPAGATING THROUGH THE ENTIRE NETWORK.
WHAT? IT'S NOT LIKE *I* DID IT.
STAY WHERE YOU ARE...
I CAN HELP.
LET HIM TRY, RICHARD. YOU CAN TRUST HIM NOW.
I'M NOT ENTIRELY SUR TRUST *YOU*
WHAT HARM COULD IT DO AT THIS POINT, MISTER WOOLSEY?
IT MAY BE PUTTING IT A LITTLE SIMPLY, BUT THE SHAPE THE PEGASUS GATE SYSTEM IS IN, HE COULD HARDLY MAKE IT WORSE.
VERY WELL. PROCEED.

HOW'D YOU DO THAT?

AH, YES... VERY INTERESTING. I WOULDN'T HAVE THOUGHT THEY COULD DO THAT.

DO THAT?

WOULD YOU MIND FILLING US IN?

THE MASTER ROUTING RECORDS ARE CORRUPTED, AS YOUR COLLEAGUES ON ATLANTIS HAVE DISCOVERED.

THANKS FOR TELLING US WHAT WE ALREADY KNOW.

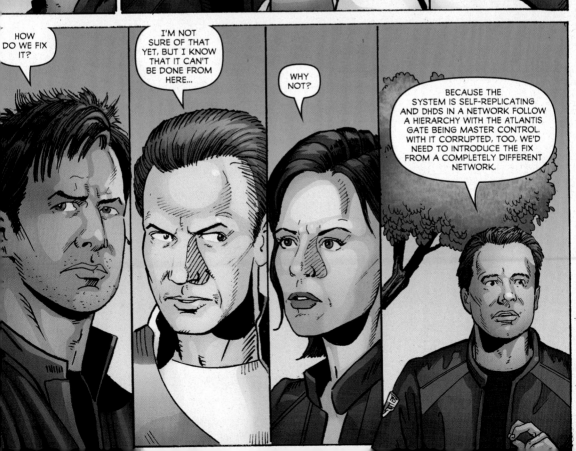

HOW DO WE FIX IT?

I'M NOT SURE OF THAT YET, BUT I KNOW THAT IT CAN'T BE DONE FROM HERE...

WHY NOT?

BECAUSE THE SYSTEM IS SELF-REPLICATING AND DHDS IN A NETWORK FOLLOW A HIERARCHY WITH THE ATLANTIS GATE BEING MASTER CONTROL. WITH IT CORRUPTED, TOO, WE'D NEED TO INTRODUCE THE FIX FROM A COMPLETELY DIFFERENT NETWORK.

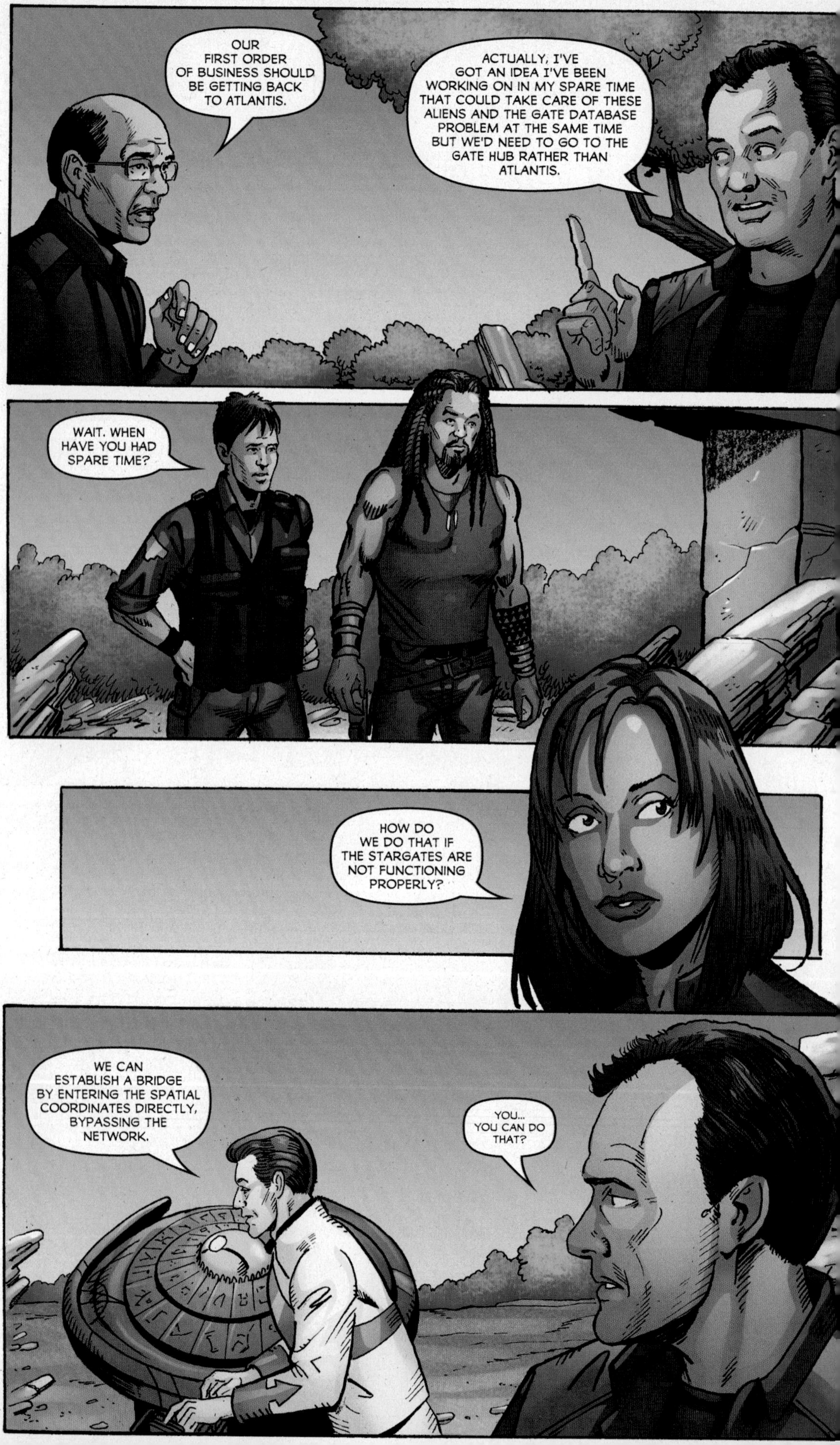
OUR FIRST ORDER OF BUSINESS SHOULD BE GETTING BACK TO ATLANTIS.
ACTUALLY, I'VE GOT AN IDEA I'VE BEEN WORKING ON IN MY SPARE TIME THAT COULD TAKE CARE OF THESE ALIENS AND THE GATE DATABASE PROBLEM AT THE SAME TIME BUT WE'D NEED TO GO TO THE GATE HUB RATHER THAN ATLANTIS.
WAIT. WHEN HAVE YOU HAD SPARE TIME?
HOW DO WE DO THAT IF THE STARGATES ARE NOT FUNCTIONING PROPERLY?
WE CAN ESTABLISH A BRIDGE BY ENTERING THE SPATIAL COORDINATES DIRECTLY, BYPASSING THE NETWORK.
YOU... YOU CAN DO THAT?

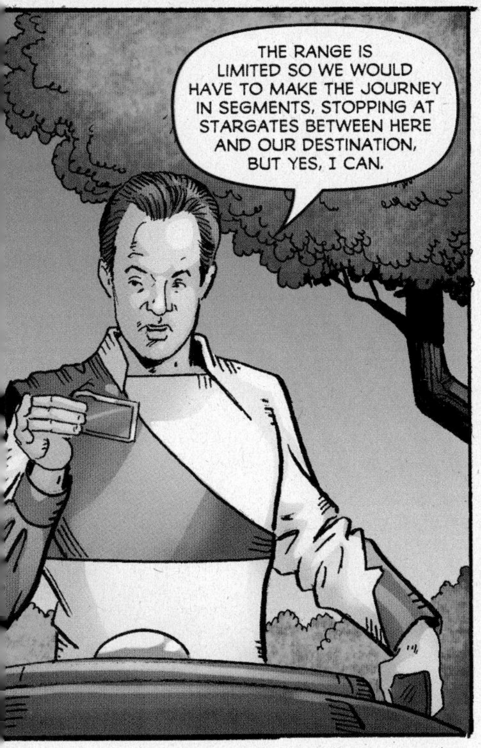
THE RANGE IS LIMITED SO WE WOULD HAVE TO MAKE THE JOURNEY IN SEGMENTS, STOPPING AT STARGATES BETWEEN HERE AND OUR DESTINATION, BUT YES, I CAN.

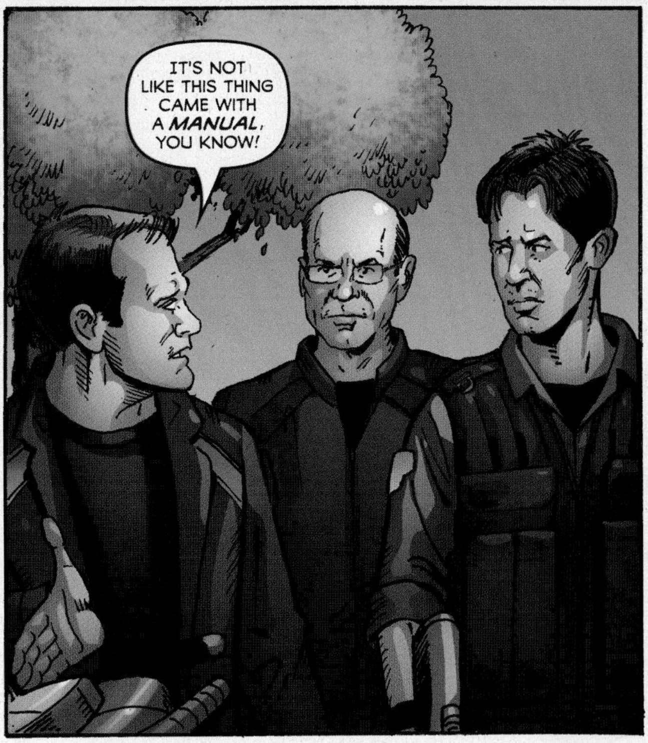
IT'S NOT LIKE THIS THING CAME WITH A MANUAL, YOU KNOW!

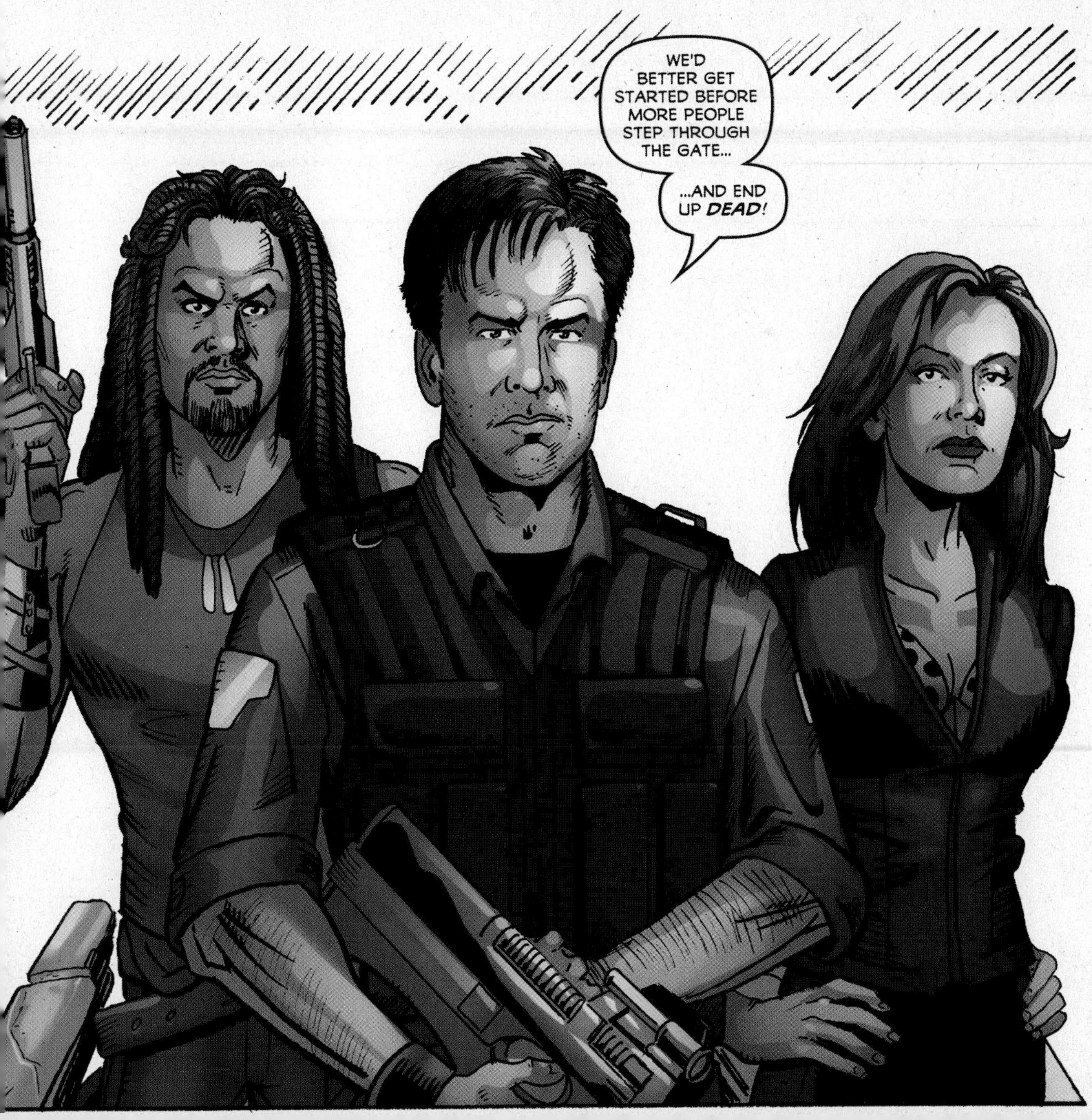
WE'D BETTER GET STARTED BEFORE MORE PEOPLE STEP THROUGH THE GATE...
...AND END UP DEAD!

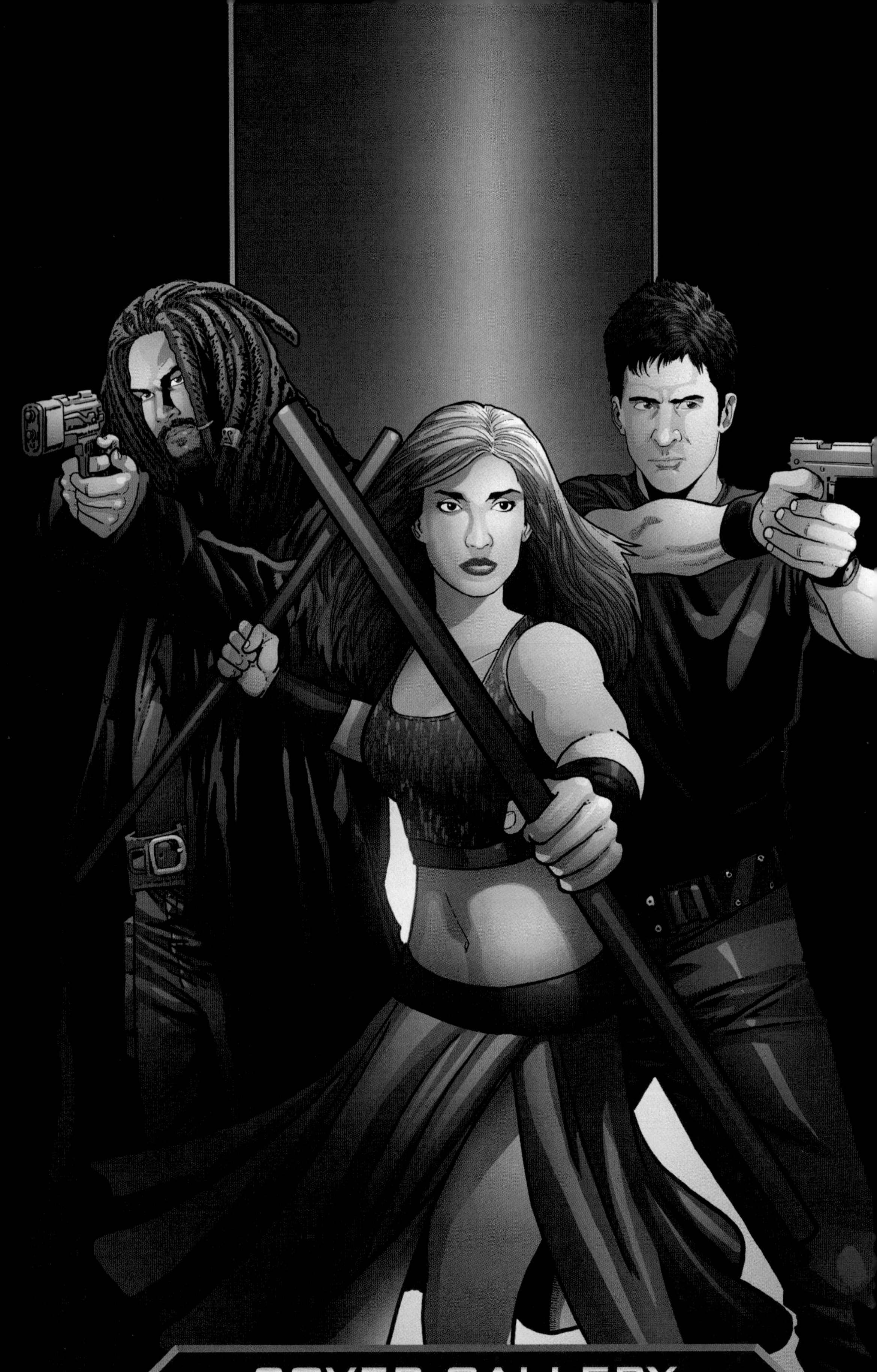

COVER GALLERY

SINGULARITY #3 MAIN COVER

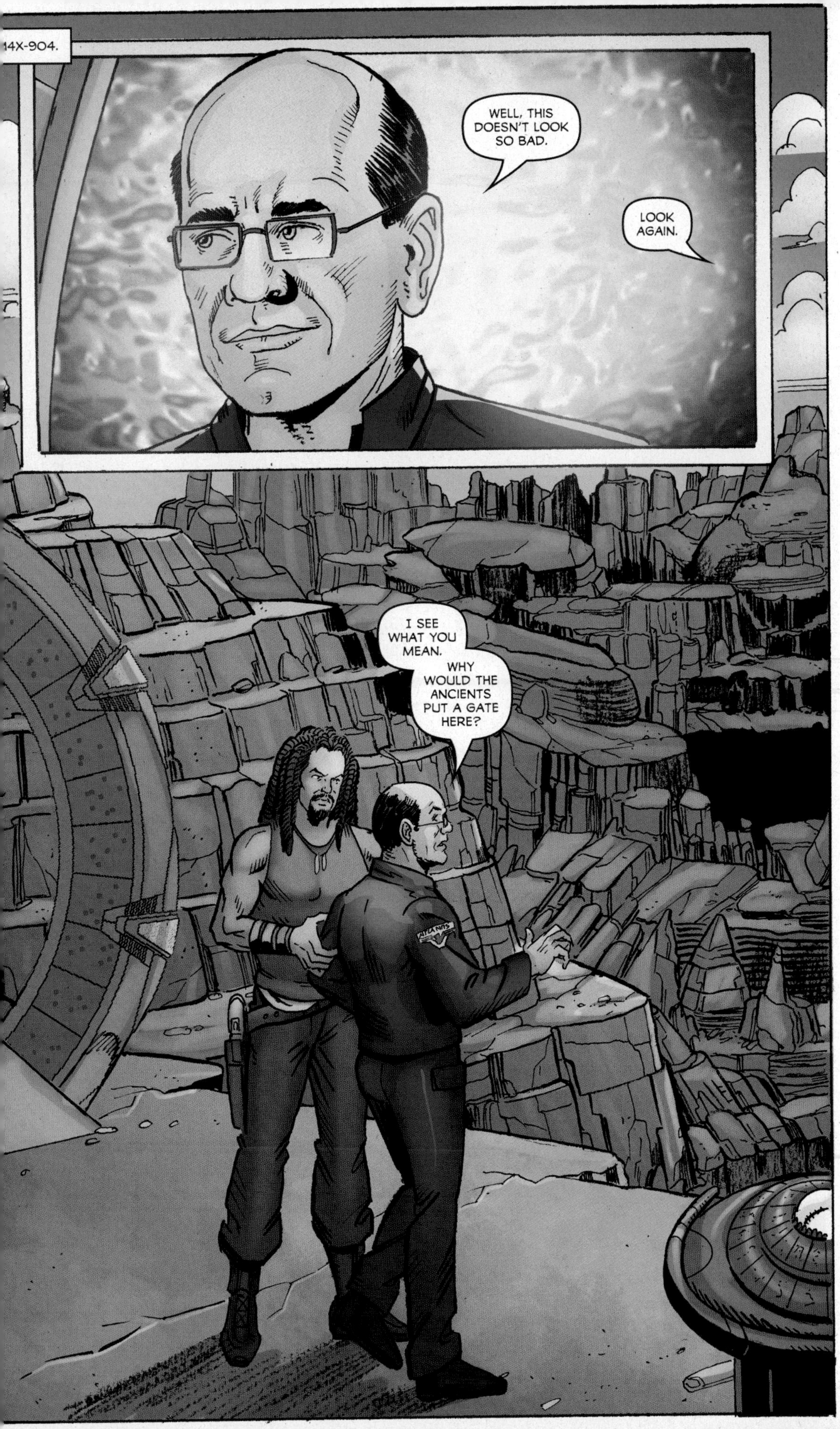

14X-904.
WELL, THIS DOESN'T LOOK SO BAD.
LOOK AGAIN.
I SEE WHAT YOU MEAN.
WHY WOULD THE ANCIENTS PUT A GATE HERE?

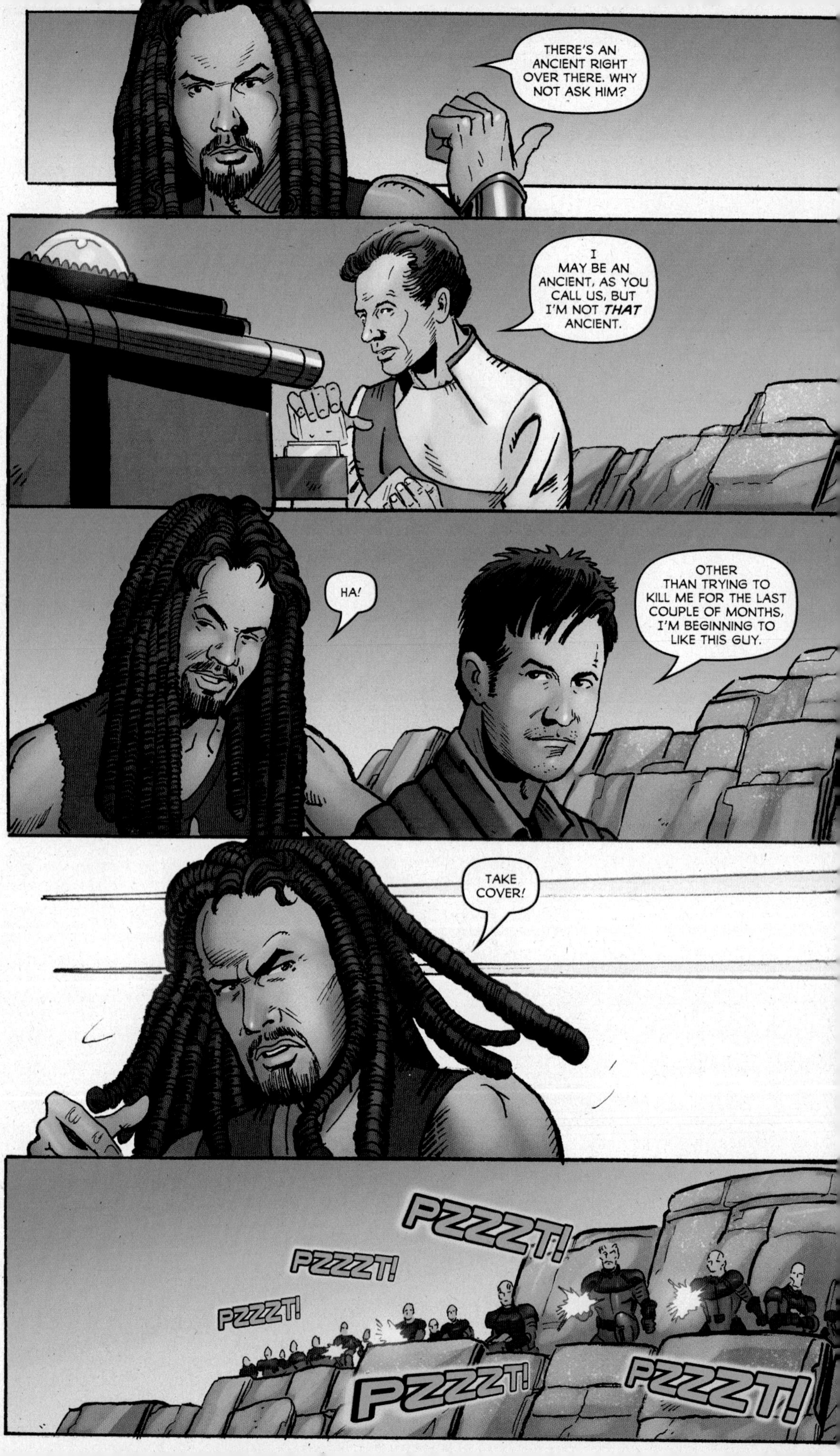
THERE'S AN ANCIENT RIGHT OVER THERE. WHY NOT ASK HIM?
I MAY BE AN ANCIENT, AS YOU CALL US, BUT I'M NOT *THAT* ANCIENT.
HA!
OTHER THAN TRYING TO KILL ME FOR THE LAST COUPLE OF MONTHS, I'M BEGINNING TO LIKE THIS GUY.
TAKE COVER!
PZZZZT!
PZZZT!
PZZZT!
PZZZT!
PZZZZT!

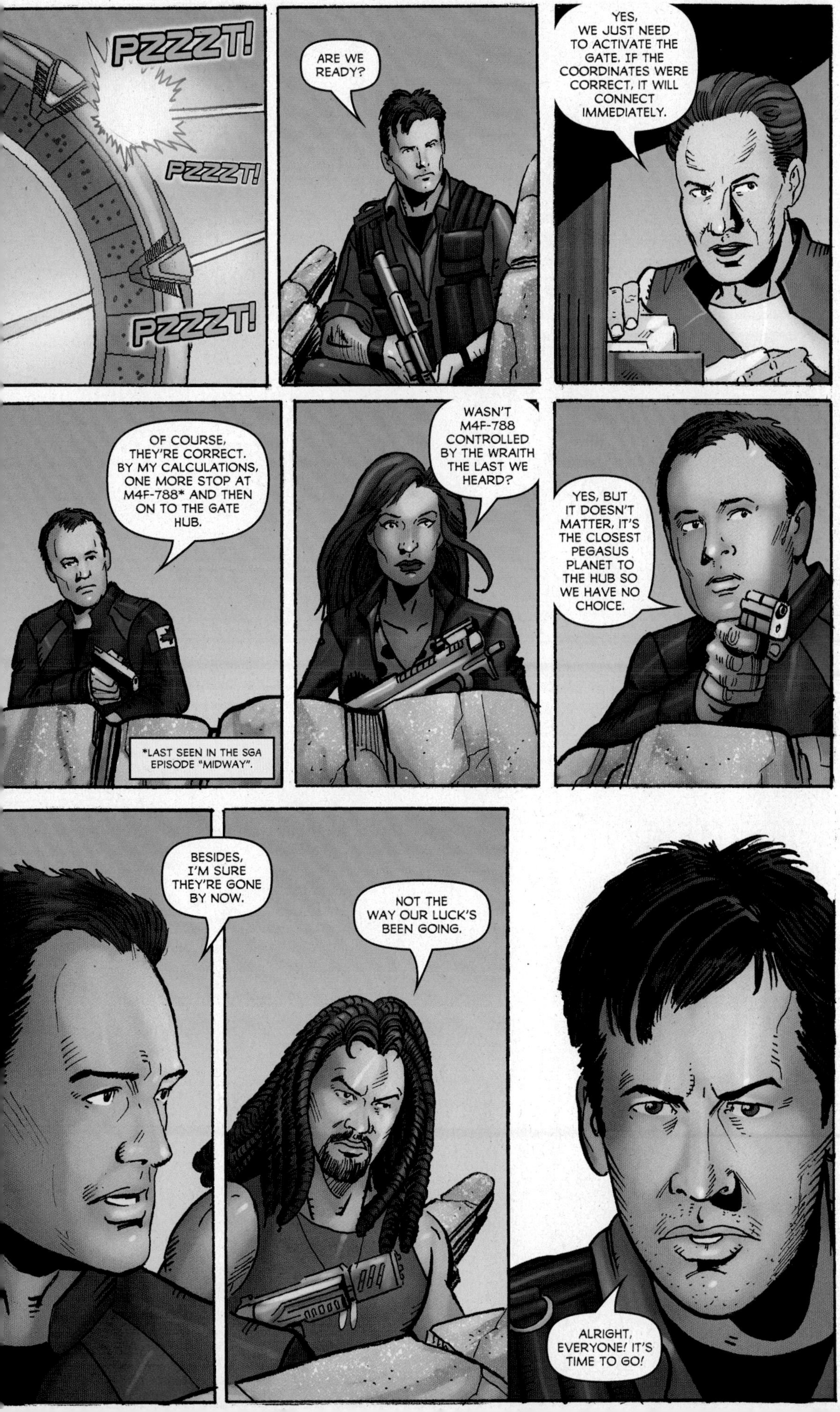
PZZZT!
PZZZT!
PZZZT!
ARE WE READY?
YES, WE JUST NEED TO ACTIVATE THE GATE. IF THE COORDINATES WERE CORRECT, IT WILL CONNECT IMMEDIATELY.
OF COURSE, THEY'RE CORRECT. BY MY CALCULATIONS, ONE MORE STOP AT M4F-788* AND THEN ON TO THE GATE HUB.
*LAST SEEN IN THE SGA EPISODE "MIDWAY".
WASN'T M4F-788 CONTROLLED BY THE WRAITH THE LAST WE HEARD?
YES, BUT IT DOESN'T MATTER, IT'S THE CLOSEST PEGASUS PLANET TO THE HUB SO WE HAVE NO CHOICE.
BESIDES, I'M SURE THEY'RE GONE BY NOW.
NOT THE WAY OUR LUCK'S BEEN GOING.
ALRIGHT, EVERYONE! IT'S TIME TO GO!

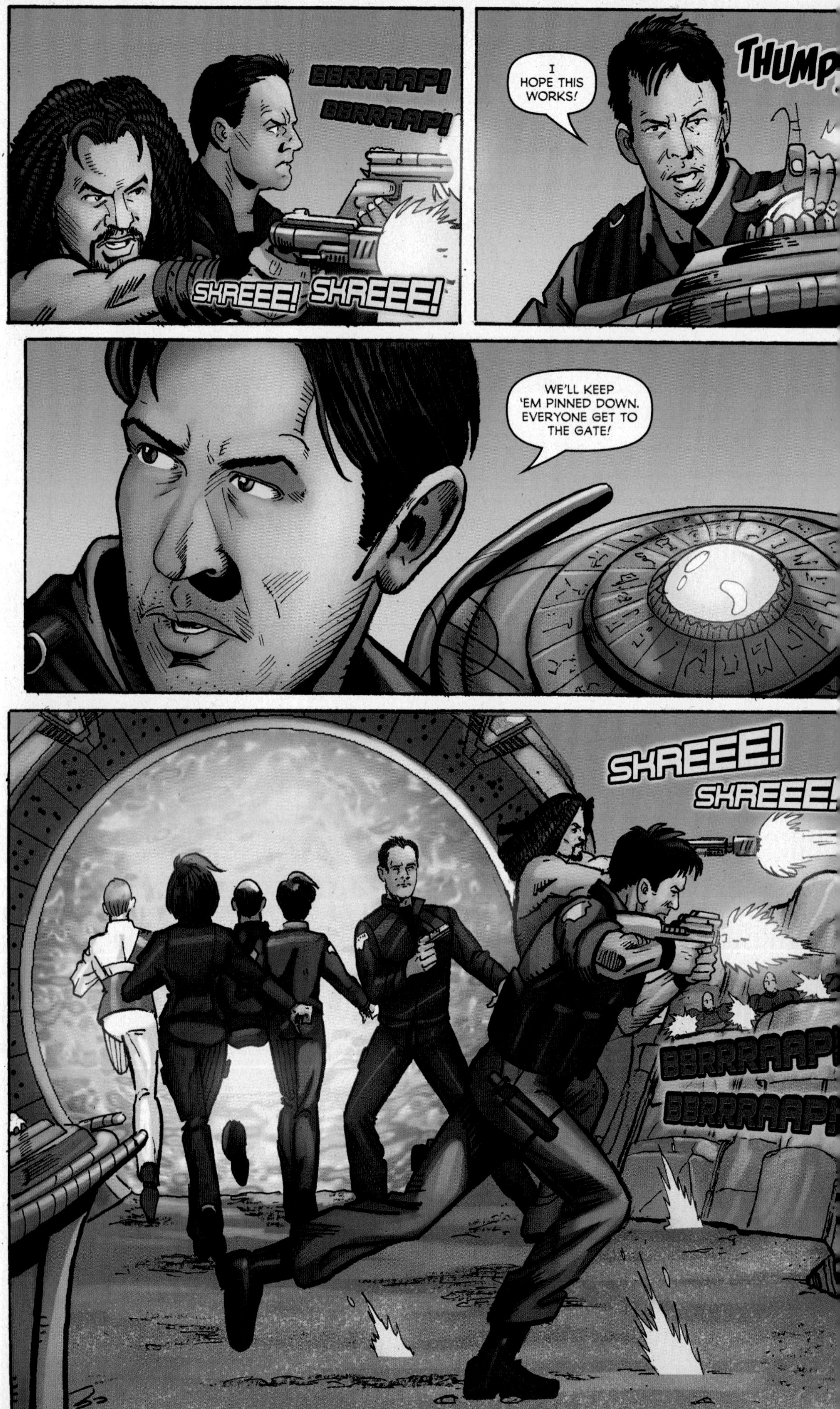

BBRRAAP!
BBRRAAP!
SKREEE! SKREEE!
I HOPE THIS WORKS!
THUMP
WE'LL KEEP 'EM PINNED DOWN. EVERYONE GET TO THE GATE!
SKREEE!
SKREEE!
BBRRRAAP!
BBRRRAAP!

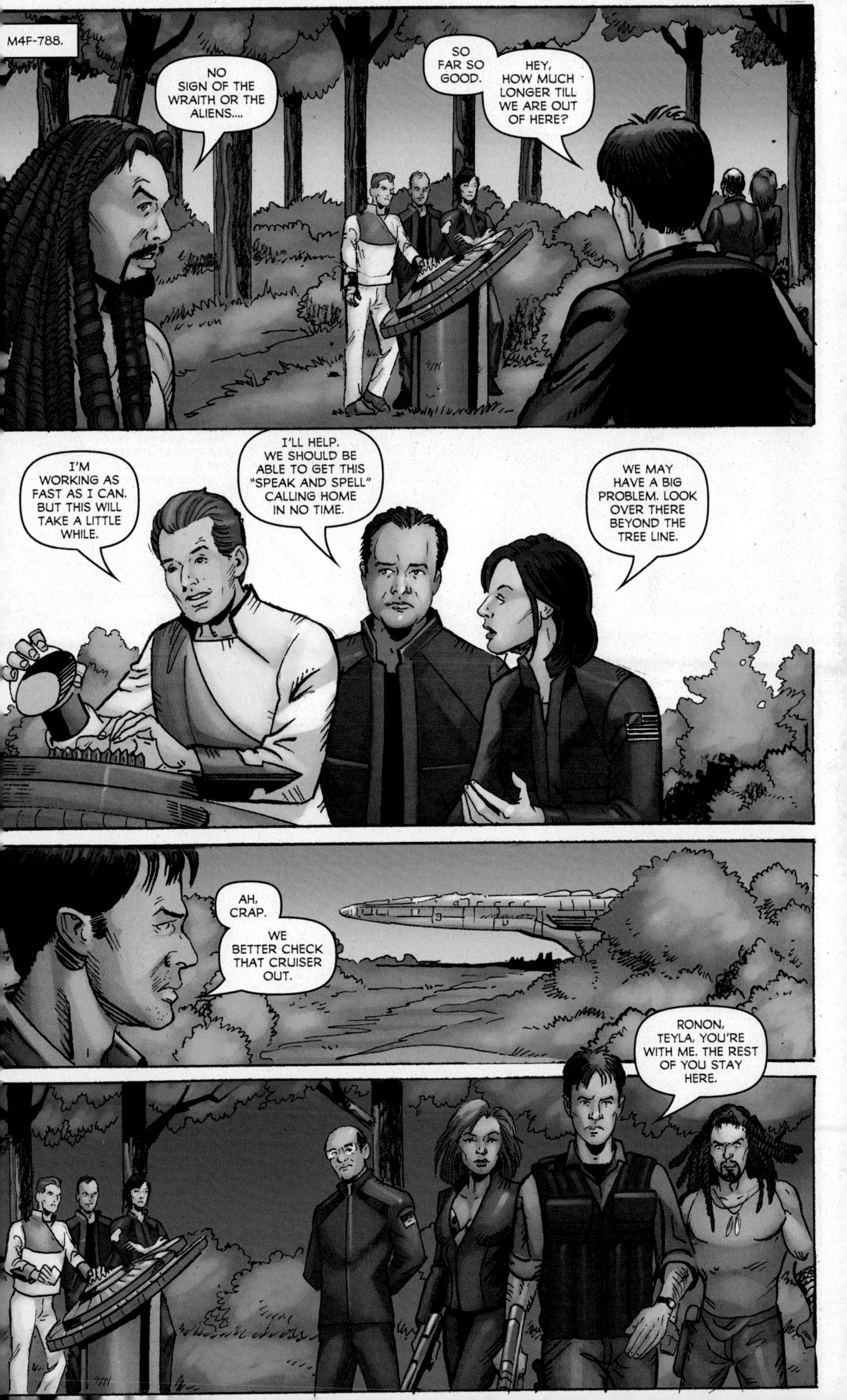
M4F-788.
NO SIGN OF THE WRAITH OR THE ALIENS....
SO FAR SO GOOD.
HEY, HOW MUCH LONGER TILL WE ARE OUT OF HERE?
I'M WORKING AS FAST AS I CAN. BUT THIS WILL TAKE A LITTLE WHILE.
I'LL HELP. WE SHOULD BE ABLE TO GET THIS "SPEAK AND SPELL" CALLING HOME IN NO TIME.
WE MAY HAVE A BIG PROBLEM. LOOK OVER THERE BEYOND THE TREE LINE.
AH, CRAP.
WE BETTER CHECK THAT CRUISER OUT.
RONON, TEYLA, YOU'RE WITH ME. THE REST OF YOU STAY HERE.

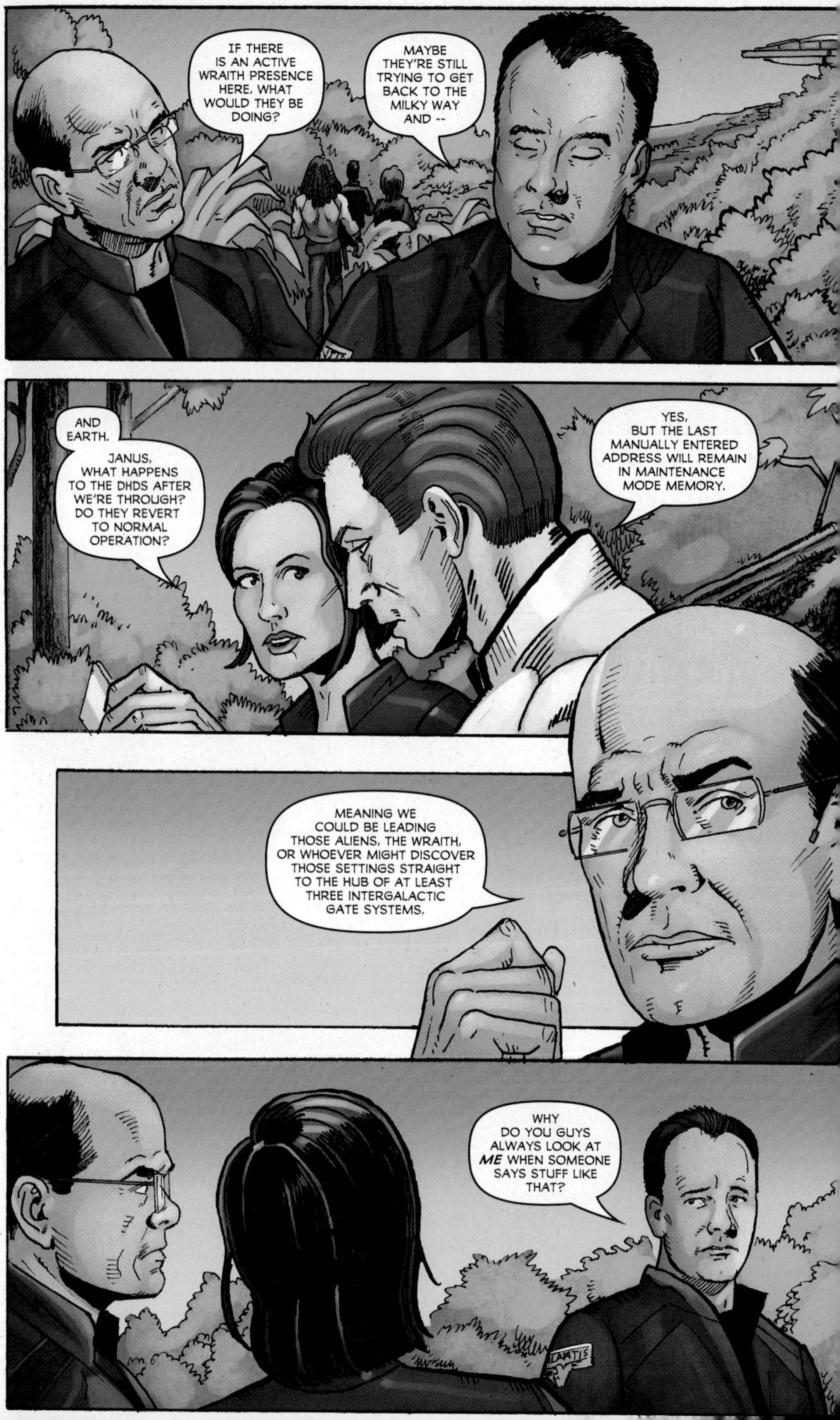
IF THERE IS AN ACTIVE WRAITH PRESENCE HERE, WHAT WOULD THEY BE DOING?
MAYBE THEY'RE STILL TRYING TO GET BACK TO THE MILKY WAY AND --
AND EARTH.
JANUS, WHAT HAPPENS TO THE DHDS AFTER WE'RE THROUGH? DO THEY REVERT TO NORMAL OPERATION?
YES, BUT THE LAST MANUALLY ENTERED ADDRESS WILL REMAIN IN MAINTENANCE MODE MEMORY.
MEANING WE COULD BE LEADING THOSE ALIENS, THE WRAITH, OR WHOEVER MIGHT DISCOVER THOSE SETTINGS STRAIGHT TO THE HUB OF AT LEAST THREE INTERGALACTIC GATE SYSTEMS.
WHY DO YOU GUYS ALWAYS LOOK AT *ME* WHEN SOMEONE SAYS STUFF LIKE THAT?

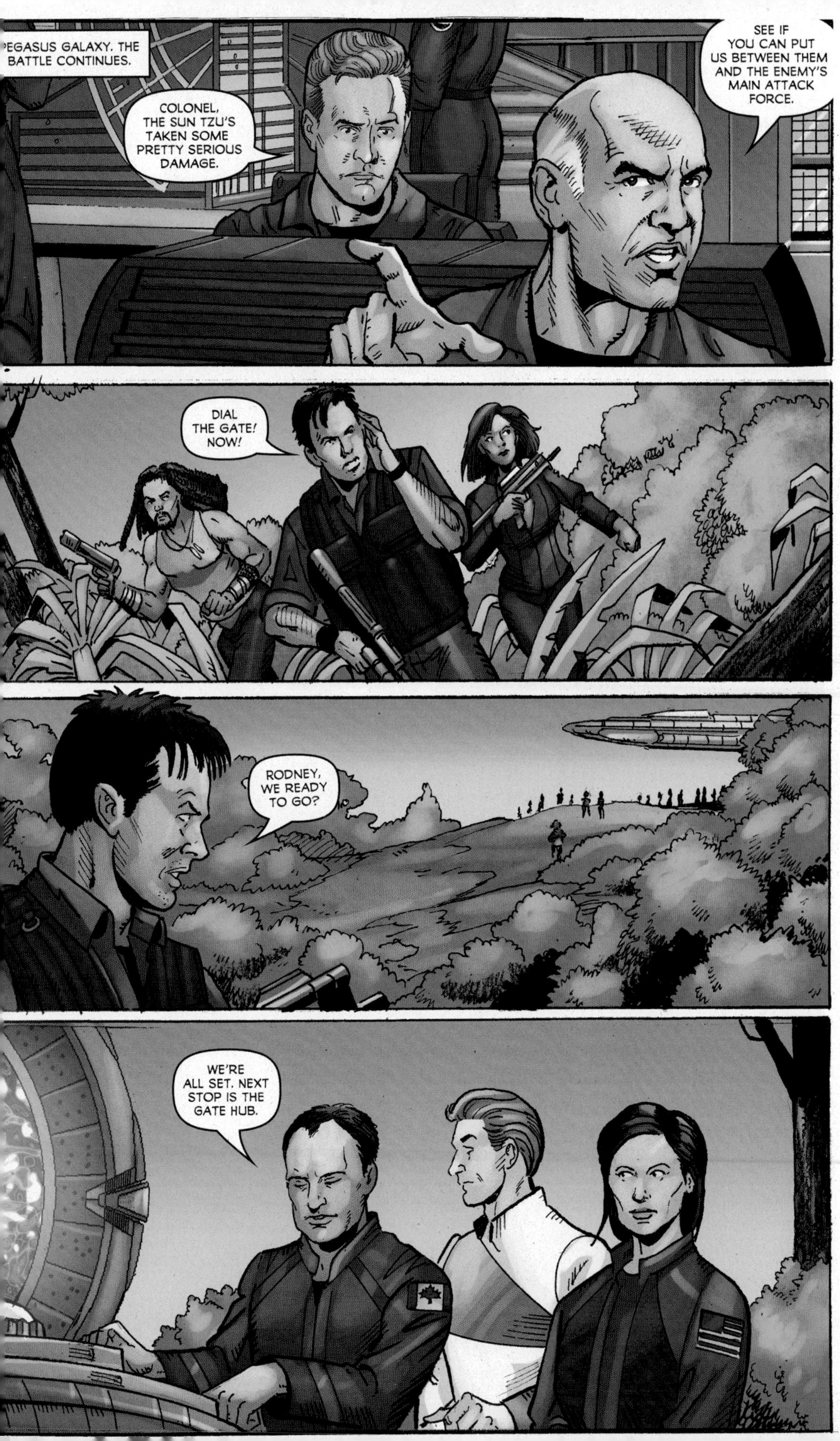
PEGASUS GALAXY. THE BATTLE CONTINUES.
COLONEL, THE SUN TZU'S TAKEN SOME PRETTY SERIOUS DAMAGE.
SEE IF YOU CAN PUT US BETWEEN THEM AND THE ENEMY'S MAIN ATTACK FORCE.
DIAL THE GATE! NOW!
RODNEY, WE READY TO GO?
WE'RE ALL SET. NEXT STOP IS THE GATE HUB.

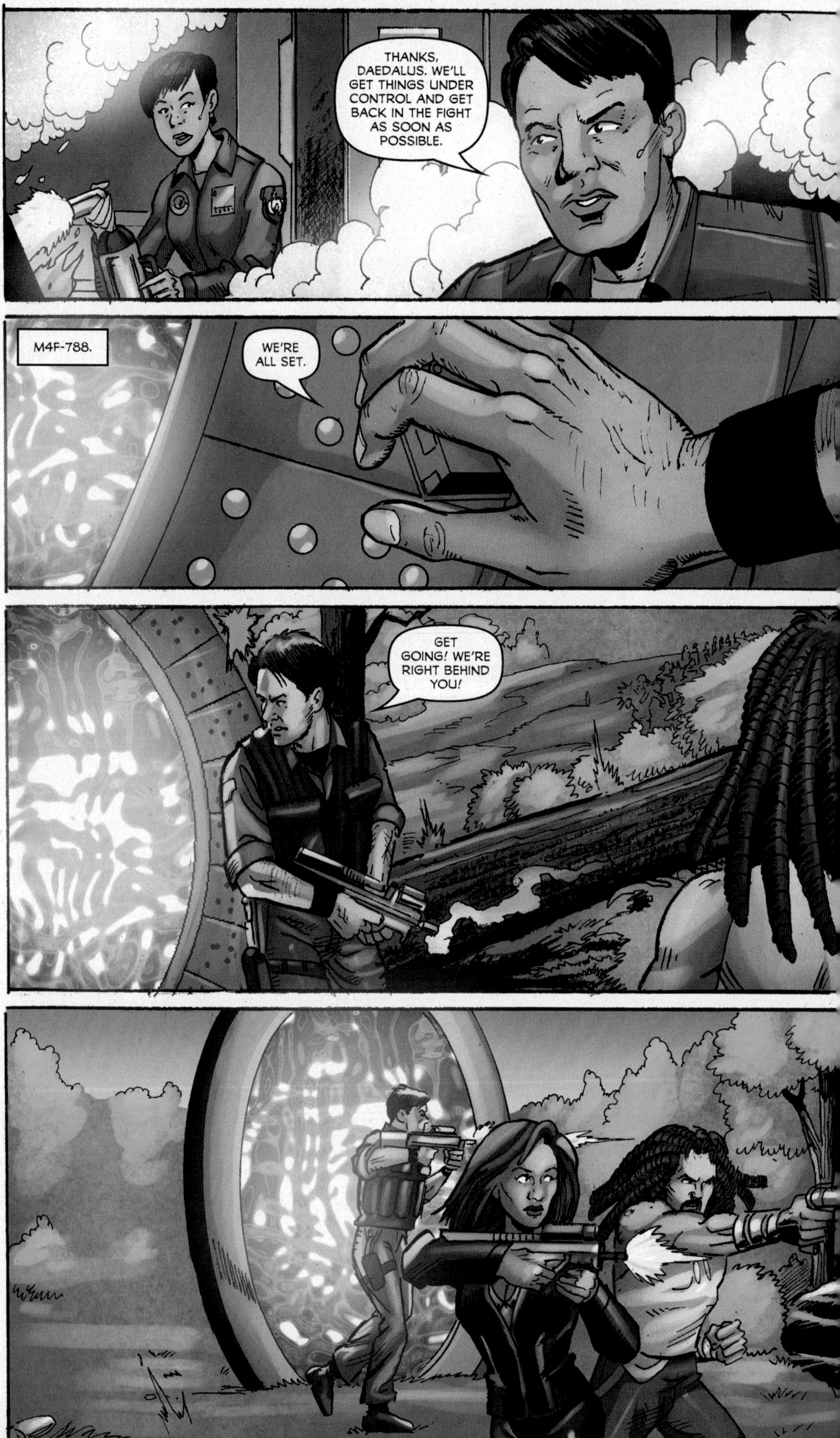
THANKS, DAEDALUS. WE'LL GET THINGS UNDER CONTROL AND GET BACK IN THE FIGHT AS SOON AS POSSIBLE.
M4F-788.
WE'RE ALL SET.
GET GOING! WE'RE RIGHT BEHIND YOU!

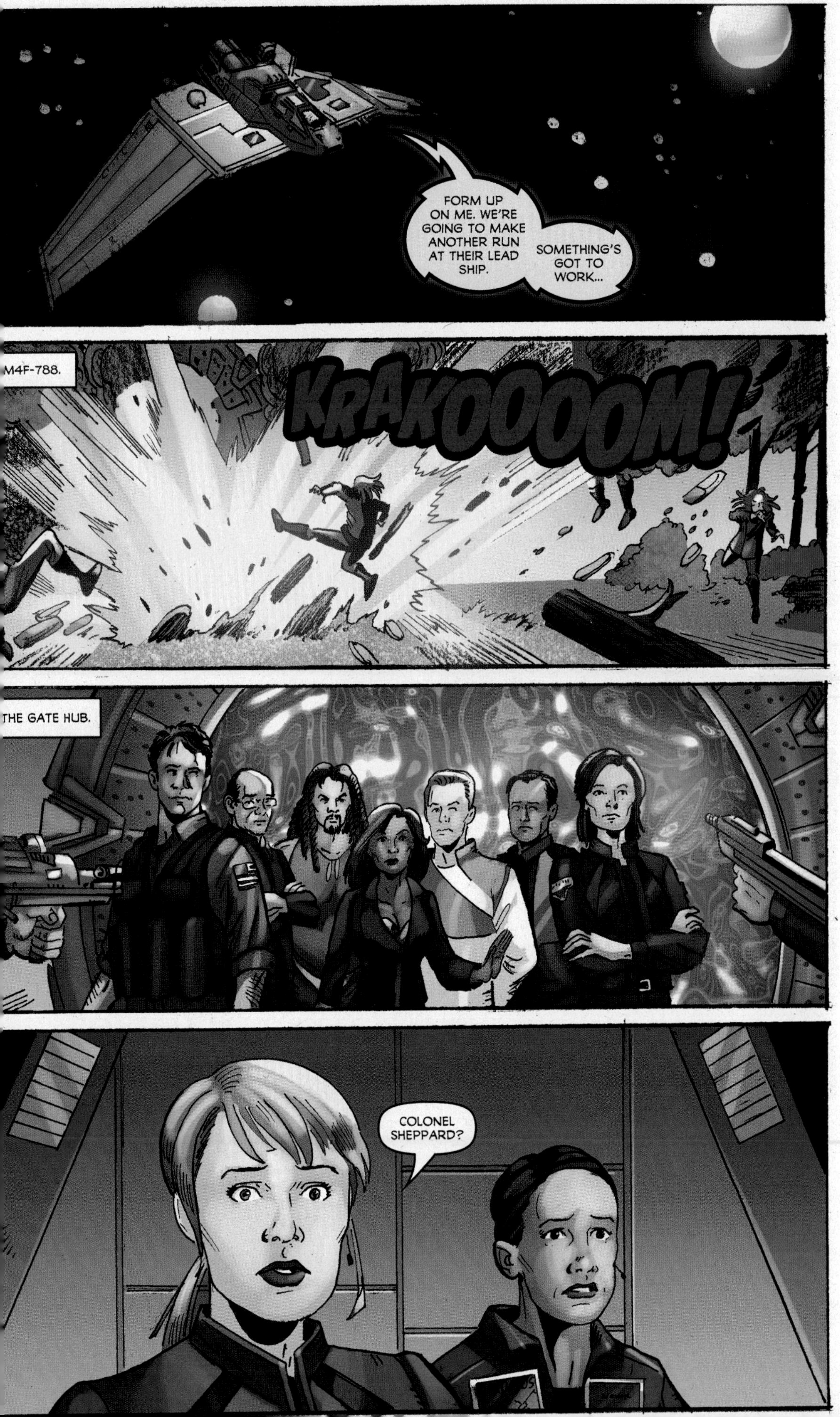
FORM UP ON ME. WE'RE GOING TO MAKE ANOTHER RUN AT THEIR LEAD SHIP.
SOMETHING'S GOT TO WORK...
M4F-788.
KRAKOOOOM!
THE GATE HUB.
COLONEL SHEPPARD?

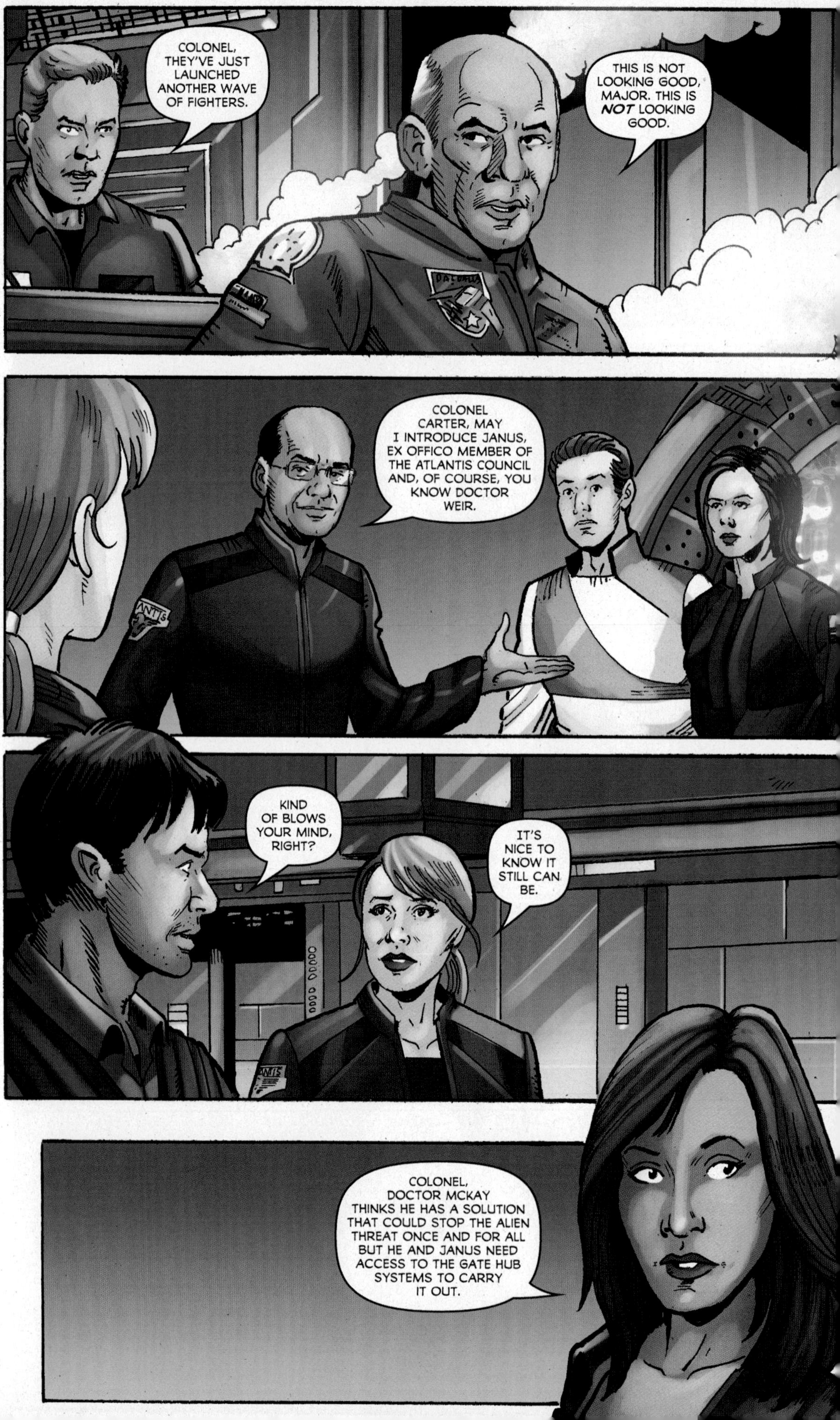

COLONEL, THEY'VE JUST LAUNCHED ANOTHER WAVE OF FIGHTERS.
THIS IS NOT LOOKING GOOD, MAJOR. THIS IS *NOT* LOOKING GOOD.
COLONEL CARTER, MAY I INTRODUCE JANUS, EX OFFICO MEMBER OF THE ATLANTIS COUNCIL AND, OF COURSE, YOU KNOW DOCTOR WEIR.
KIND OF BLOWS YOUR MIND, RIGHT?
IT'S NICE TO KNOW IT STILL CAN BE.
COLONEL, DOCTOR MCKAY THINKS HE HAS A SOLUTION THAT COULD STOP THE ALIEN THREAT ONCE AND FOR ALL BUT HE AND JANUS NEED ACCESS TO THE GATE HUB SYSTEMS TO CARRY IT OUT.

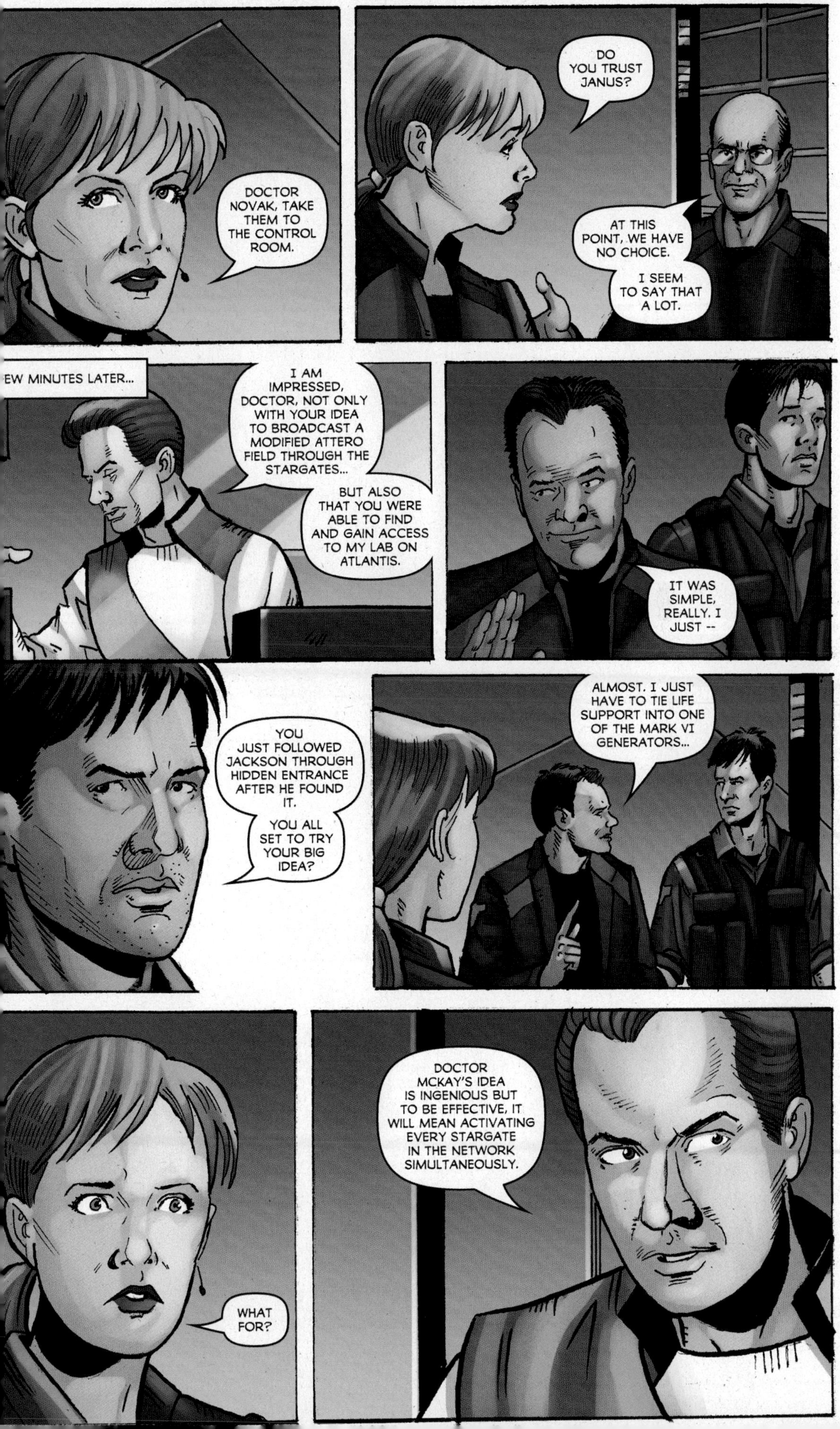
DOCTOR NOVAK, TAKE THEM TO THE CONTROL ROOM.
DO YOU TRUST JANUS?
AT THIS POINT, WE HAVE NO CHOICE.
I SEEM TO SAY THAT A LOT.
EW MINUTES LATER...
I AM IMPRESSED, DOCTOR, NOT ONLY WITH YOUR IDEA TO BROADCAST A MODIFIED ATTERO FIELD THROUGH THE STARGATES...
BUT ALSO THAT YOU WERE ABLE TO FIND AND GAIN ACCESS TO MY LAB ON ATLANTIS.
IT WAS SIMPLE, REALLY. I JUST --
YOU JUST FOLLOWED JACKSON THROUGH HIDDEN ENTRANCE AFTER HE FOUND IT.
YOU ALL SET TO TRY YOUR BIG IDEA?
ALMOST. I JUST HAVE TO TIE LIFE SUPPORT INTO ONE OF THE MARK VI GENERATORS...
WHAT FOR?
DOCTOR MCKAY'S IDEA IS INGENIOUS BUT TO BE EFFECTIVE, IT WILL MEAN ACTIVATING EVERY STARGATE IN THE NETWORK SIMULTANEOUSLY.

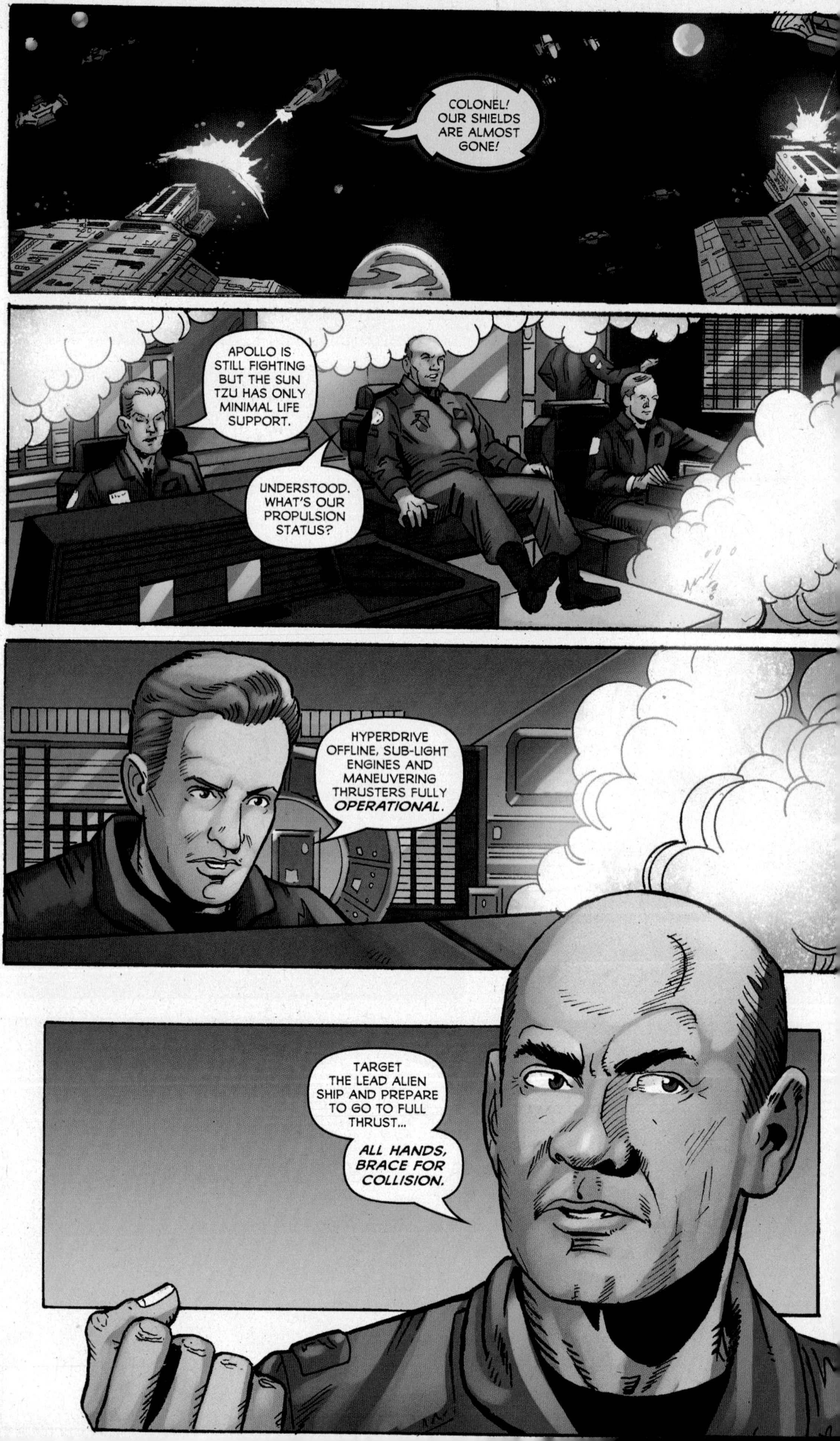

COLONEL! OUR SHIELDS ARE ALMOST GONE!
APOLLO IS STILL FIGHTING BUT THE SUN TZU HAS ONLY MINIMAL LIFE SUPPORT.
UNDERSTOOD. WHAT'S OUR PROPULSION STATUS?
HYPERDRIVE OFFLINE, SUB-LIGHT ENGINES AND MANEUVERING THRUSTERS FULLY *OPERATIONAL*.
TARGET THE LEAD ALIEN SHIP AND PREPARE TO GO TO FULL THRUST...
ALL HANDS, BRACE FOR COLLISION.

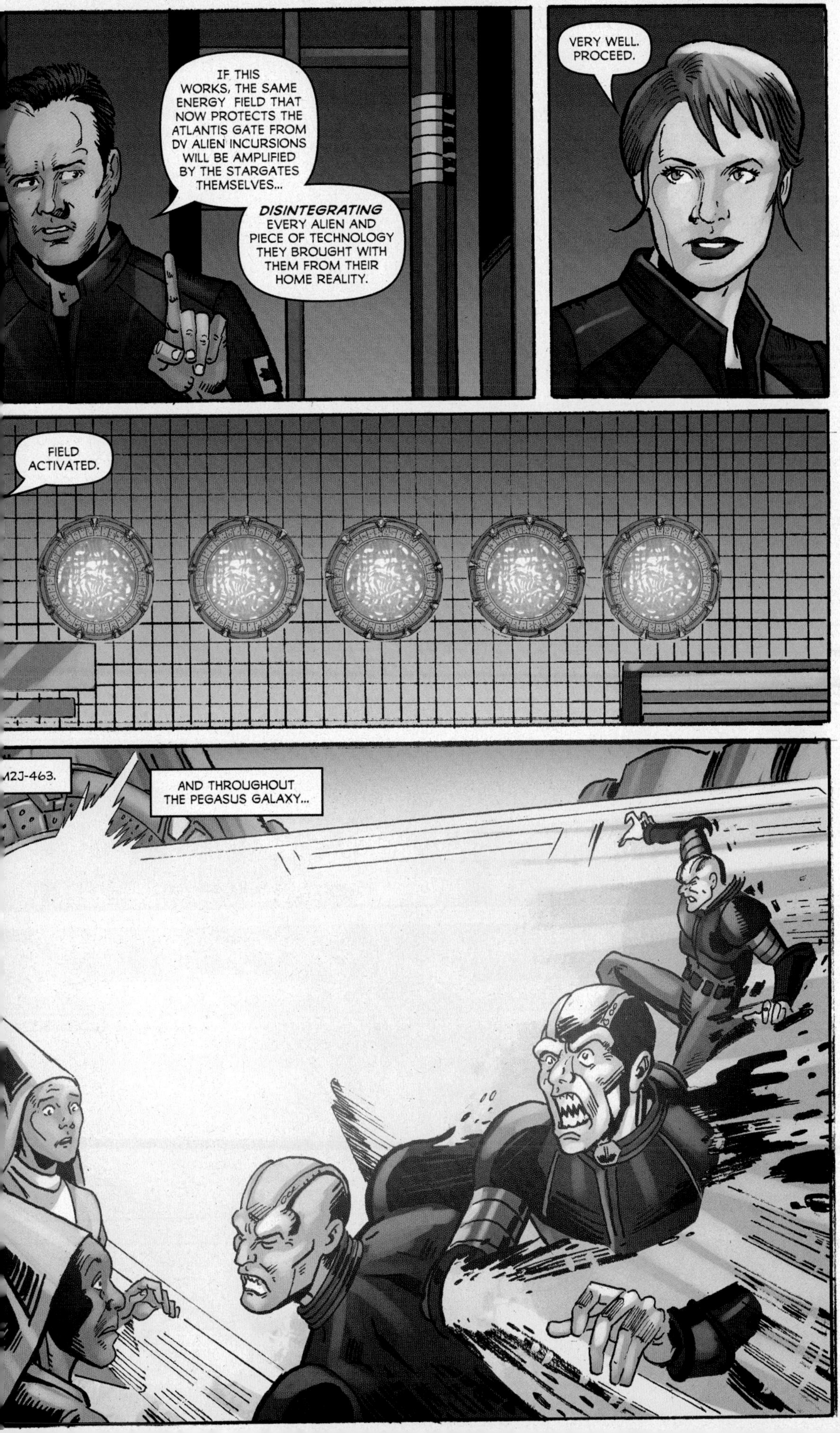
IF THIS WORKS, THE SAME ENERGY FIELD THAT NOW PROTECTS THE ATLANTIS GATE FROM DV ALIEN INCURSIONS WILL BE AMPLIFIED BY THE STARGATES THEMSELVES...
DISINTEGRATING EVERY ALIEN AND PIECE OF TECHNOLOGY THEY BROUGHT WITH THEM FROM THEIR HOME REALITY.
VERY WELL. PROCEED.
FIELD ACTIVATED.
M2J-463.
AND THROUGHOUT THE PEGASUS GALAXY...

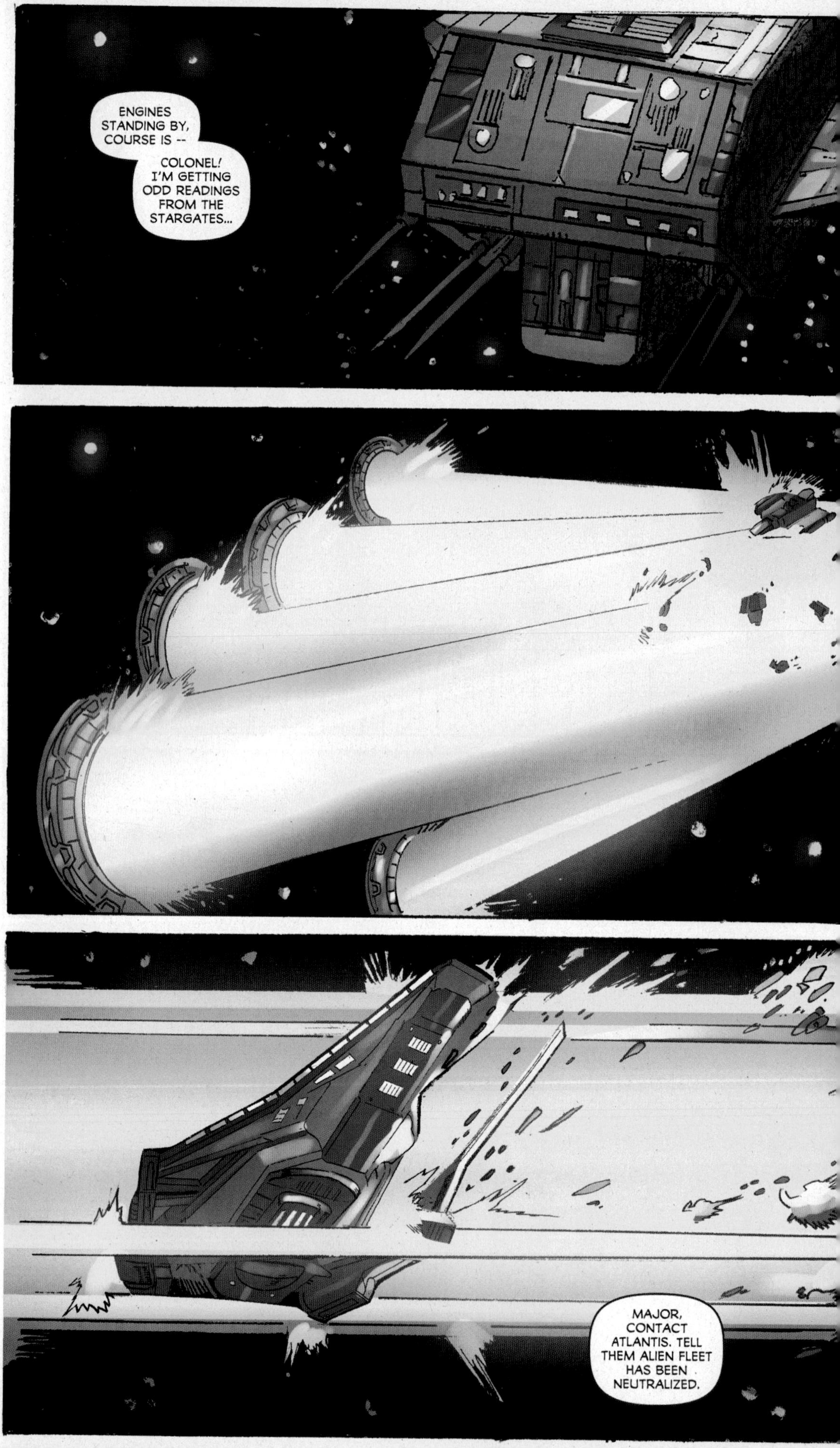
ENGINES STANDING BY, COURSE IS --
COLONEL! I'M GETTING ODD READINGS FROM THE STARGATES...
MAJOR, CONTACT ATLANTIS. TELL THEM ALIEN FLEET HAS BEEN NEUTRALIZED.

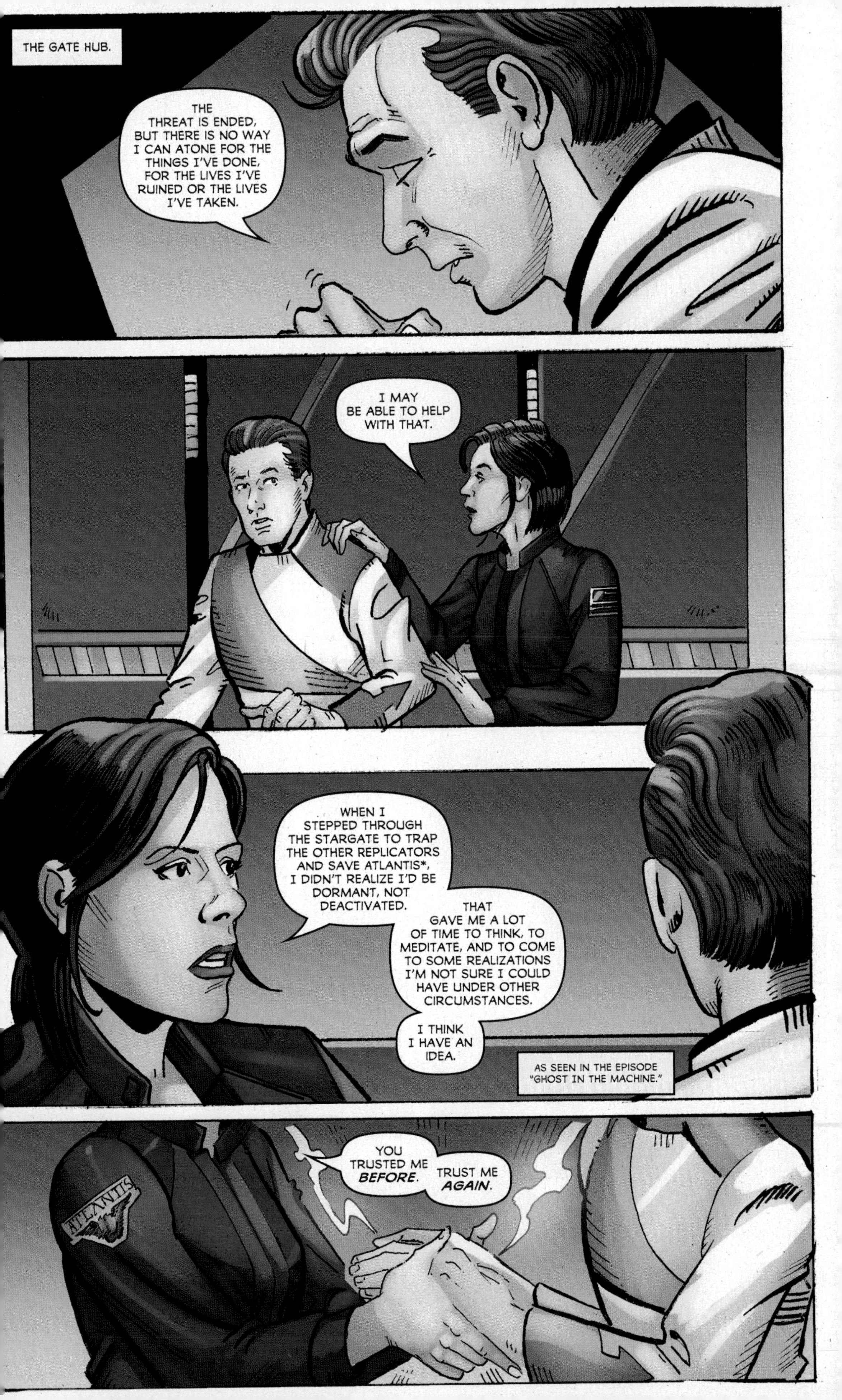
THE GATE HUB.
THE THREAT IS ENDED, BUT THERE IS NO WAY I CAN ATONE FOR THE THINGS I'VE DONE, FOR THE LIVES I'VE RUINED OR THE LIVES I'VE TAKEN.
I MAY BE ABLE TO HELP WITH THAT.
WHEN I STEPPED THROUGH THE STARGATE TO TRAP THE OTHER REPLICATORS AND SAVE ATLANTIS*, I DIDN'T REALIZE I'D BE DORMANT, NOT DEACTIVATED.
THAT GAVE ME A LOT OF TIME TO THINK, TO MEDITATE, AND TO COME TO SOME REALIZATIONS I'M NOT SURE I COULD HAVE UNDER OTHER CIRCUMSTANCES.
I THINK I HAVE AN IDEA.
AS SEEN IN THE EPISODE "GHOST IN THE MACHINE."
YOU TRUSTED ME ***BEFORE***.
TRUST ME ***AGAIN***.
ATLANTIS

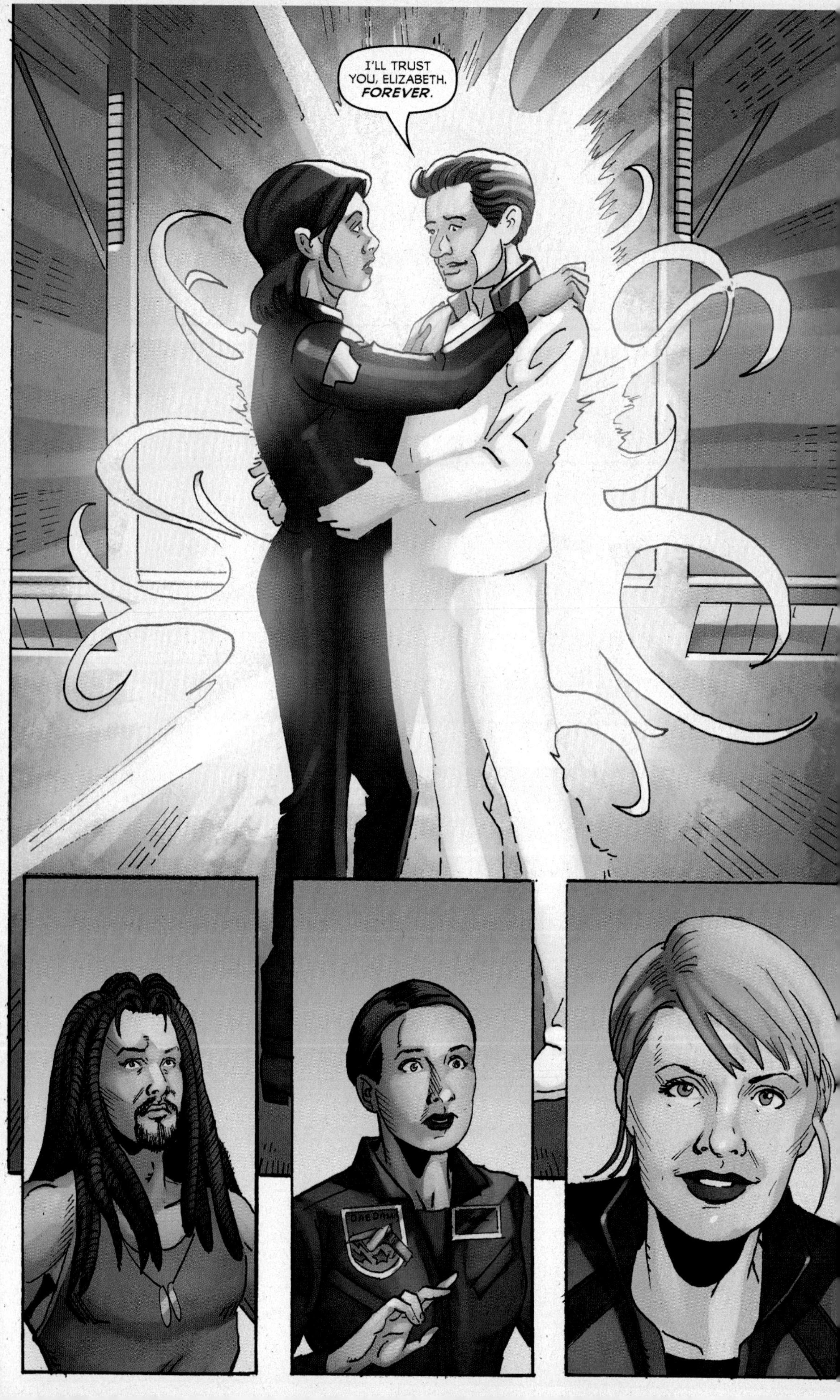
I'LL TRUST YOU, ELIZABETH. *FOREVER*.

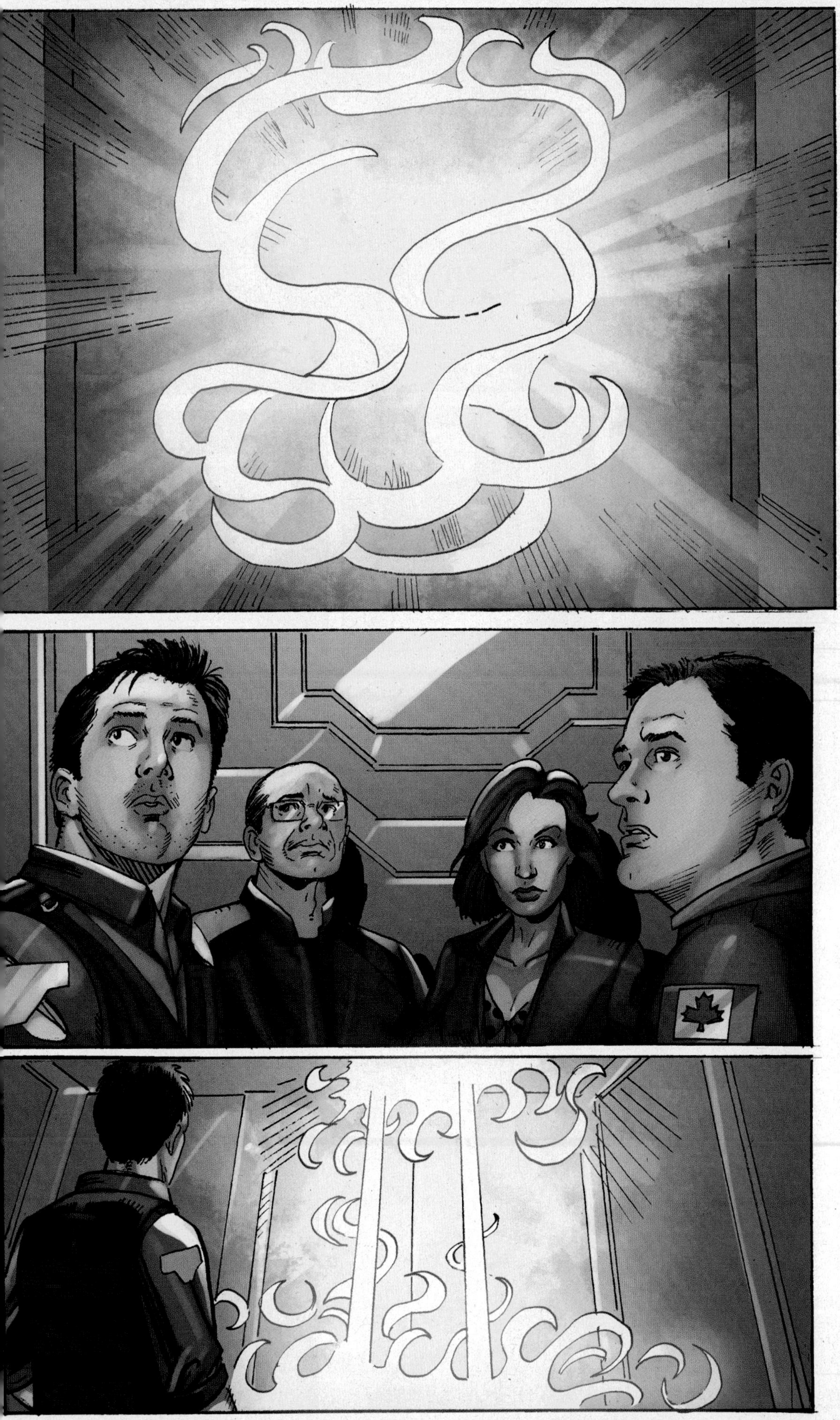

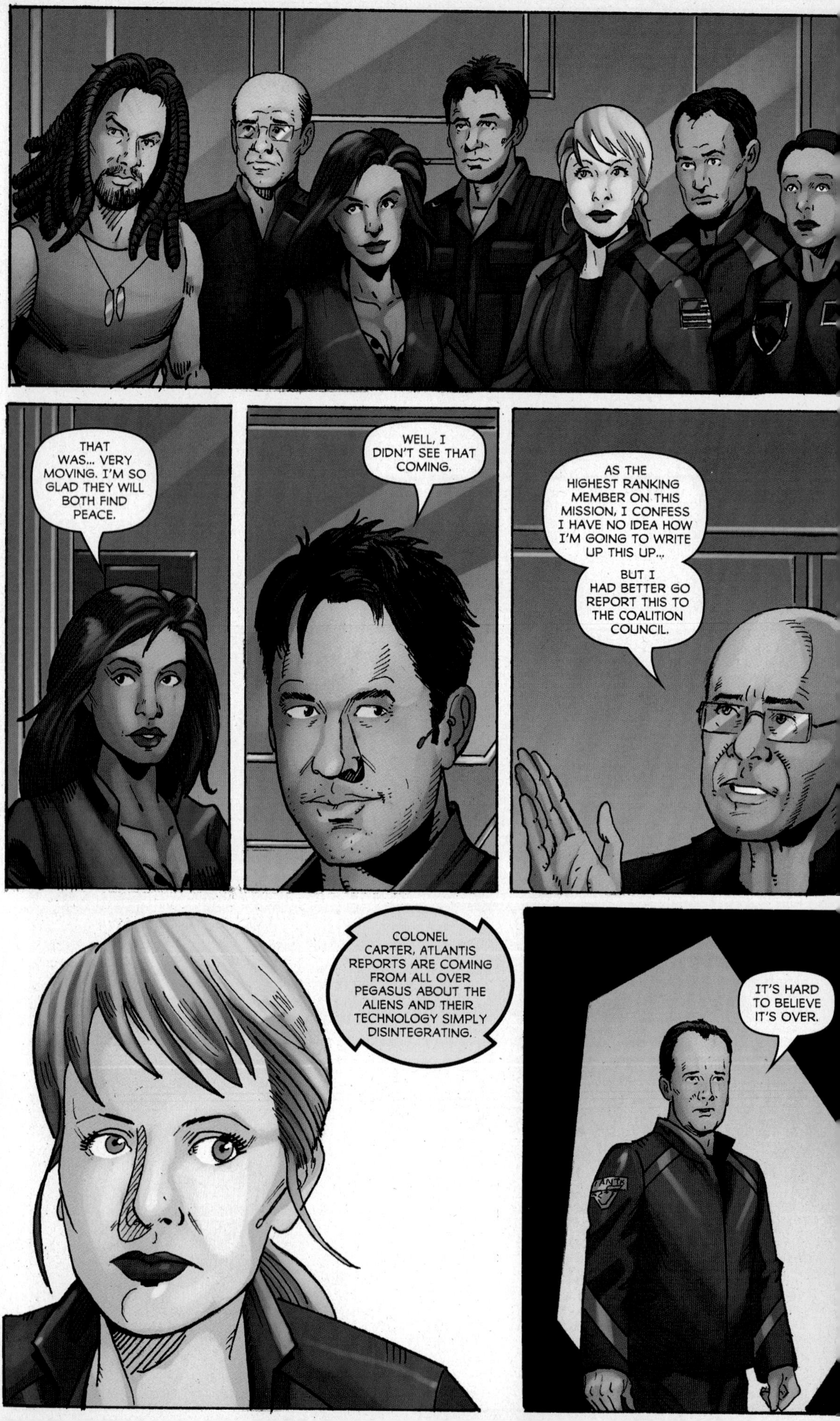
THAT WAS... VERY MOVING. I'M SO GLAD THEY WILL BOTH FIND PEACE.
WELL, I DIDN'T SEE THAT COMING.
AS THE HIGHEST RANKING MEMBER ON THIS MISSION, I CONFESS I HAVE NO IDEA HOW I'M GOING TO WRITE UP THIS UP...
BUT I HAD BETTER GO REPORT THIS TO THE COALITION COUNCIL.
COLONEL CARTER, ATLANTIS REPORTS ARE COMING FROM ALL OVER PEGASUS ABOUT THE ALIENS AND THEIR TECHNOLOGY SIMPLY DISINTEGRATING.
IT'S HARD TO BELIEVE IT'S OVER.

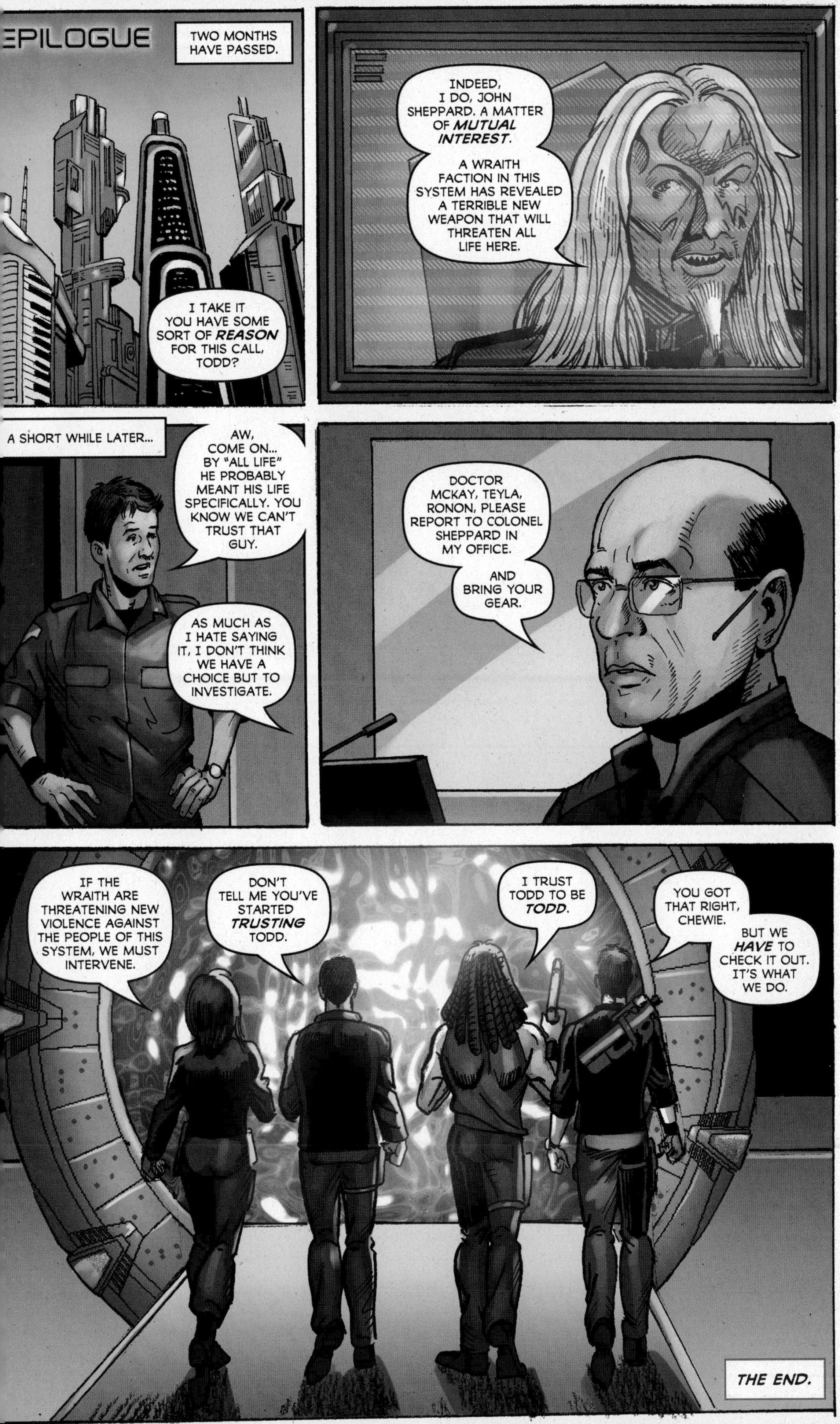
EPILOGUE
TWO MONTHS HAVE PASSED.
I TAKE IT YOU HAVE SOME SORT OF REASON FOR THIS CALL, TODD?
INDEED, I DO, JOHN SHEPPARD. A MATTER OF MUTUAL INTEREST.
A WRAITH FACTION IN THIS SYSTEM HAS REVEALED A TERRIBLE NEW WEAPON THAT WILL THREATEN ALL LIFE HERE.
A SHORT WHILE LATER...
AW, COME ON... BY "ALL LIFE" HE PROBABLY MEANT HIS LIFE SPECIFICALLY. YOU KNOW WE CAN'T TRUST THAT GUY.
AS MUCH AS I HATE SAYING IT, I DON'T THINK WE HAVE A CHOICE BUT TO INVESTIGATE.
DOCTOR MCKAY, TEYLA, RONON, PLEASE REPORT TO COLONEL SHEPPARD IN MY OFFICE.
AND BRING YOUR GEAR.
IF THE WRAITH ARE THREATENING NEW VIOLENCE AGAINST THE PEOPLE OF THIS SYSTEM, WE MUST INTERVENE.
DON'T TELL ME YOU'VE STARTED TRUSTING TODD.
I TRUST TODD TO BE TODD.
YOU GOT THAT RIGHT, CHEWIE.
BUT WE HAVE TO CHECK IT OUT. IT'S WHAT WE DO.
THE END.

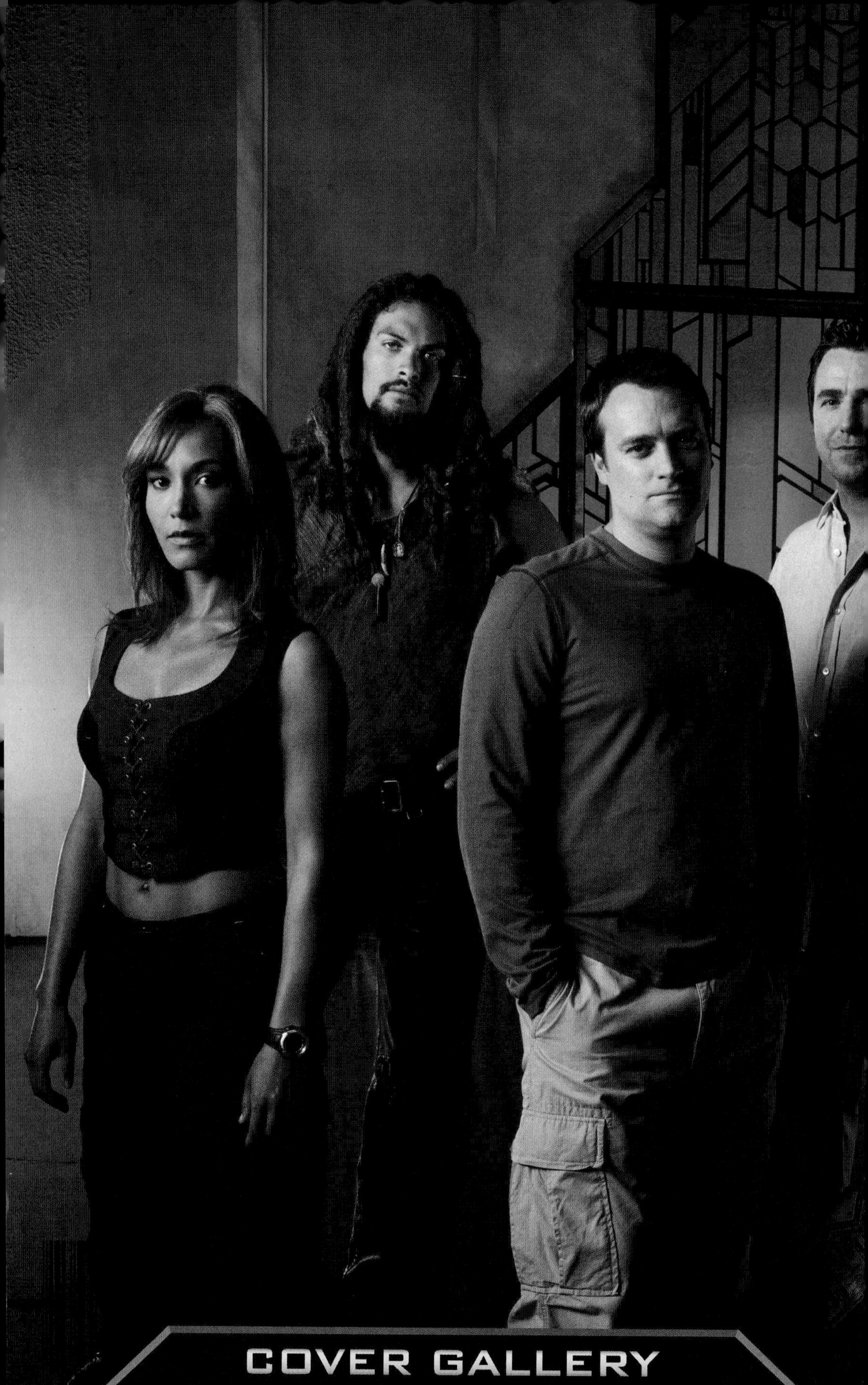

COVER GALLERY

HEARTS & MINDS #1 INCENTIVE COVER

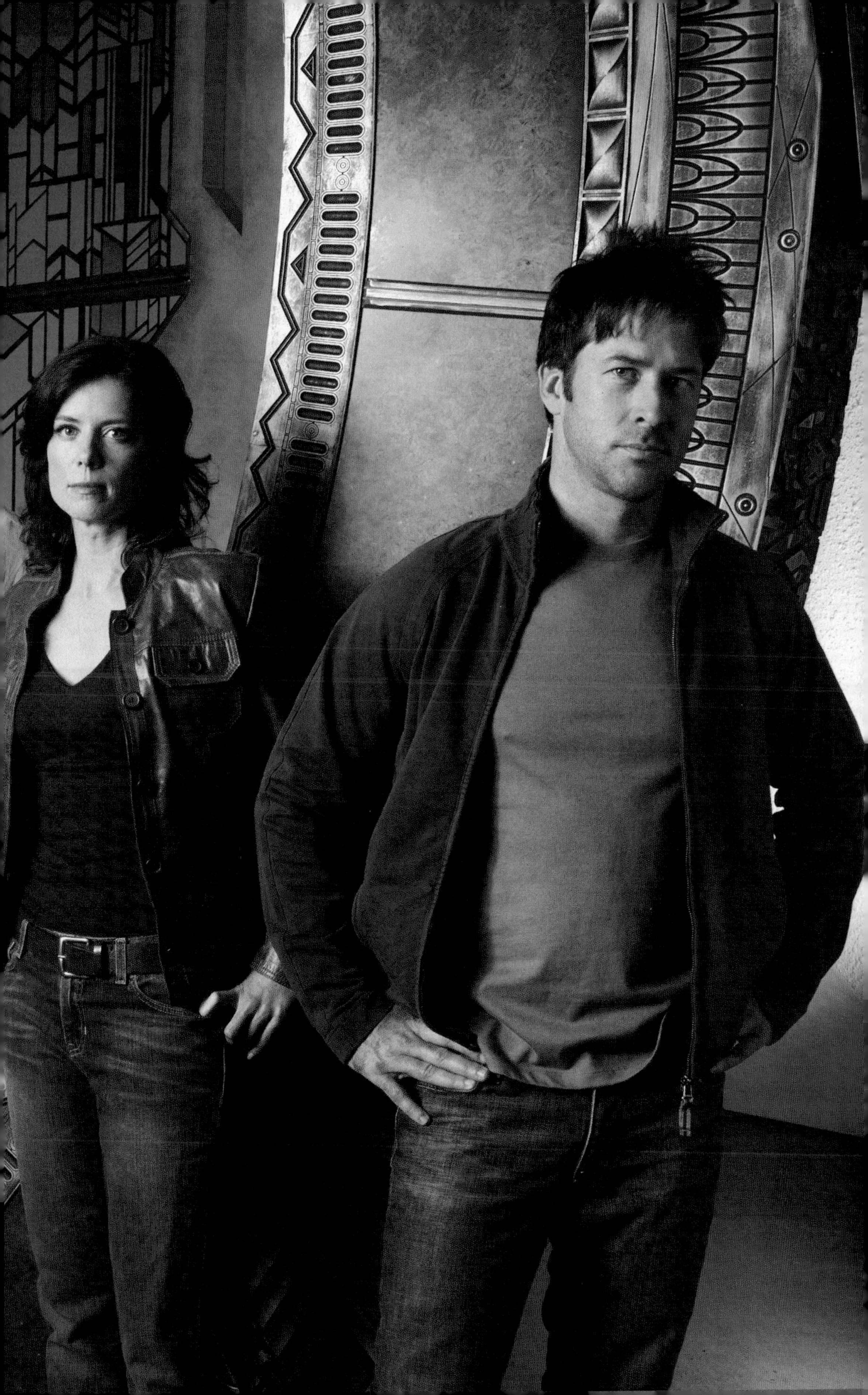

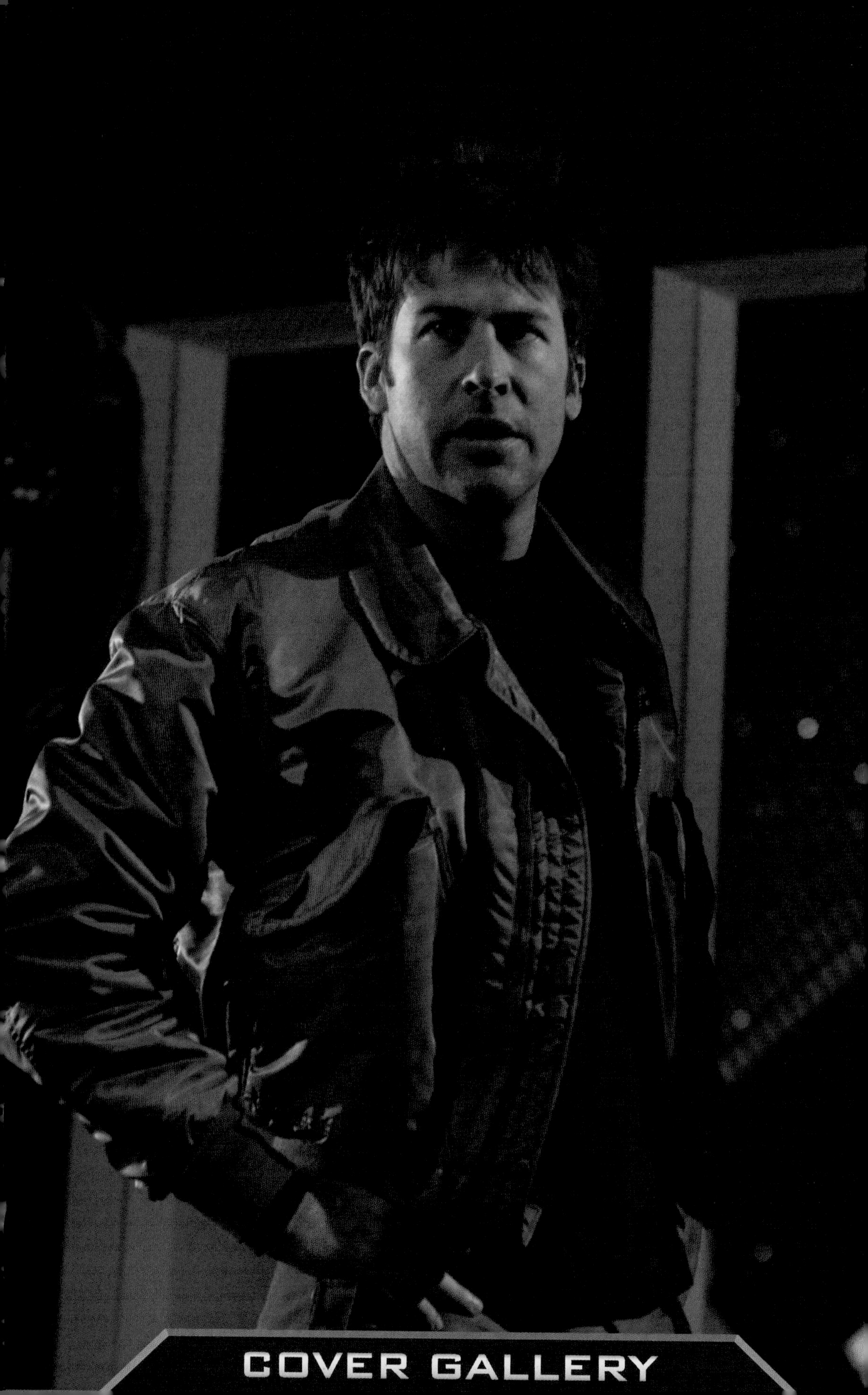

COVER GALLERY

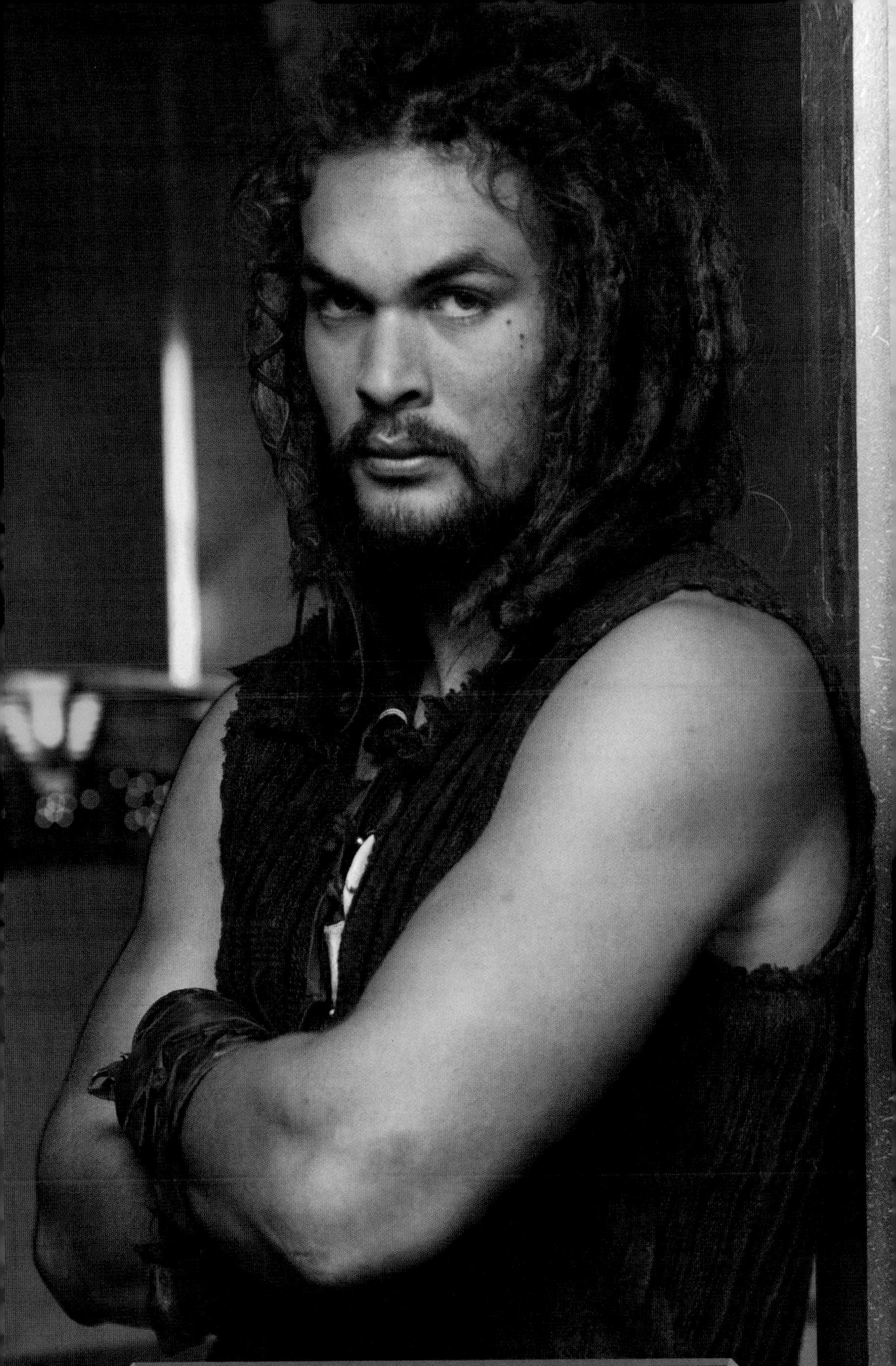

COVER GALLERY

HEARTS & MINDS #2 PHOTO COVER

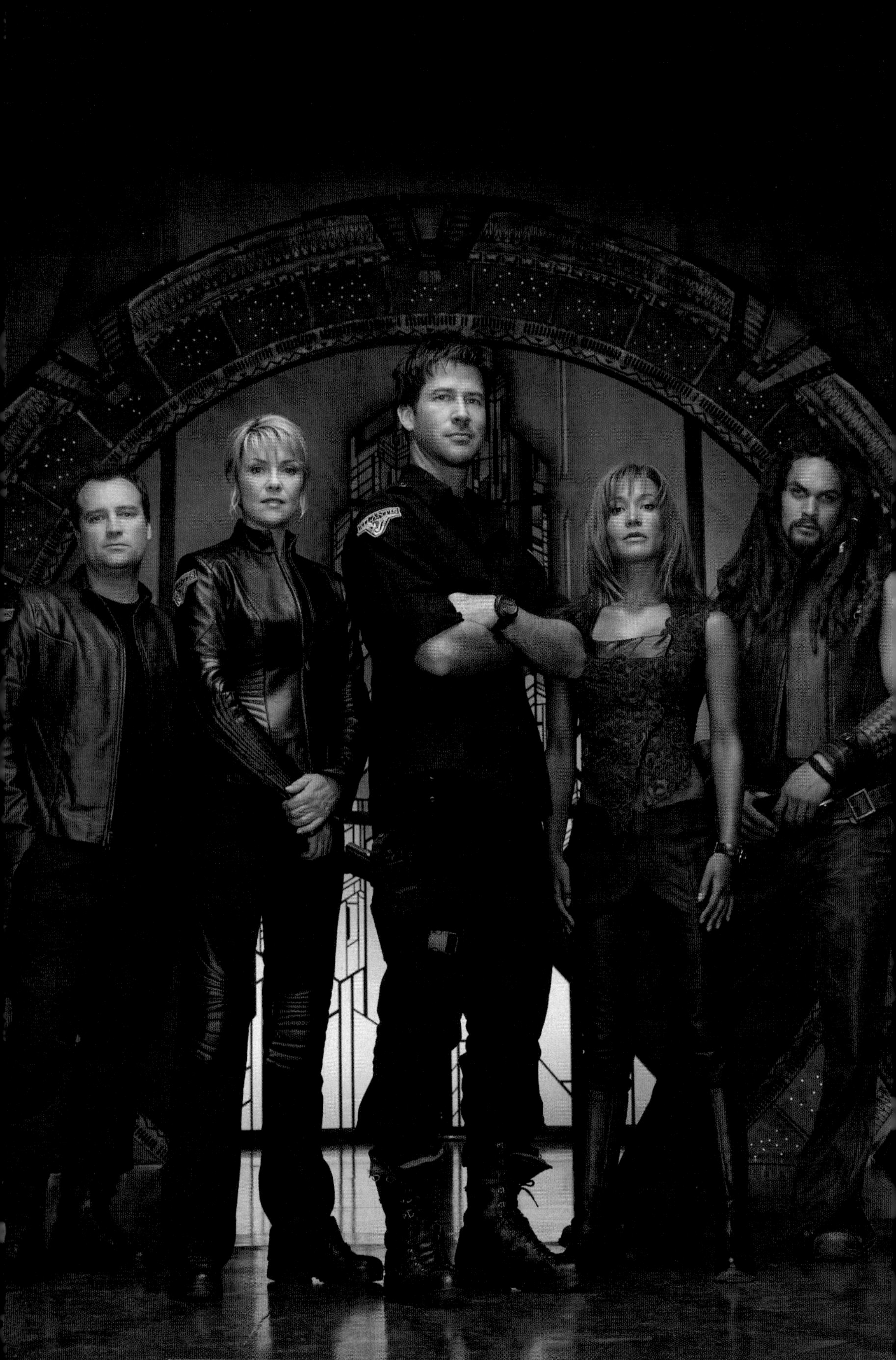

COVER GALLERY

HEARTS & MINDS #3 INCENTIVE COVER

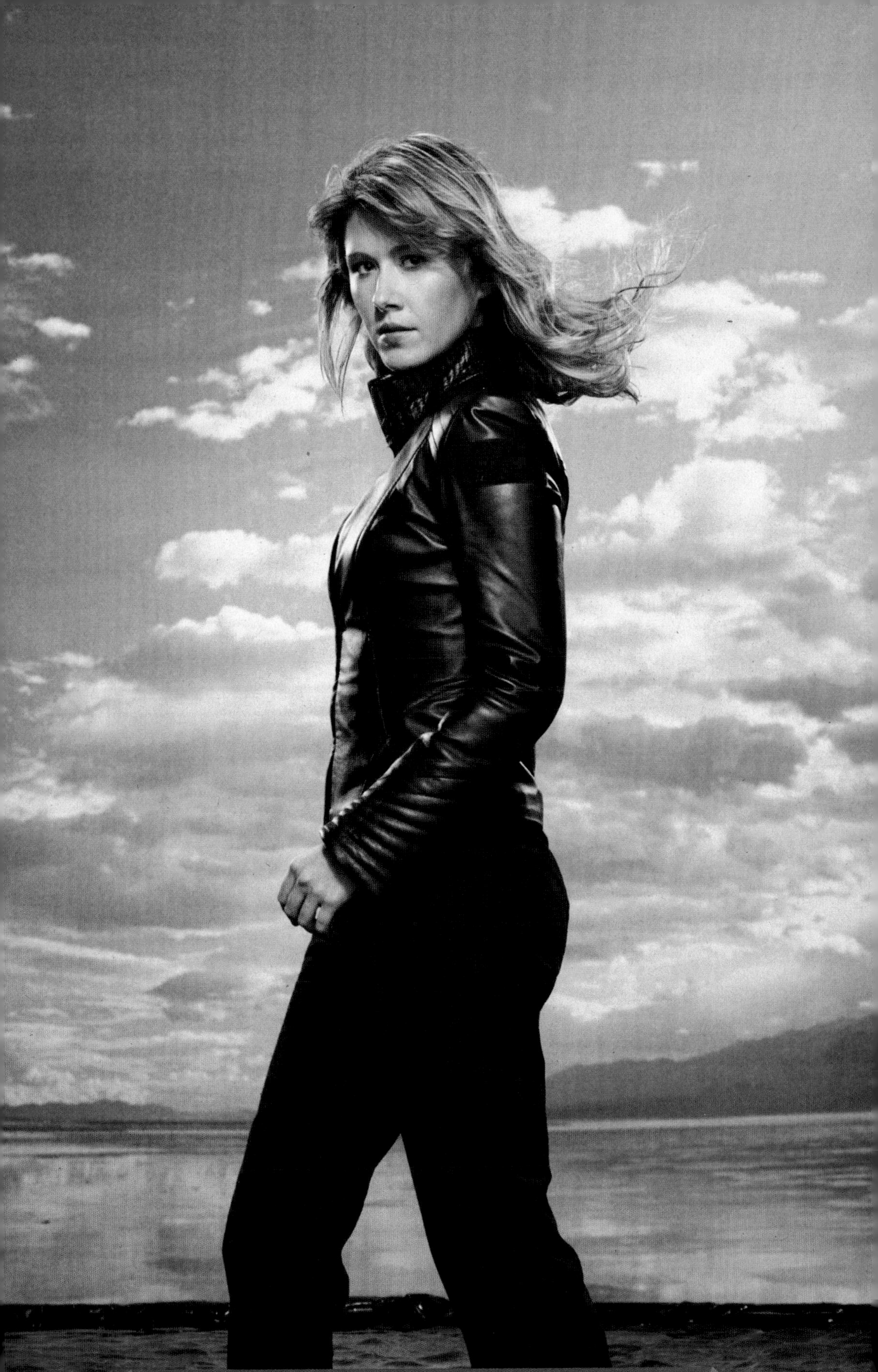

COVER GALLERY

HEARTS & MINDS #3 PHOTO COVER

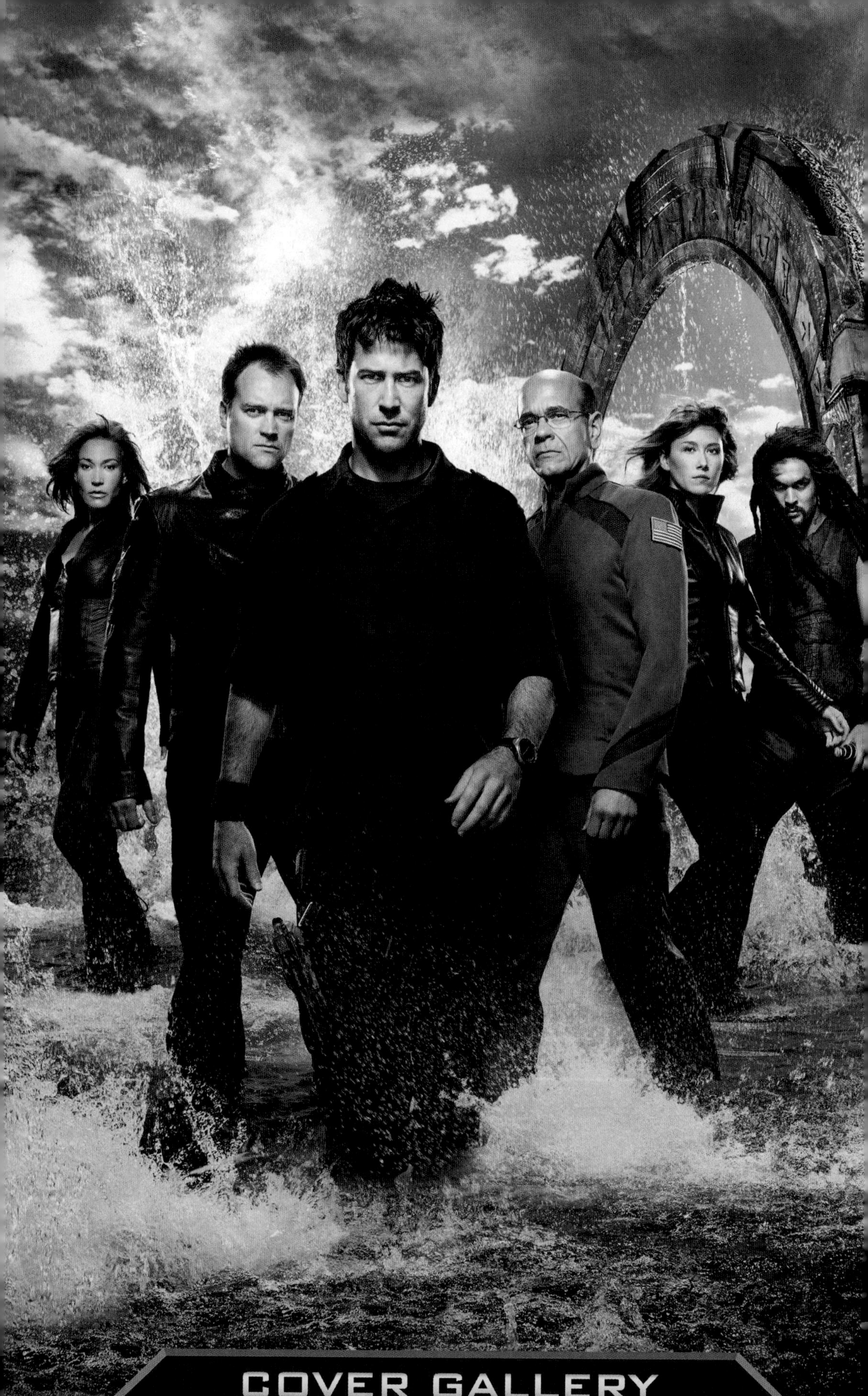

COVER GALLERY

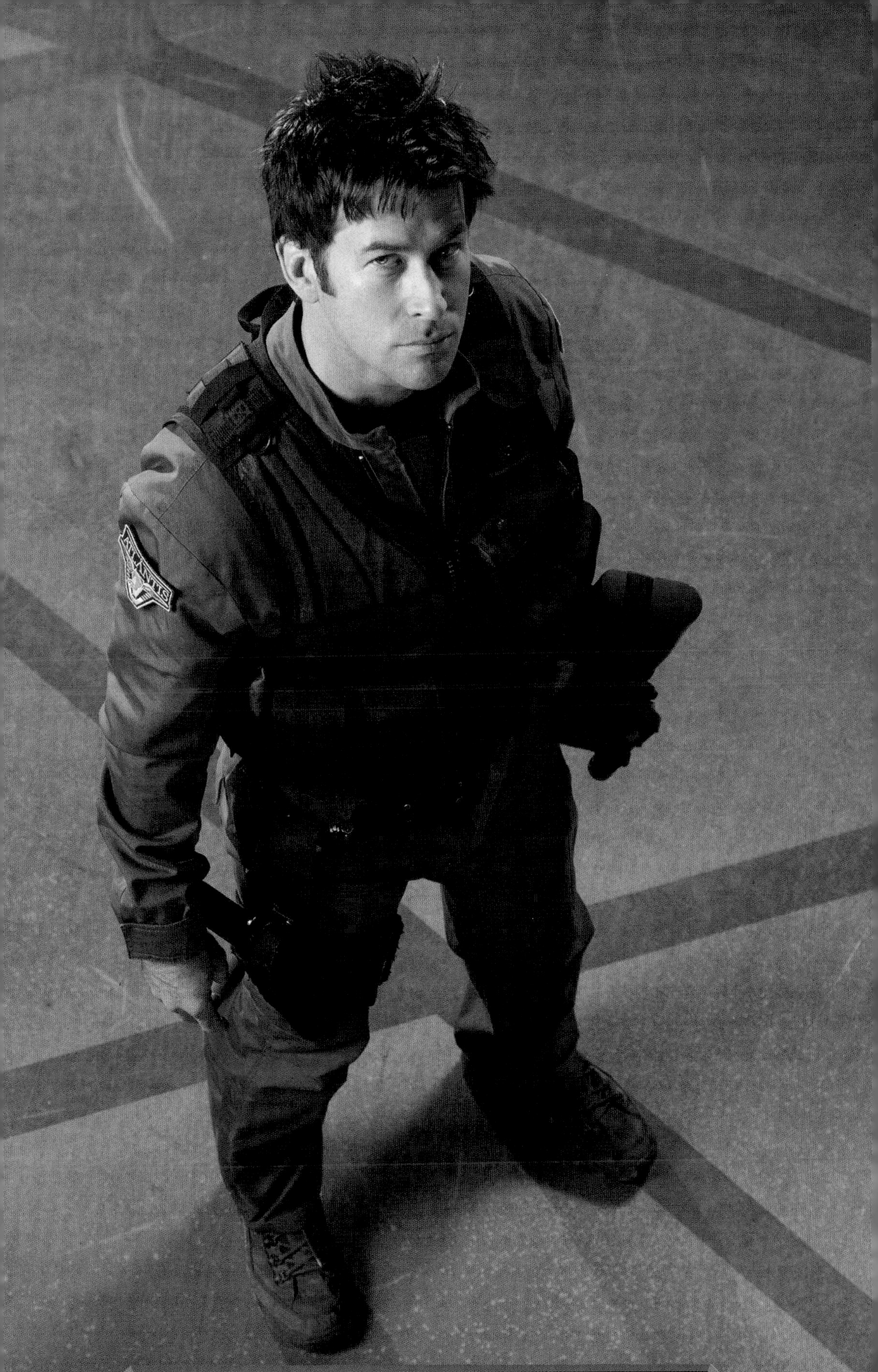
ATLANTIS

COVER GALLERY

SINGULARITY #1 PHOTO COVER

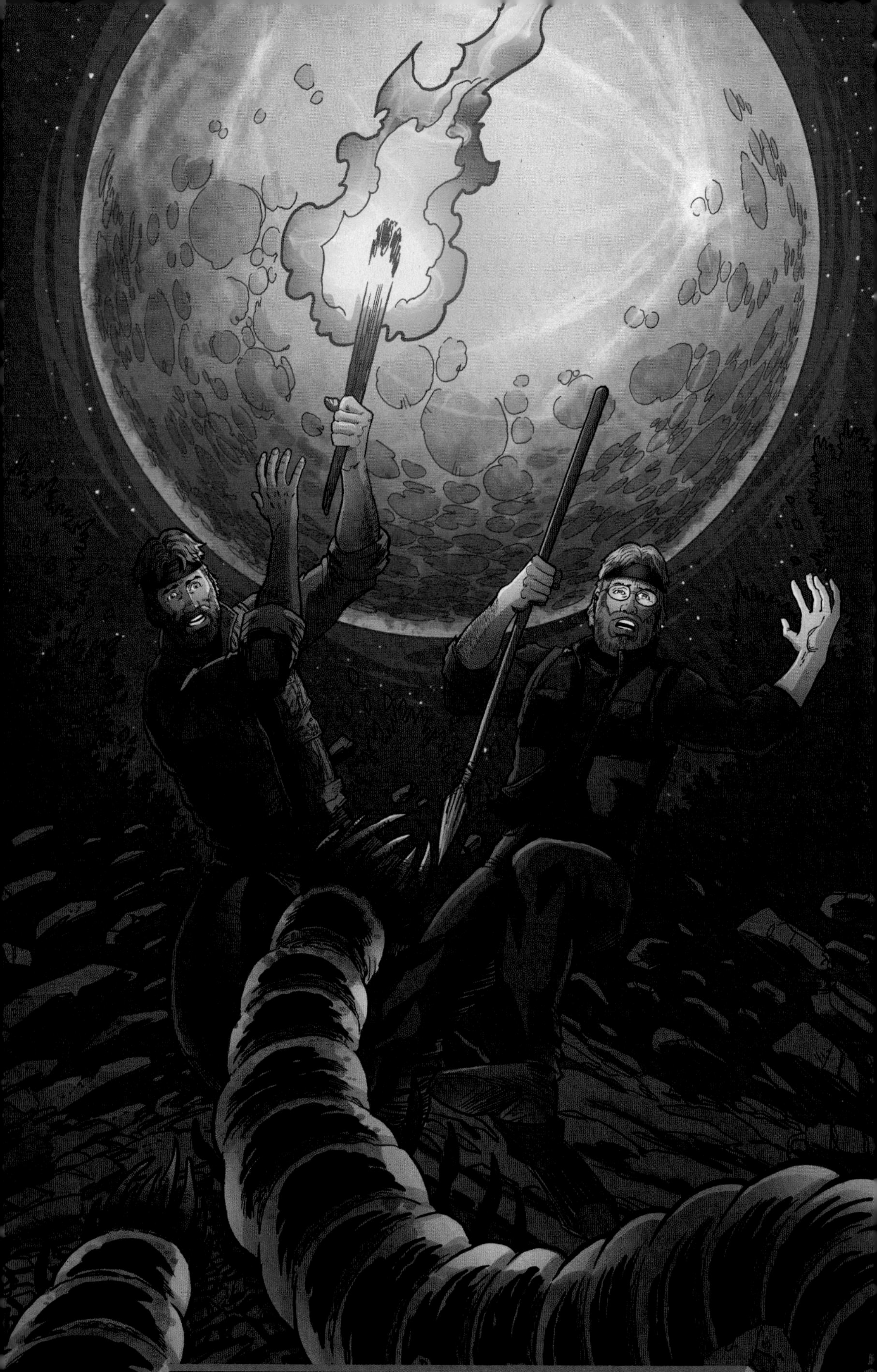

COVER GALLERY

SINGULARITY #1 PREMIUM COVER

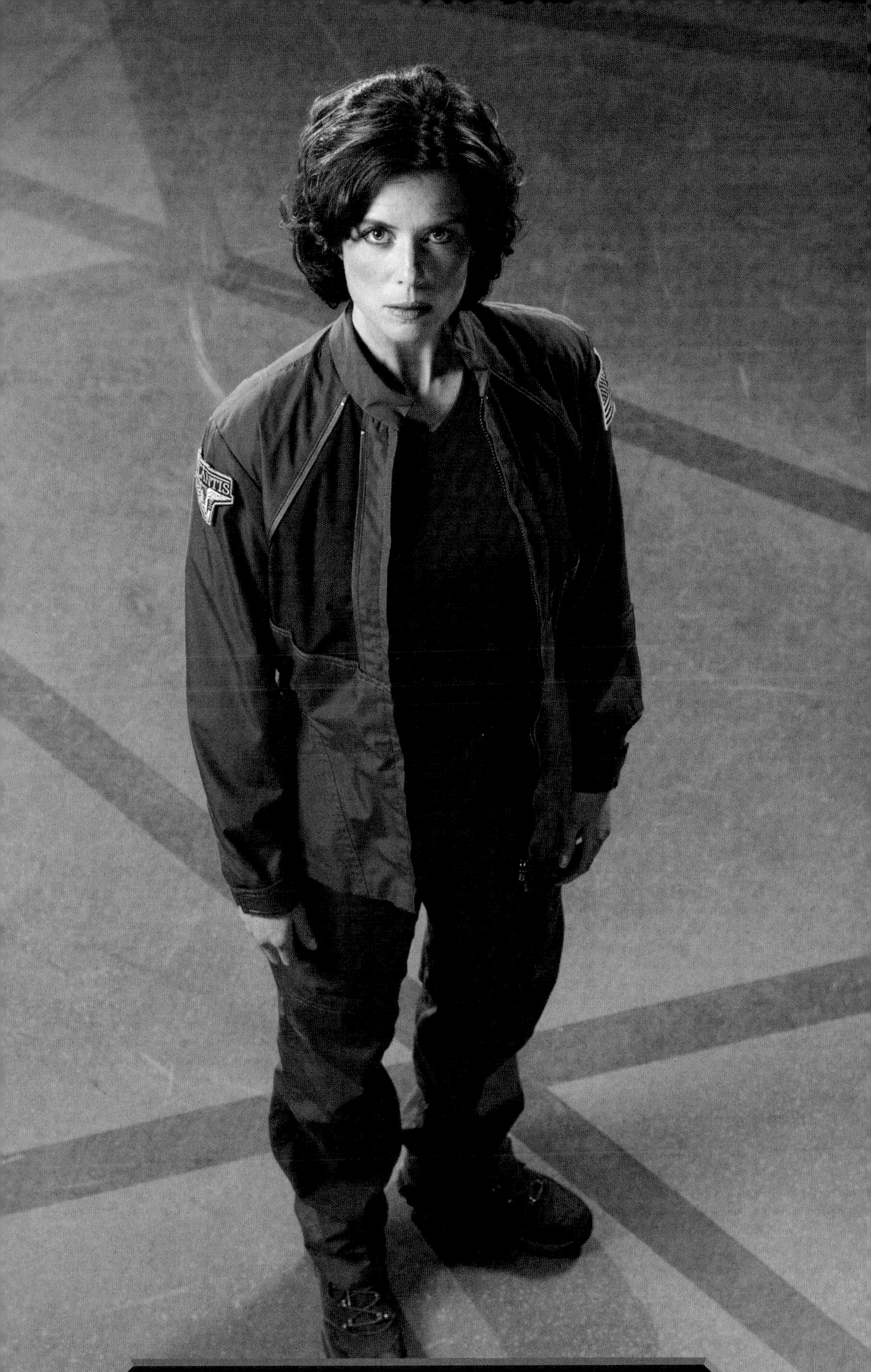

COVER GALLERY

SINGULARITY #2 PHOTO COVER

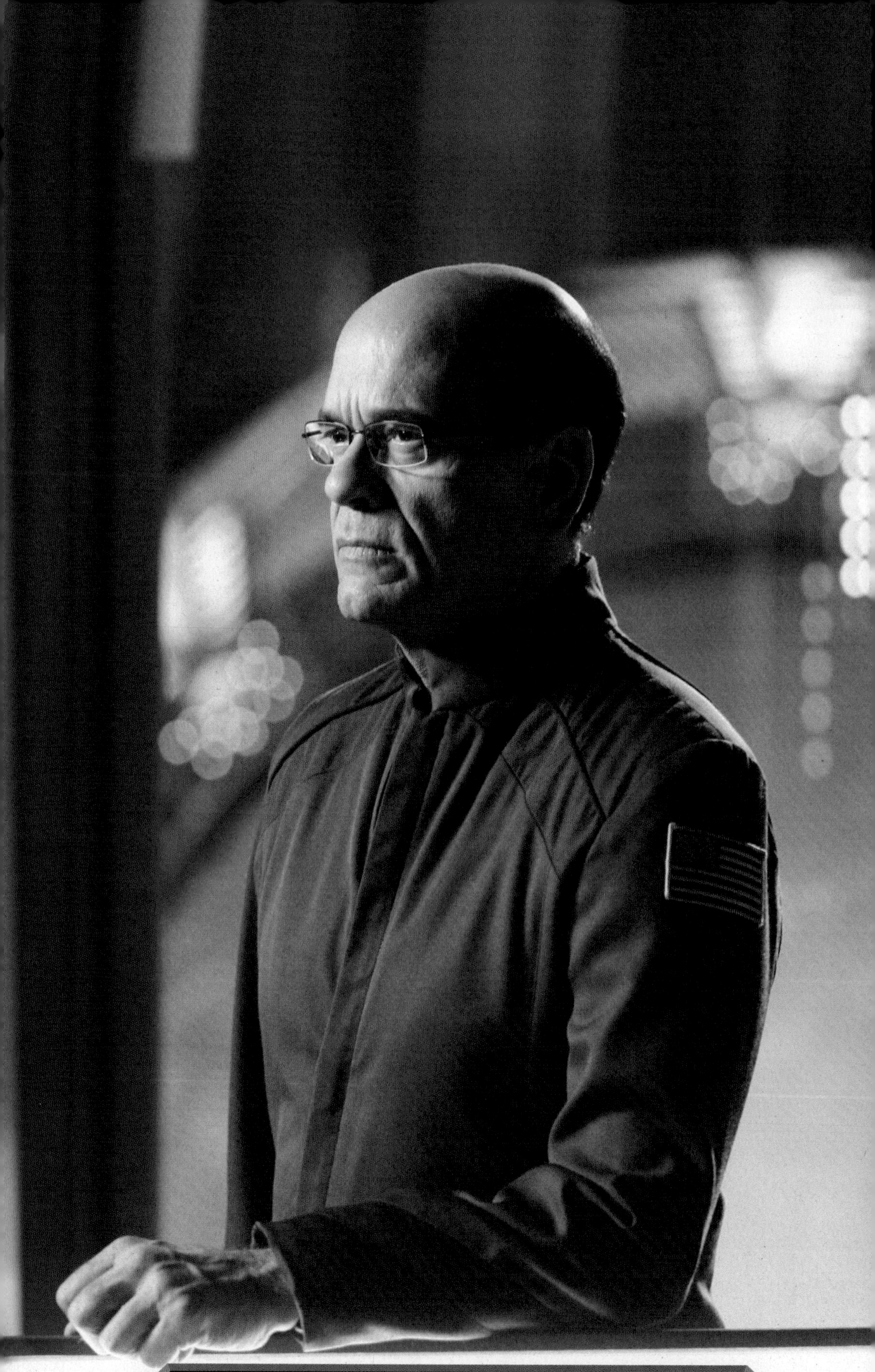

COVER GALLERY

SINGULARITY #2 PREMIUM COVER

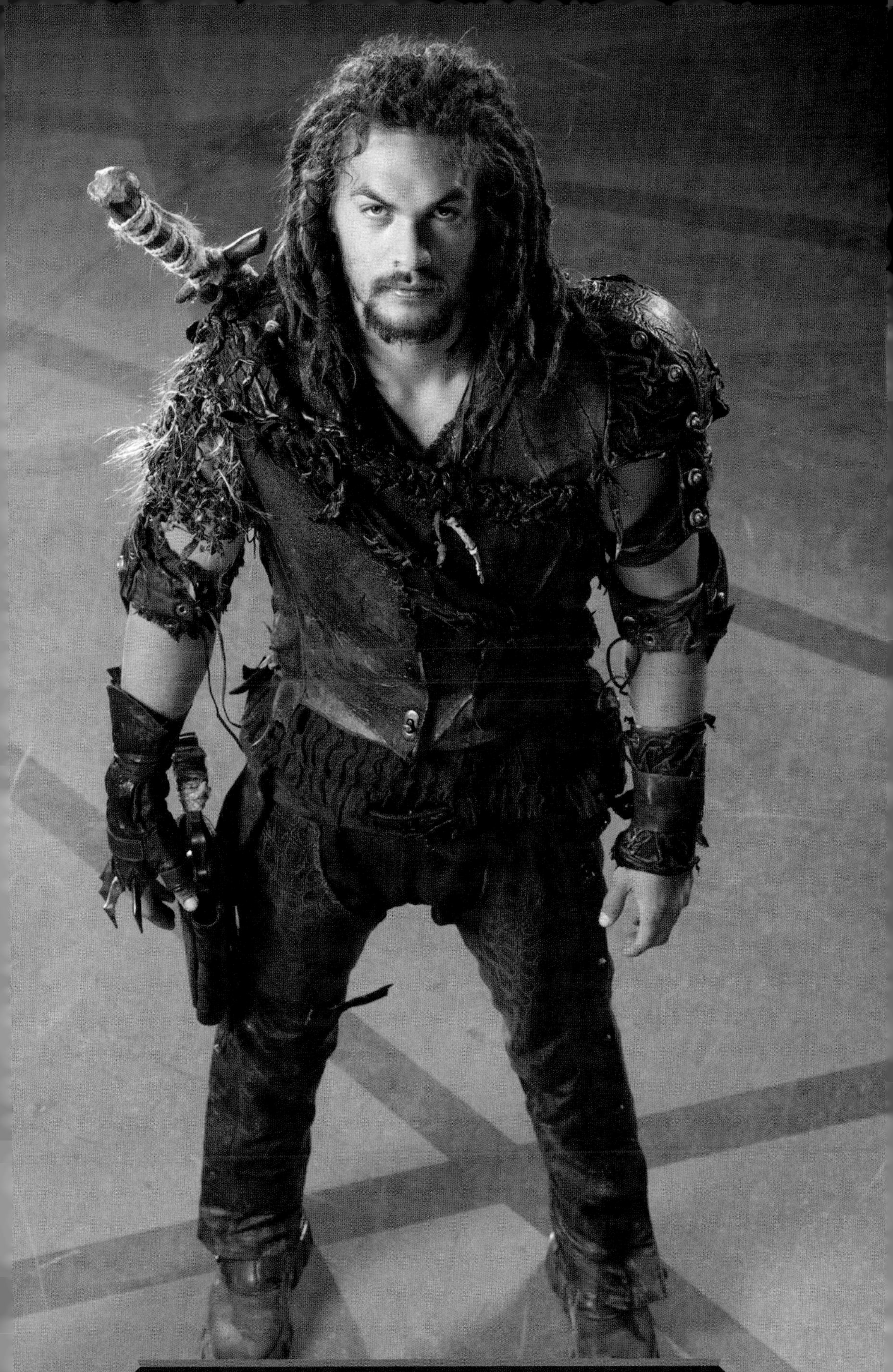

COVER GALLERY
SINGULARITY #3 PHOTO COVER

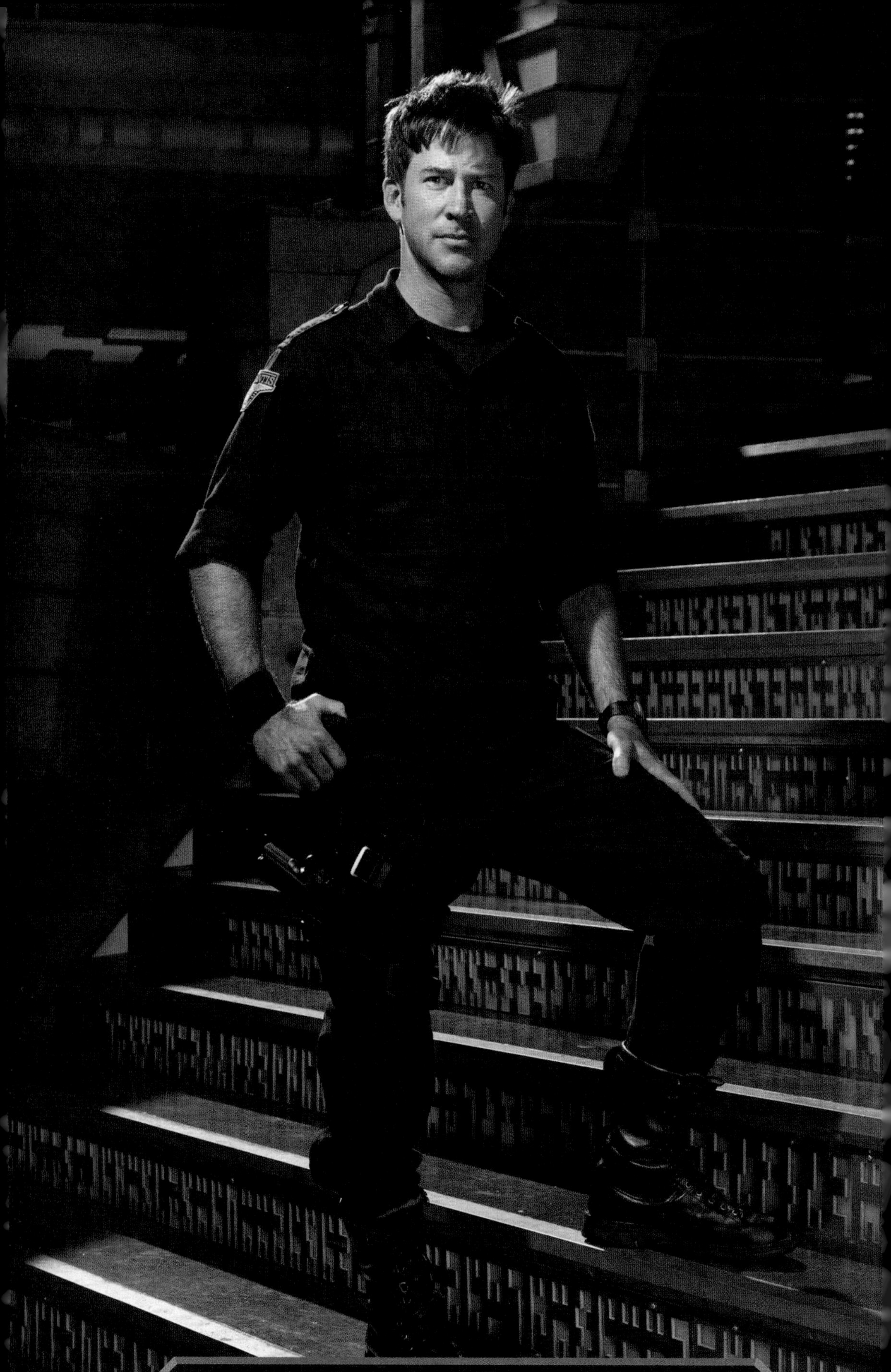

COVER GALLERY

SINGULARITY #3 PREMIUM COVER

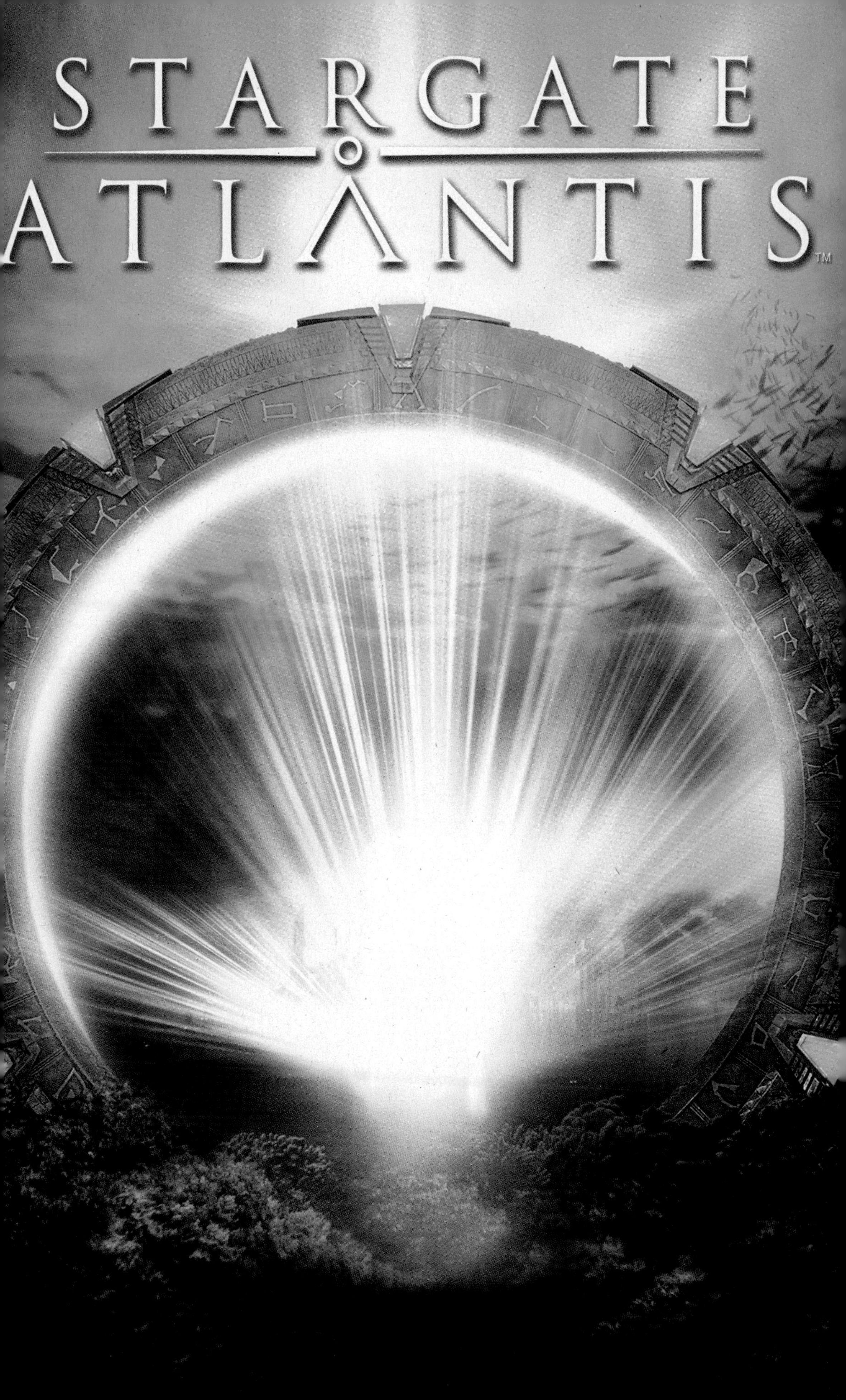
STARGATE
ATLANTIS™

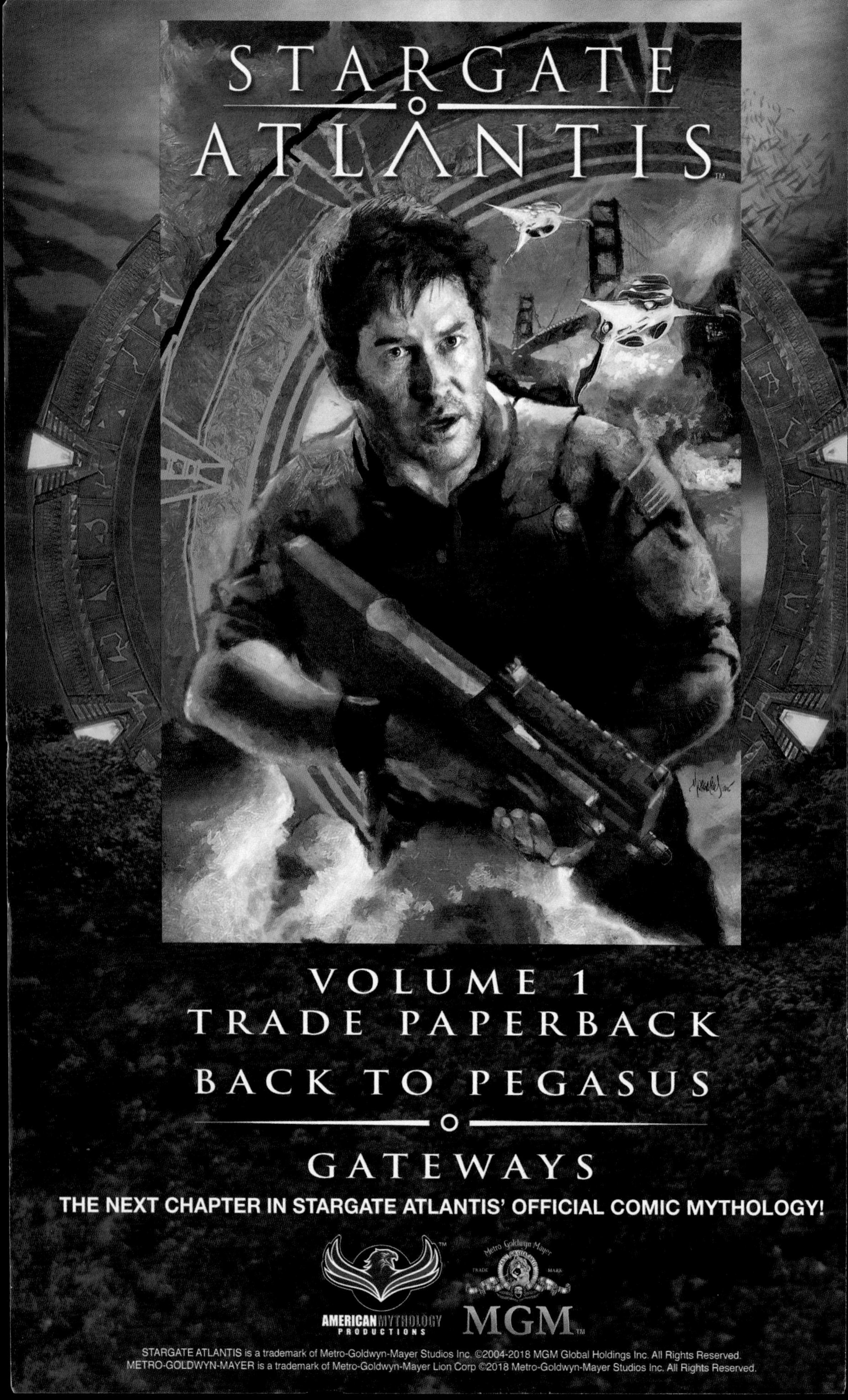
STARGATE
ATLANTIS
VOLUME 1
TRADE PAPERBACK
BACK TO PEGASUS
GATEWAYS
THE NEXT CHAPTER IN STARGATE ATLANTIS' OFFICIAL COMIC MYTHOLOGY!
AMERICAN MYTHOLOGY PRODUCTIONS
Metro Goldwyn Mayer
MGM
STARGATE ATLANTIS is a trademark of Metro-Goldwyn-Mayer Studios Inc. ©2004-2018 MGM Global Holdings Inc. All Rights Reserved.
METRO-GOLDWYN-MAYER is a trademark of Metro-Goldwyn-Mayer Lion Corp ©2018 Metro-Goldwyn-Mayer Studios Inc. All Rights Reserved.